Getting the Message

A Plan for Interpreting and Applying the Bible

Daniel M. Doriani

P&R
P U B L I S H I N G
P.O BOX 817 • PHILLIPSBURG • NEW JERSEY 08865-0817

© 1996 by Daniel M. Doriani

Unless otherwise indicated, Scripture quotations are from the HOLY BIBLE, NEW INTERNATIONAL VERSION. Copyright © 1973, 1978, 1984 International Bible Society. Used by permission of Zondervan Bible Publishers. Italics indicate emphasis added.

Printed in the United States of America

Library of Congress Cataloging-in-Publication Data

Doriani, Daniel M., 1953–
     Getting the message : a plan for interpreting and applying the Bible / Daniel M. Doriani
          p.   cm.
     Includes bibliographical references and index.
     ISBN-10: 0-87552-238-6 (paper)
     ISBN-13: 978-0-87552-238-8 (paper)
     1. Bible—Hermeneutics. 2. Bible—Study and teaching. I. Title.
BS476.D67   1996
220.6'01—dc20   96-33770

Getting the Message

Contents

Preface

With this book I hope to equip Christian leaders for the arduous but exhilarating task of interpreting and applying the Scriptures with facility and confidence. Since it seeks to inculcate skills, this book is for doers, for those who teach biblical truth week by week. Whether you read primarily to remind yourself of familiar principles, to organize scattered efforts, or to prepare for a teaching ministry, remember that exegesis is a skill, and we grow in skills by practicing them. To master the art of interpretation, one must practice that art in the hours available to you each week.

Perhaps this book's chief innovation is that it presents the steps of interpretation in the order in which students of Scripture actually use them. In the acronym CAPTOR, each letter stands for a phase of interpretation: C = Context, A = Analysis, P = Problems, T = Themes, O = Obligations, R = Reflection. After two introductory chapters, chapters 3–12 explore the six phases of interpretation. The final chapter then offers concrete suggestions for getting started. By offering models of exegesis, book lists, and more detailed information, the five appendices also seek to make the principles of this book usable.

You need not have unlimited time to follow this plan since you need not follow all the procedures described here for a single study. Rather the book outlines principles you can use over the years for various studies. For example, chapter 8, "Developing Themes," presents the steps necessary for a topical Bible study. Chapter 4, "The

Historical Context," describes the research one does at the beginning of a book study. Once it is done, you will use it repeatedly for months.

This project was conceived in upper-level biblical studies classes at Geneva College, when I learned that motivated students can acquire substantial exegetical skills even if they have not learned the biblical languages. The success and enthusiasm of those students, and of the people of Faith and Berean Presbyterian Churches, led me to believe that even nontechnical training can give motivated people substantial skill in English Bible interpretation. Since I have taught seminary students and pastors for the last several years, I hope the final form of this book is sophisticated enough to interest them. Yet I have pursued a form that should make it accessible to the college students, Bible study leaders, elders, and deacons whom I kept in mind as I wrote.

A word about my convictions. First, I believe that the Bible is the inspired, true, reliable record of both God's acts in history and their meaning. Second, while this book essentially follows the grammatical-historical method of exegesis, it also uses analytical techniques from all of life. The Bible is essentially the story of redemption, but the biblical drama is rooted in and touches every sphere of life, and so it is only sensible to use tools from all of life. Because the Bible is a literary work that uses rhetorical methods to gain a response from its readers, it makes sense to use literary and rhetorical tools. There is no need for a general fear of those "critical" methods.[1] If the interpreter has a high view of Scripture, such methods are simply tools we used to understand the various facets of the Bible. From shovels to telephones to the Internet, the effect of most tools depends chiefly on the intentions of the people using them.

In the process of completing this book, I acquired many debts. I am grateful to the board and administration of Covenant Theological Seminary for granting the sabbatical leave in which I completed this book. I thank my colleagues at the seminary for fostering an academic community where each member hopes and acts for the success of the rest. I especially thank Robert Peterson for his detailed editorial comments on the initial drafts of most chapters, and Bob Yarbrough, Bryan Chapell, Phil Long, and Jack Collins for being constant partners in conversation about the enterprise of biblical interpretation. Dozens of students have a fingerprint in this book; among them Daryl Madi stands out for his timely assistance.

I owe the deepest debt to my wife, Debbie, who condensed the possessions of a family of five into a package that fit in the back of two cars, moved to New Haven for several months, and made a small apartment into a home and day school for three bright young girls while I hid in the bowels of Yale's libraries.

I dedicate this book to my parents, Max and Marjorie Doriani, and my brothers Paul and Chris, who taught me to love the life of the mind. Perhaps our best hours as a family came as we sat at table after dinner, testing ideas and learning to use words to good effect.

Notes

[1] Of course, some methods do tend to put the reader in the position of a judge of Scripture. Therefore, I must reject methods that say that we cannot grasp the meaning of a text and that each reader must construct the meaning for himself. I also oppose the "hermeneutic of suspicion," which declares that whatever the surface meaning of a text, at root all authors use texts to take or to legitimate power over others.

1

Introduction

Is There an Interpreter in the House?

Anyone who loves God and believes that he has spoken with unique authority in the Bible has ample reason to learn the methods of effective Bible study. And yet, Bible study takes work, and we all have more than enough work to do, a reality that tests our motivation to learn how to interpret Scripture.

Sometimes God uses troubling situations to kindle our desire for a better understanding of his Word. Imagine that it is Sunday morning and your pastor is away. A guest speaker has read some texts in the Old Testament that feature polygamy, and the sermon begins.

> My experiences in Africa and my study of Scripture have convinced me that it is time to reevaluate the church's teaching on polygamy. Like many teachers, I held the traditional line and blustered my way through when students asked me how God could have allowed his leaders to be polygamists during the old covenant if polygamy is a sin. Then, when I began my work in Africa, the Lord granted me some success with village chiefs in Burkina Faso. When they confessed Christ and were baptized, I made them give up all but their chief wife and send the others and their children away. But, instead of preserving the dignity of marriage, it destroyed the

1

former wives, who were reduced to begging and prostitution, and their children, who became orphans and outcasts. Some chiefs, seeing the shame it brought to their children, refused to become Christians, though they were drawn to Christ. Lesser men, with only one wife, became leaders of the church, but no one in the village respected them, and the church lost its standing. What's more, the women there do not mind polygamy. One told me, "The day my husband took a second wife was the happiest of my life. Now I have someone to share the work, and she is a friend, like a sister."

Then I began to study the question of polygamy. Abraham, Jacob, and David were all polygamists. The Lord rebuked all three men for their sins, but he never condemned them for polygamy. Genesis and Samuel even portray the second marriage of Jacob, to Rachel, and the fourth marriage of David, to Abigail, as positive, even romantic events. Furthermore, even though Jesus condemns oaths, divorce, and other Old Testament practices, he never forbids polygamy, and neither does any of the apostles.

Yes, polygamy has been rare in the history of the church, but that is primarily because the Catholic church hardly even approved of marriage. When the Reformation came and began to present a positive view of marriage, theologians quickly raised the possibility of polygamy. Martin Luther even urged the Lutheran political leader, Philip of Hesse, to take a second wife, since he could not live chastely with but one.

There are many reasons to reconsider the issue of polygamy today. Yes, monogamy is ideal, but we hardly live in an ideal world. What shall we say, for example, to Christian women who long to marry but cannot find a suitable mate because so many men are immature, immoral, unbelievers, or uninterested in women? Many men can support two or more wives, both financially and emotionally. Isn't polygamy better for everyone than a life of loneliness for their potential second wives?[1]

Sermons like that can keep people on the church steps for a long time while small bands of children whirl about in ever-more-disheveled clothes, and Sunday dinners threaten to burn. Though disturbing, the stories about Africa and Luther can seem persuasive. If no one can show biblically where the guest speaker was wrong, that inability can prove more troubling than the sermon itself.

Is it enough to say that the pastor will have an answer when he returns? Or should believers be able to formulate at least a rudimentary response on their own? After all, don't we often hear speakers or read books that claim to disclose forgotten truths or elucidate passages misunderstood by the church for hundreds of years? Their views may sound interesting—almost persuasive. Yet something doesn't seem right. But unless we own a massive library or can call the pastor right away, often we're at a loss. And we can wonder, is it just that our old ideas die hard, or is there something wrong with the message we hear, something we can't quite put our finger on? Though we may never go to seminary, shouldn't we know how to distinguish between true and false teaching?

How often have you wished you could handle the Bible more confidently? Perhaps you have been confused when Bible teachers contradict each other, or when a sermon soars far beyond your simple thoughts on a text. Or you realize that the stock Sunday school material you have will not work for your class, but you have no idea how to prepare your own lesson.

Why are Christians unable to evaluate sermons, or to gain much from devotional reading, or to prepare lessons on their own? It is because they lack a method for studying the Bible. This book presents a straightforward method for effective Bible study. The goal of that study is not simply to understand the Bible better, but also to apply it to life.

Our Need for Training

In many fellowships, Bible study consists of reading a passage of Scripture and asking, "What does this passage say to me?" In other words, "When I read this text, what thoughts or feelings does it stir up in me?" Putting the question in that subjective form allows people to "find" almost any idea they like in a text. Christians are thus encouraged to seize upon a snippet of truth—a moralism or a proof text for a favorite doctrine—while ignoring everything else. When we observe this practice in others (it's hard to catch ourselves at it), we notice that the Bible tends to "say" safe, trendy, or self-serving things.

Yes, believers should expect to hear God's voice through their Bible study. Yes, all believers are priests (1 Peter 2:5, 9; Rev. 5:10) and have direct access to God and his Word without the intervention of priests or experts. Yes, God is the ultimate teacher of everyone who knows him (Jer. 31:33–34). His anointing leads us into the truth (1 John 2:27). But we abuse this privilege if we let our impressions drown out the prophets and apostles. Because we believe in the authority of the Bible, we need an objective method for determining, as best we can, what the Bible originally meant and what it means today.

We need training because we live in a world far removed from the world of the Bible—in time, in language, and in customs. We speak English, Spanish, or German. They spoke Hebrew, Aramaic, or Greek. We live in a technological society, shaped by cars, refrigerators, telephones, videos, and computer networks, all ruled by elected officials, convertible currencies, and global markets. They lived in an agrarian society shaped by donkeys, wooden plows, clay pots, and dirt roads, all ruled by a Roman emperor and his armies.

Because of the differences between biblical times and our age, we need training in biblical *language* and *customs*. As for language, how many of us know precisely what the terms *atonement, justification, redemption,* and *propitiation* mean? As for customs, even casual readers of the Gospels can see that, contrary to the habits of "religious" people in his day, Jesus associated with outcasts, sinners, and people of other races; but readers miss Jesus' violation of some other social customs. For example, in current Western culture, men and women converse freely in nearly every setting, and so we hardly notice it when the Gospels show Jesus talking to women.

In fact, when the disciples found Jesus talking to a Samaritan woman in John 4, the text says that they were surprised, not to find him talking to a despised Samaritan, but to find him talking to a woman (4:27). The disciples were shocked because the rabbis believed that teaching women was a waste of time. One rabbi even said, "It is better that the words of the Law should be burned, than that they should be given to a woman."[2] In their opinion, all women were dangerously seductive. Unless we are aware of such attitudes, we cannot appreciate that Jesus' conversation with the Samaritan woman was bold and risked condemnation.

For reasons such as this, we need to know about Jewish life and religion to get the most from reading the Bible. In fact, the issue of cultural distance had already arisen by the time the New Testament was written. That is why Mark, Luke, and John, writing for gentile audiences, explained Aramaic terms and Jewish customs that arose in their gospel narratives. For example, Mark interrupted his story of a conflict over ritual cleanness between Jesus and the Pharisees to explain to his gentile readers that the Jews had traditions that called for ceremonial washings (Mark 7:1–5). He also explained Aramaic terms that came up during the crucifixion of Jesus (15:22, 34; for similar asides, see 5:41; 7:19; 9:6; 11:32; 15:16). John interprets even common Jewish terms such as *rabbi, Messiah,* and the name Cephas (John 1:38–42). Thus, strange customs and terms already impeded communication to people living perhaps a few hundred miles away and just a few decades after the events. How much more do we need instruction now, two thousand years later and in an alien culture, if we hope to understand the language and culture of the Bible!

Training the mind also helps us apply the Bible to new situations. For example, who stands in the position of the Samaritan woman in our society? In a different vein, Christians who work with medical technology have to wrestle with the morality of such things as artificial insemination or the use of "heroic measures" on the terminally ill. Every disciple has to decide how to use television and radio. Should we watch programs that have quality actors and writers, but regularly feature lewd language and immorality? May we watch such a program if the immorality is occasional and incidental? If it is chronic? In popular music, does vulgarity matter if we cannot make out the words? Or is the whole popular music industry corrupt and unworthy of our support?

The Bible never addresses these or many similar questions *directly.* In a way, it cannot, if it is to speak to all ages and cultures. If God had chosen to dictate instructions about computers or life-support systems to Peter or Ezekiel, they would have been nonsense to all but late–twentieth-century readers. Thus, single proof texts rarely answer questions that stem from new, contemporary situations. "Thou shalt not kill" does not solve every ethical quandary that comes up in a hospital. We need to search the whole Bible to find relevant principles, and training will help the search go faster.

So far, we have been saying that successful interpretation depends on sound methods of interpretation. Yet we must add that it also depends upon sound interpreters. The bulk of this book focuses on techniques used to interpret or "exegete" the Bible. But we must turn to the interpreters from time to time because the spirit they have as they exegete the Bible is just as important as the skills they possess.

State of the Heart:
What About the Interpreter?

Serious inquirers must use proper methods, but the mastery of methods does not, by itself, guarantee that God will bless their labors. At its best, Bible study is an encounter with the personal God, not just with a text. Only when we join skillful methods to a receptive heart can we expect Bible study to bear fruit in the lives of individuals and the church.

Personal receptivity is vital because the proper goal of interpretation is application.[3] As the apostle Paul says, "All Scripture is God-breathed and is useful for teaching, rebuking, correcting and training in righteousness, so that the man of God may be thoroughly equipped for every good work" (2 Tim. 3:16–17). People prove they have understood a concept when they apply it to new situations, especially in their own lives. A disciple demonstrates an understanding of the principle of speaking the truth in love when he or she expresses a difficult truth without hurting anyone. On the other hand, if a man claims to understand the biblical teaching on marriage, yet drives his wife from their home, divorces her, and swiftly marries another woman, we have to question his understanding.[4]

So, we must say, "Beware of method alone!" Believers and unbelievers can both acquire valid techniques of interpretation. Many of them apply to any book, essay, or poem. Skeptics can understand the grammar and terminology of the Bible perfectly well. Investigators can temporarily enter the biblical world to gain information.[5] But unless God grants a willingness to submit to biblical authority, they can read all day and profit nothing. Unless they are repenting of their sins, they will resist and refuse to apply God's Word, even as they read it. As a result, they will use inappropriate methods, such as trying to find purely natural explanations for supernatural events, or systematically doubting everything until they establish an unshakable core of reliable facts. Unfortunately, their reliable facts about Jesus may amount to little more than saying that he taught, healed people, and was executed by the Romans.

The half-committed Christian occupies an awkward position, too. He weaves his way through the Bible like a child picking his way through the vegetables while dining with Aunt Alberta, not quite sure if the goal is to eat or avoid eating. So much in the text seems unpalatable: "This can't mean what it appears to say. . . . Surely that no longer applies today," he mutters to himself when biblical statements offend his tastes. The half-committed Christian can hardly have a hunger for Bible study. He is not sure he *wants* to know its message.

What advantage, then, does a believer have over skeptics and waverers? Is it his general spirituality? A sensitivity to spiritual things? A capacity for religious empathy? A belief that supernatural events can occur?[6] The believer's essential advantage is that he takes the right posture before the Bible. He does not look it in the eye, as if he were an equal who has the right to criticize it at any point.[7] He does not merely encounter it, expecting to meet new horizons, new worlds of thought that may or may not break in and change him.[8] He *submits to its authority*, for he holds it to be the very Word of the sovereign Lord whom he loves.

Christians have an advantage because their higher commitment to the Bible may make them work longer and harder on the text. Still, *the Christians' advantage lies less in the work they do on the text than in the work God does in them* as they bow before it.[9] Again, a skeptic using proper methods can discover the ideas presented in the Bible. Believers have no mystical advantage in grasping the grammar or customs of the Bible. But because God operates on the heart, convicting of sin and of God's greater grace, the Christian is willing to receive the message, even if it stings.

The believer's advantage lies in his willingness to apply the Bible. That is no small advantage, if, as we said, the goal of interpretation is application. Skeptics may misconstrue the Bible for many reasons, but surely their unwillingness to submit to the God who gave Scripture counts most in the end.

The subject of prayer illustrates that we must join heart and method. Some authors emphasize the right methods of prayer—the proper times (early morning) and places (perhaps a secluded corner), and the correct content (adoration, confession, thanksgiving, and supplication). Wise as they may be, such instructions do not get to the heart of the matter, for one can establish the proper time, place, and structure of prayer and still have a poor prayer life. For this reason, whenever Jesus taught his disciples *what to pray* (an aspect of method), he also taught them *how to pray*—how to have the right attitude toward God (Matt. 6:5–15; Luke 11:1–13).

With biblical interpretation, as with prayer, three elements are necessary: proper methods, proper heart conditions, and proper goals. Methods without devotion can breed pride or a quest for selfish advantage. "The proper goal of the study of hermeneutics," says D. A. Carson, is not the accumulation of elite knowledge, but "the better understanding of and obedience to holy Scripture."[10] Before proceeding, therefore, each reader should ask, "What kind of a reader am I?" To be sure, the Bible is not the sort of book that critics and loafers are likely to read. Still, self-examination has its place. Are you committed to believing and applying whatever you discover as you study the Bible, regardless of the cost?[11]

Three Forms of Heart Failure

Although the question above invites a simple yes or no, there is more to it. Even if we give a provisional yes, we might still fail because of immaturity or spiritual insensitivity, if not rebellion.

Immaturity. Immaturity impedes one's ability to interpret Scripture. As people mature and learn fundamental principles, they gain a capacity to learn more. For example, one must have a certain level of maturity to comprehend biblical teaching on love. While little children like to talk about love, it is pointless to discuss much beyond the love of family and friends. Children may gladly give away all their money—but then, they have no concept of the power of money. And how do you talk about selfless love to a child who joyfully shares a favorite food with his parents, but screams when his sister so much as breathes toward his dish?

Similarly, the concept of church discipline boggles the minds of some new converts, because it runs contrary to popular ideas about the tenderness of God and the "right" to keep others from interfering in our lives. So, unless we understand our sin and the holiness of God, biblical teaching on church discipline makes little sense. Thus, immaturity hampers our ability to receive scriptural teachings.

Insensitivity. Insensitivity resembles immaturity, but stems more from laziness or a stubborn trust in false ideas than from pure ignorance or rebellion. For example, Jesus' disciples misunderstood his predictions of his crucifixion because of their attachment to false ideas about the Messiah. Although Jesus often told them about his coming death, they never accepted it until after the event. When he foretold his crucifixion, they could not grasp it and were afraid to ask about it (Luke 9:45). Peter even rebuked Jesus for talking about his death (Matt. 16:13–23). The disciples could not hear Jesus because his concept of a suffering Messiah clashed with their hopes for a triumphal Messiah.

We often do the same thing when the Bible says something that seems strange to us. We may feel confused for a while, but in time we either ignore the passage or reinterpret it so that it fits more comfortably into our thinking. For example, during the period of the Crusades, Christians in western Europe believed it was their obligation to conquer or at least stop the Muslims. There is no record of any evangelistic impulse toward them until St. Francis of Assisi and his followers began to move in the thirteen century. Why did no one preach to the Muslims until then? Christians were not ignorant of the biblical basis for missions; they simply believed it did not apply to the Saracens, whom they regarded as subhuman and destined for destruction.[12] Thus, they let preconceptions nullify the biblical message.

Sadly, future Christians will no doubt shudder at our insensitivity, too. What will make them shake their heads? Our materialism and indifference to the poor? Our easy acceptance of denominations? The excesses of the church-growth movement and the marketing of the church? There is no simple cure for spiritual blind spots, but it helps to have a method of Bible study that gives us confidence to declare, "I may not fully understand it yet, but I know and accept what the Bible says."

Rebellion. When Cornelius greets Peter at his door in Acts 10, he manifests the spirit that leads to profitable hearing and study of the Word. He declares, "Now we are all here in the presence of God to listen to everything the Lord has commanded you to tell us" (Acts 10:33). Sadly, if many supposed Christians told the truth, they would admit, "Now we are all here in the presence of mankind to hear everything that meets a felt need, maintains our comfort zone, and confirms our preexisting opinions."

Rebellion, whether naive or deliberate, breeds many distortions of Scripture. A woman awakens in a cold sweat one morning, decides her marriage is an icy road with no visible exits, and starts planning a divorce. There is no infidelity, abuse, or desertion; she just wants to escape. She may study the Scripture, change her mind, and work to improve her marriage, or she may proceed with a divorce even though the Bible forbids it. She clutches a single phrase, "God is love," and reasons to herself, "If God is love, he does not want me to suffer in this miserable marriage for the rest of my life."

Or perhaps someone in the family embraces Buddhism or enters a homosexual relationship. And suddenly family members are tempted to bend Scripture toward a more tolerant view of other faiths or lifestyles. Before long, the art of twisting the biblical text becomes as sophisticated as advanced origami. In the end, if the Bible does not agree with their goals, so much the worse for the Bible! They have learned to dismiss it whenever it challenges them, and it has slowly become a closed book to their hard hearts.

Ultimately, the Spirit of God is the only remedy for immaturity, insensitivity, and rebellion. But the Spirit is pleased to use his Word to cure souls. For this reason, the church still needs skillful, hardworking teachers of the Word—such as some of you (Eph. 4:11; 1 Tim. 5:17). But before you can teach others, you need to be teachable yourself.

Why This Book? A Plan of Action

This book is far from the first to present a method of Bible study. What sets it apart from the rest? First, it is a primer in Bible interpretation. It is written for those who are ready to move from casual and devotional reading of Scripture to a more theological and exegetical reading.[13] There is nothing wrong with reading the Bible devotionally, but the kingdom needs some leaders who have acquired higher skills. This book is a first-level guide for those who want to get serious about exegesis.

Second, as a primer, this book uses an easily remembered plan for interpretation. Many books scatter the basic principles for interpretation through many chapters, arranged according to the "genres" of Scripture, such as law, poetry, prophecy, and letters.[14] This book presents the steps of interpretation in the order in which you will actually use them. It summarizes the main principles for interpretation in a single word, the acronym CAPTOR:

C = Context
A = Analysis
P = Problems
T = Themes
O = Obligations
R = Reflection

There are two aspects of *context* (chaps. 3 and 4). The historical context is the culture and circumstances in which a book or passage was written. The literary context of a passage is the text before and after it. In *analysis* we study the flow of events in a story or the flow of ideas in a teaching (chaps. 5 and 6). Our *problems* are the words, customs, phrases, or names that we may not understand in the text (chap. 7). *Themes* are the major ideas of a passage—which may run through the whole Bible (chap. 8). *Obligations* are the things our passage requires us to do (chaps. 9 and 10). In *reflections* we attempt to discover the main point and application of our passage (chaps. 11 and 12). Reflection includes a consideration of how our passage presents Jesus and his redemption. Using these six concepts, anyone who is willing to read carefully, think hard, and discipline himself to follow a method can interpret the Bible with substantial accuracy, even if he has limited formal education.

Third, this book is distinct in its emphasis on application. Far too many books assume that application takes care of itself if we just listen to the promptings of the Holy Spirit and speak honestly to the troubles we see in ourselves and others. Unfortunately, it is not that simple. Consistently strong application requires both heart and mind (method).

Fourth, this book has exercises. No one can gain or master skills in exegesis without practice. If you treat a work on interpretation like any other book, it will profit you little. Exegesis is a skill, an art, and we only acquire skills through practice. If we want to learn to fix plumbing, to cook, or to play golf, books help, but genuine progress begins when we have equipment in our hands and a project before us. Remember how you learned to ride a bicycle: not through your father's instructions, but by climbing on and falling off again and again until you mastered it. How do we learn to cook omelets? By overheating the pan and scorching the eggs once, by adding too many fillings the next time, and so forth, until we know how to get it right, at least for our tastes. Perhaps you like recipe books, but reading cannot compare to cooking and eating. The same is true of biblical interpretation. For this reason, I urge you to do the exercises at the end of each chapter in order to realize lasting profit.

Conclusion

This chapter and the next one are about the conditions that foster good biblical interpretation. First, one must believe in, or at least be open to, the God of the Bible. One must also believe that he has revealed himself to humanity in the Bible. Second, one must desire a direct engagement with the Word and with the Lord who gives it. You must long to be able to evaluate sermons and books and to produce worthwhile studies on your own. That aspiration will motivate you to read and practice the principles in this book. I hope you are reading with a desire to know the living Lord and his truth better, and to share your knowledge with many whose lives you touch. I pray that in some small way this work will help you become a worker who handles the Word of Truth well, and that you will find treasures both new and old to share with God's people.

Notes

[1] The sermon is fictitious, but it is based on reports from Bill Myers, a missionary to Togo, Bishop Francis Ntiruka and Rev. Angolwisye Malumbugi, both of Tanzania, and African missiologist Adrian Hastings. None of them advocated this view.

[2] The Jerusalem Talmud, cited by James B. Hurley, *Man and Woman in Biblical Perspective* (Grand Rapids: Zondervan, 1981), 72.

[3] Many works on interpretation seem to assume that the goal of interpretation is application, but relatively few state it. See Gerhard Maier, *Biblical Hermeneutics,* trans. Robert Yarbrough (Grand Rapids: Baker, 1994), 57–58, 62; Bernard Ramm, *Protestant Biblical Interpretation,* 1st ed. (Boston: W. A. Wilder, 1950), 88ff.; Jay Adams, *Truth Applied: Application in Preaching* (Grand Rapids: Zondervan, 1990), passim; Bryan Chapell, *Christ-Centered Preaching: Redeeming the Expository Sermon* (Grand Rapids: Baker, 1994), 199–204. In secular hermeneutics, Hans-Georg Gadamer took a similar stance in *Truth and Method,* trans. Garrett Barden and John Cumming, 2d ed. (New York: Seabury Press, 1965), 289–99. Calvin constantly implies the centrality of application without precisely asserting it. See chap. 9, note 17.

[4] Of course, it is possible to understand what the Bible says and disagree with it, but we are speaking of taking biblical teaching to heart, not simply comprehending it abstractly.

[5] George Lindbeck, "Scripture, Consensus and Community," *This World* 23 (Fall 1988): 19–24. For an extended discussion of the role of the heart in theological work, see John Frame, *The Doctrine of the Knowledge of God* (Phillipsburg, N.J.: Presbyterian and Reformed, 1987), 319–28.

[6] For a survey of views on this issue, see Maier, *Biblical Hermeneutics*, 47–63.

[7] For a sympathetic description of exegesis that does not flow from religious commitment or special respect for the authority of Scripture, see James Barr, *Holy Scripture: Canon, Authority and Criticism* (Philadelphia: Westminster Press, 1983), 110–16, and James Barr, *The Bible in the Modern World* (New York: Harper & Row, 1973), 5–12, 23–34.

[8] Gadamer, *Truth and Method*, 236–74.

[9] See John Calvin, *Institutes of the Christian Religion*, ed. John T. McNeill (Philadelphia: Westminster Press, 1960), 1.7.4–5; Maier, *Biblical Hermeneutics*, 53–55.

[10] D. A. Carson, "Hermeneutics: A Brief Assessment of Some Recent Trends," *Themelios* 5 (January 1980): 20.

[11] Calvin briefly addresses this question in his *Institutes*, 1.7.4–5; 1.8.1, 11–13, and assumes the central importance of an affirmative answer to this question in his description of the Christian life as self-denial, in the *Institutes*, 3.6–8.

[12] William Carver, *The Course of Christian Missions: A History and an Interpretation*, rev. ed. (Westwood, N.J.: Revell, 1969), 83–85; Kenneth Latourette, *A History of the Expansion of Christianity*, vol. 2: *The Thousand Years of Uncertainty: A.D. 500–A.D. 1500* (New York: Harper and Brothers, 1938), 400.

[13] For a short analysis of the different ways to read the Bible, see Richard Longenecker, "On Reading the Bible Devotionally, Homiletically, and Exegetically," *Themelios* 20 (October 1994): 4–8.

[14] Of course, there is nothing intrinsically wrong with explaining interpretation genre by genre; appendix D does that very thing. Nonetheless, beginners need a method that will work for every genre before they learn the special steps necessary for more advanced work.

2

Observing What Is There

Now Watch This!

Perhaps you have heard the story about the science professor and his eager band of freshmen. Holding up a beaker filled with a yellowish liquid, the professor began his first class: "The essence of the scientific method, from electron microscopes to the Hubbell telescope, is observation. Whatever tools we devise, the human senses remain the conduit for all information. Furthermore, even the unaided human senses have enormous power. For example, we have a vial of horse sweat before us; let us see what we can learn from it. Please do as I do." He then dipped his index finger into the beaker and licked his finger. Dismayed, but under the spell of authority, the students dutifully dipped their index fingers into the vile beaker and licked them. "What have you learned from this?" the professor asked, surveying their startled faces. "You have already discovered the importance of observation! You see," he said, holding up his fingers, "I licked my *ring* finger."

The fundamental skill for biblical interpretation, as in much of life, is observation. All other skills depend upon it. As in life, we miss a great deal of the Bible because we examine it hastily and carelessly. We glance at a tree in October, resplendent in yellow, orange, purple, and dark green, and say, "Oh, how pretty!" Then we turn away without really having seen it. We miss the message of the Bible in the same way. We read in haste, perhaps thinking, *I know what this passage says and means.* Not *expecting* to see anything that will grip us, we glance at texts and notice only what we already know or what someone once told us we ought to see. So the beauty and subtlety of the Bible go unrecognized.[1]

Children can instruct adults in this regard. They see the world as it is, not as someone has told them it should be. I took my oldest daughter for a walk in the snow late one winter afternoon when she was three and a half years old. The shadows lay long on the ground as sunset approached. "What color is the snow, Abigail?" I asked. An adult would answer, "White." But my little girl looked at the snow in the shadows and failing light, and then slowly and deliberately said, "Blue. The snow is blue." I replied, "Is that all? Is the snow any other color?" She looked again and answered observantly, "It's gray; the snow is gray—and a little bit purple, too."

In the same way, we need to learn to describe what we actually see when we read the Bible, not simply what someone once told us to see.

> ▶ **Principle 1: Beware of preconceptions. Observe what biblical texts actually say.**

For example, observe the account of John the Baptist's questions about Jesus' identity as the Messiah. Jesus is already enduring opposition from Jewish leaders when John's disciples approach him.

> After Jesus had finished instructing his twelve disciples, he went on from there to teach and preach in the towns of Galilee. When John heard in prison what Christ was doing, he sent his disciples to ask him, "Are you the one who was to come, or should we expect someone else?" Jesus replied, "Go back and report to John what you hear and see: The blind receive sight, the lame walk, those who have leprosy are cured, the deaf hear, the dead are raised, and the good news is preached to the poor. Blessed is the man who does not fall away on account of me." (Matt. 11:1–6)

Since John was the first one to testify that Jesus was indeed the "one to come," people are often puzzled by John's question. How could the prophet who prepared the way for the Lord, who introduced Jesus as the Lamb of God who takes away the sin of the world, now have doubts? He baptized Jesus, confessed Jesus' sinlessness, saw the heavens open, watched the Spirit descend on him like a dove, and heard the Father say, "You are my Son, whom I love; with you I am well pleased" (Luke 3:22). Now he is not even sure that Jesus is the Christ!

In the early church and the Reformation era, many commentators denied that John asked a genuine question, reasoning that the prophet could not falter so badly. They suggested, instead, that John actually inquired for the benefit of his disciples. He wanted *them* to hear Jesus' answer, but he had no doubts himself.[2] Our first principle cautions us against dismissing John's question on the basis of a traditional interpretation. We observe that the text depicts John as asking a question, something we ought not to overlook. But what should we think of the traditional interpretation? Our second guiding principle helps us answer that question.

> ◆ **Principle 2: Observe the text first, then explain it. As explanation proceeds, be sure it fits your observations.**

Was John's question genuine or not? We observe, first, that Jesus took the question seriously, at face value (11:4). When Jesus answers, he does not merely inform John's disciples, but instructs them to take his answer back to John. Second, the text never hints that John was insincere, and we must expect Matthew to give his readers some indication if John lacked genuine doubts.

Someone might object, "It makes little difference to us whether John truly doubted or not. The passage teaches us the same thing either way: Jesus is the Christ, as proven by his fulfillment of Messianic prophecies." This remark is half true as theology; the Christology of the passage is the same either way. But it is all wrong as an approach to the Bible. If John truly wavered, the text implies that almost anyone can have doubts. Notice also Jesus' response to John's messengers. Although John should have known better, Jesus honored the question by answering it and then praising John for his fearless and strategic service. These points can help doubters put their troubles in perspective, but we miss them if we see the episode as a charade performed only for the benefit of John's disciples.

The Role of Theology

Our brief look at John's questions reminds us not to let theological preferences unduly influence the way we read the Bible. We must admit that John had doubts, even if that makes him look bad. If his doubts show that the most courageous leader can falter, then so be it. Further, we must incorporate this lesson into our theology of faith and leadership, even if we find it uncomfortable at first. By the same token, we dare not say that John did doubt just because we like the theology of doubt it entails.

> ▶ **Principle 3: Resist reshaping your observations so that they support your preferred theology.**

If we "know" what a passage *must* say, and allow that to overrule our observations, how can we learn what it *does* say? If we are too committed to a certain theology, it becomes impossible to correct any flaws in the system. It becomes harder and harder to learn anything new. Eventually, if we refuse to let the Bible speak for itself, our theological system can become a tradition whose authority supersedes that of the Bible itself.

Of course, we must listen to theologians of the past. To act as if we were the first insightful or unbiased readers of Scripture would be sheer arrogance. Even if past teachers erred or perceived only part of the truth, they had enormous wisdom and, at a minimum, interesting reasons for views we may reject. Unfortunately, by the time the wisdom of past teachers reaches the average Christian, it has often been tamed, systematized, and simplified. It may seem stale if it addresses the hot topics of a distant generation. Therefore, although we respect past scholars, nothing can substitute for fresh interpretation of the Bible by each Christian in each generation. Each generation must observe the text of God's Word, learning to hear all that it says to the questions of the day.

The Importance of Details

But how does one observe a text? Basically, the rest of this book answers that question. Here we will focus on observing the details and subtle points of a text.

Observation begins with our motivations for paying attention. When two young people date, for example, they observe everything about each other if they believe their relationship may have a future. A woman, so my wife says, notices a man's clothes, shoes, hair, manners, fragrance, hands, and even his fingernails (clean or dirty, smooth or rough?). What story do the details tell? Both genders listen carefully for comments that reveal warmth, humor, and romantic interest.

We should begin our study of a passage of Scripture with no less interest in the details. That means reading it as if for the first time—slowly, attending to the exact terms, phrasing, and details. Read it with pen and paper (or computer) at hand, jotting down everything noteworthy or mysterious.

> ▶ **Principle 4: Make note of any details that are for any reason especially striking.**

Attend to all unexpected details. Notice details that appear to be unimportant at first. Remember anything that reveals the motives and feelings of people. Observe figures of speech and unusual words or grammatical forms, such as pronouns and verb tenses. Take the time to consider the importance of details.

Details That Count: Umbrellas and Hair

A playwright once said that if a character lays a gun on the table in the first act, someone had better use it before the end of the last act. For example, the fictional hero Indiana Jones has a slightly eccentric father who carries an umbrella with a flourish in the early scenes of the film *Indiana Jones and the Last Crusade*. Why is the umbrella in the movie? Merely because umbrellas and canes signify oddity? We find out when Indiana and his father walk on a beach, thinking themselves safe from the evil men who pursue them. Suddenly a fighter plane zeroes in on Indiana and his father, ready to gun them down as they stand defenseless on the open sand. But instead of running away when he sees the plane coming, Indiana's father walks straight toward a nearby flock of sea gulls, rapidly opening and closing his umbrella. Frightened, the fowl take off, fly into the path of the plane, and foul its engines so that it crashes. Now we know why the dramatist had the father carry the umbrella.

Likewise, biblical details often come into play some time after we first see them.[3] Of course, the Bible is more sparing with details than modern drama, which uses many details simply to flesh out a story. The Bible records fewer details, but they usually make a difference before the story ends.[4] Take hair as an example. The Bible rarely describes the hair of its characters, so it is easy to recall the few occasions when it does describe someone's hair: Esau was a hairy man; Samson had long hair, then no hair; Absalom had long, thick hair; Elisha was bald. In Daniel we read of the unsinged hair of Shadrach, Meshach, and Abednego, and of Nebuchadnezzar's long hair (Dan. 3 and 4). In Luke we meet a woman who washed Jesus' feet with her hair.

None of these details about hair lacks significance, but in a few cases hair plays a crucial role. The beauty of Absalom's hair is essential to his story. It contributes to his superiority complex, and possibly to his rebellion against his father, David. Then, when his forces fight with David's, it contributes to his downfall. Fleeing on his mule after his army loses its pivotal battle, his flying hair becomes entangled in the branches of a tree, and he hangs there, unable to free himself. Eventually David's men find him, and Joab, David's general, kills him. Samson's rebellion turns on his long hair, too. When he lets Delilah cut it off, he is rejecting God, his vows, and his role as a judge. Later, the return of his hair is part of his repentance and vindication.

Sometimes, details about hair simply fill out a scene. For example, because Esau was a hairy man, his brother Jacob had to cover his own skin when he went to steal the blessing of his blind father, lest Isaac touch and discover him. That little deception adds to the picture of Jacob as a calculating liar. The hair rounds out Isaac's sin, too. Isaac began by neglecting God's decree that Jacob should lead. He ended up with all five senses failing him as he tried to make spiritual decisions by natural means: blind eyes, ears failing to distinguish voices, nose smelling Esau's clothes, fingers feeling for hairiness, and the final decision made on the basis of taste.[5]

Details That Are Everything: Bethel and Baldness

Occasionally, we can make sense of a biblical narrative only through the details. Such an episode marked the beginning of Elisha's prophetic career. Shortly after Elijah went up to heaven, leaving his mantle behind, Elisha performed a miracle, "healing" the water of Jericho. Next we read,

> From there Elisha went up to Bethel. As he was walking along the road, some youths came out of the town and jeered at him. "Go on up, you baldhead!" they said. "Go on up, you baldhead!" He turned around, looked at them and called down a curse on them in the name of the LORD. Then two bears came out of the woods and mauled forty-two of the youths. And he went on to Mount Carmel and from there returned to Samaria. (2 Kings 2:23–25)

How can the details help us comprehend an unsettling passage that seems, at first glance, to show a peevish prophet using his powers to inflict a disproportionate punishment on rude youths? First, we notice the setting. Elisha was walking along the road leading to Bethel. Bethel was one of the two cities where Jeroboam I, the first king of the northern kingdom, set up centers of worship to prevent his people from worshiping at Jerusalem. The people supposedly worshiped the Lord but did so at altars of golden calves under the supervision of illegal priests. The city quickly descended into idolatry and paganism. Moreover, after several generations, the priests of Bethel viewed the temple there as "the king's sanctuary and the temple of the kingdom" (Amos 7:13). The king expected pleasant messages and paid the priests to make it so (1 Kings 22; Amos 7:10–17). The prophetic messages of Elijah, however, had been a thorn in the side of the northern kings. They viewed him as their enemy (1 Kings 18:17) and everyone viewed Elisha as his successor (2 Kings 2:15, 19). So, when we read that youths from Bethel mocked Elisha, we doubt that they were merely poking fun at a bald man.

Second, we need to investigate the boys' taunt, "Go on up, you *baldhead.*" Elisha was a younger man at this time, and, judging by surviving representations from the ancient Near East, baldness was rare among young men. Furthermore, because travelers ordinarily covered their heads, the boys could not have seen that Elisha was bald. The youths knew (or thought they knew) he was bald for other reasons. Perhaps they recognized Elisha and knew he was in fact bald. His clothing may also have marked him as a prophet.[6] The prophets of many ancient Eastern religions shaved their heads, as some monks do today.[7] The religion at Bethel was eclectic, and since the boys grew up around prophets, they had probably seen many who were bald-headed. So, whether Elisha actually was bald or not, the youths taunted him and the God he represented.[8]

Third, the wording of the taunt indicates that the lads taunted Elisha for his role as God's prophet. They said "Go on up," not "Go out" or "Go away." Assuming they recognized Elisha, the taunt "Go on up!" urged him to imitate the recent "going up" of Elijah. Thus, the details of the story explain why the prophet called down judgment on the gang. Elisha was not a mean-spirited prophet unleashing his power against teasing children. Rather, idolaters from a rebellious city mocked the Lord's prophet, and the Lord sent judgment on them and their families.

Details That Enrich: Verb Tenses, Pronoun Choices, and Cultural Details

Rarely will details play such a vital role as they do in the Elisha story. More often they enrich our appreciation of a text that we already comprehend. For example, consider the familiar parable of the prodigal son (Luke 15). How miserable is the prodigal before he returns to his father? Every detail answers the question. He has taken one of the lowest occupations in Jewish eyes, herding. Worse yet, he cares for pigs—unclean animals. Yet his agony becomes clearest when we notice the verb tenses in verse 16: "He kept longing to fill his stomach with the pods that the pigs were eating, but no one was giving him anything."[9] He keeps longing to eat the pig's food, but, the verb tense intimates, he can never quite bring himself to it. There he is, torn between terrible hunger and the desire to preserve a hint of dignity.

When the prodigal returns home, several cultural details fill out the father's welcome (15:22). For example, he orders someone to put sandals on his feet because slaves often went barefoot in Jesus' day, but sons wore sandals. This act, along with the giving of the robe and the ring, shows that the father disregards the son's request to be a hired man and reinstates him as a son.

Finally, the pronouns and other words in the exchange between the father and the older son deepen our understanding of the second, climactic phase of the parable. Notice the derisive pronouns in the older son's protests of the father's welcome of the prodigal: "When *this son of yours* who has squandered your property with prostitutes comes home, *you* kill the fattened calf for him!" (v. 30). The father replies, "My son, you are always with me, and everything I have is yours. But *we* had to celebrate and be glad" (v. 31). "My son" is warm and engaging, next to the cold, angry son. Then, by saying "*We* had to celebrate," rather than "*I* had to celebrate," the father gently invites his son to join the party.

Pronouns also help to interpret the encounter between Samuel and Saul in 1 Samuel 15. After Saul defeats the Amalekites at Samuel's command, does he honestly report that he spared only the best of the Amalekite herds in order to offer them as sacrifices? Notice three pronouns from Saul's self-defense in verse 15: "The soldiers brought them from the Amalekites; they spared the best of the sheep and cattle to sacrifice to the LORD your God, but we totally destroyed the rest." First, Saul attempts to pin the blame on his soldiers—"*They* spared"—even though the decision was his (see v. 9). Second, he tries to claim the credit for what was done correctly: "*We* totally destroyed the rest." Finally, Saul betrays his own faithlessness when he says he intends to sacrifice to "the LORD *your* God," rather than "my God" or "our God."[10]

Incidentally, I learned to pay close attention to pronouns when I was a pastor. I knew visitors had made a decision to join our church, at least informally, when they stopped saying "your church" and began to say "our church." And, in family counseling, I shuddered if children were "yours" rather than "ours."

Do All Details Matter?

Details also illumine 2 Samuel 9, a chapter describing the relationship between David and Mephibosheth, the son of David's friend Jonathan. This episode shows that the weight of details varies. We can distinguish details that one might call essentials, accidentals, and teasers. A detail is *essential* if the story could hardly stand without it. *Accidental* details have little or no role in a text. *Teasers* might or might not be important. Please read 2 Samuel 9 before you go on and jot down details that seem essential or accidental.

Mephibosheth's lineage is an essential detail. Unless we know that Mephibosheth is Jonathan's son and Saul's grandson, the story has scant impact. David took an interest in the man precisely because of his ancestry. His kindness is striking because Mephibosheth, as a potential heir to Saul's throne, could have been used against David by one of his rivals. David's kindness also shows his faithfulness to a promise he had made long before to Jonathan, Mephibosheth's father. He swore he would show kindness to Jonathan's sons, even if it was inconvenient (1 Sam. 20), and now he is doing it. The servant Ziba is also essential because his service constitutes part of the honor given to Mephibosheth.

Lo Debar is an accidental detail. Mephibosheth's location at Lo Debar does not advance the story. Lo Debar had no special role in Saul's day, and no symbolic importance. The reference to it states a fact, but it bears no special meaning.

Ziba's sons and Mephibosheth's lameness are teasers. These are "guns on the table," apparently pointless, yet intriguing, perhaps for that very reason. If Ziba had fifteen sons and twenty servants (verse 10), he was a prominent man. If David made this prominent man the personal servant of Mephibosheth, then David was setting Mephibosheth up for life. So the magnitude of David's generosity increases. Second, Mephibosheth was lame in both feet. Crippled people could do little in those days. Prosthetics were unknown; "desk jobs" were rare. Since a cripple was such a burden, David's generosity grows again. Taken together, the details lift David's act from the realm of routine kindness into that of self-sacrifice, loyalty, and righteousness. In some ways it says more about him than his military conquests do.

Some readers may be uneasy with the suggestion that we categorize details as essential and accidental, as significant and insignificant. Indeed, there is good reason for this discomfort. For the process of observation to be most fruitful, we need to stop discussing the method of observation and start talking about the attitude of the observer, which is the subject of the next section.

Observations and Observers

As we saw in chapter 1, interpreters need to approach the biblical text with faith and humility. That faith may recede as we begin to view the text as a mere artifact, an object to be scrutinized with a detached, critical eye. Faith can fade as we acquire ever-longer lists of things to analyze. Such lists are an indispensable part of theological education. Just as trained public speakers cannot help but notice phrasing, gestures, vocal inflection, cadence, and structure in every talk they hear, so trained interpreters cannot help but notice certain things in a text. The greater the training, the harder it is to return to a simple, devotional reading of the Word. The fully trained person has lost his or her naïveté.

For the sake of the household of the faith, some trained interpreters—scholars, pastors, and even lay theologians—have to give up the pleasures of passive devotional listening. These interpreters must acquire analytical skills; effective teaching comes no other way. The church needs experts, people who have acquired the knowledge and methods to understand the Bible more deeply. Such leaders teach the church, reapplying the historic truths of the faith to the issues of the day. They detect and resist the encroachment of the spirit of their age into the thought and life of the church. But the price of their service is the loss of innocence, the end of casual reading.[11]

We gain nothing by denying this difficulty. But we need to be on guard against coldness or arrogance. While sophisticated analytical methods can deepen our faith as they deepen our understanding, the danger is that they may also squeeze out piety. With the growth of analytical skills, some interpreters cease to stand under the text's authority and begin to stand over it as critical analysts.

Humility teaches us to admit the limits of our perception. We always miss a great deal of a text's message because our ability to observe is limited by our culture and our tradition.

Our *culture*, first, implicitly directs our attention toward some aspects of a text and away from others. We easily miss the most common things, the points on which everyone agrees.[12] But it is difficult to observe things that are "always before our eyes." As we saw in the last chapter, we assume that women can be educated, so we hardly notice it when the Gospels show Jesus talking to women. But a first-century reader would have been astonished to hear Jesus tell Martha that Mary had chosen the better course by leaving the kitchen to sit at his feet (Luke 10:38–42). Similarly, when a woman cries out to Jesus, "Blessed is the mother who gave you birth and nursed you" (11:27), her statement reflects the notion that women found greatness or blessedness in marrying a great husband or having a great son. She complimented Jesus by praising his mother. But

Jesus replies that women can have blessedness in their own right, saying, "Blessed rather are those who hear the word of God and obey it" (v. 28). Again, most Westerners never notice the radicalism of this interchange, since it has become the common perspective. The most important things can be hidden because they are so simple and familiar.[13]

Our *traditions* also limit our perceptions. By *tradition* I mean the presuppositions or foundational beliefs we use to categorize and analyze ideas. Theological traditions do this, as does a broader Western mentality that includes ideas about human nature, property, the good life, what counts as evidence, and so on. The human mind cannot operate in the abstract, without traditions or presuppositions. Thus, we bring certain commitments and preconceptions to every text we read.

These commitments lead us to make judgments about texts before all the elements that determine the case have been given. They limit our ability to listen to a text. They lead us to make preliminary predictions or projections about what the text is saying. These prejudgments can be true or false. They ultimately cause no harm *if we remain willing to revise them,* so that the text can still catch us and astonish us. Traditions are not the enemies of the mind. They are part of us and we think within them. But we must be aware of our biases and test them for truthfulness; we must beware of the tyranny of hidden presuppositions.[14]

Traditions can serve us well or poorly. Positively, they are mental anchors that keep us from being driven here and there by the gust of each new idea. They give us mental tools, including a terminology that allows us to notice, label, and remember things. Negatively, traditions are dangerous if (1) we immediately reject anything that appears to be contrary to them, (2) we quickly reinterpret new ideas to make them fit our tradition, or (3) we are so immersed in our traditions that we cannot see them. We cannot shed our culture and tradition like an old coat, nor should Christians even attempt to do so. But we should filter them, "distinguishing the true prejudices, by which we understand, from the false ones, by which we misunderstand."[15]

Traditions and cultures are like microscopes. A microscope is very effective for viewing small things nearby, but to look through a microscope is to cut off, at least momentarily, every other way of seeing things. A striking instance of this appears in an account written by a seventeenth-century American woman of her capture by the Pequot Indians. Describing her meeting with Philip, the Indian chief who was leading devastating attacks against the English colonies, she reports nothing of strategic interest for the war, such as the strength of his forces or the location of his camp, and almost nothing that would interest an anthropologist or historian today, such as his beliefs, his ecology, or the social structure of his tribe. Instead, her report dwells almost exclusively on the chief's invitation to join him in smoking tobacco, a habit she once shared, then rejected, and heartily disapproved at the time. Why an outburst on the evils of tobacco? Because smoking was a moral issue that was hotly debated within her Puritan tradition. Her tradition taught her to see tobacco, but not ecological or military matters.[16]

We may shake our heads at the power of tradition to blind someone, but we too will be blinded unless we labor to expand our horizons. The goal of observation is to overcome our own blind spots as much as possible. Here are some suggestions:

1. Remember the distance between your culture and biblical cultures. There is both continuity and discontinuity between the two. Learn as much as you can about biblical times, so that you will neither naively read Western ways into the biblical world, nor lazily assume that "everything was different back then."

2. Try to understand biblical writers on their own terms. Enter their culture, their way of thinking, their tradition. Join the world of the Bible as best you can.

3. Look beyond your comfortable certainties—the things we repeat over and over—in order to expand your range of vision. The goal is not to abandon your tradition but to let it grow as it encounters new ideas, accepting some and developing a response to others.[17]

Conclusion

This chapter has continued to examine the conditions necessary for effective Bible study. The first condition, which we have not argued, but assumed on the basis of the biblical doctrine of inspiration, is a *belief* that the authors of Scripture were skilled, inspired men. All that they wrote is true, and it all "matters." Therefore, it deserves and rewards close study. The second condition is an *attitude* of diligence and attentiveness. The opposite attitudes, laziness and pride, undermine everything. Diligence means reading slowly, observing small details and precise choices of wording. The lazy man reads rapidly, thinking he already knows it all. The diligent stay with a text. Holding off preconceptions about what a passage "must" say, they let it speak for itself. Laziness and pride make the text fit preconceived notions of what it says.

Some Bible study guides urge Christians to read the Bible and ask, "What does this text say *to me?*" It might be better to ask, "What does this passage say *against me*—against my preconceptions and prejudices? What does it say, not strictly to me, but to everyone who diligently observes its every word?"

Exercises

Before you read the next chapter, observe the details in the following passages. Each has significant details; see if you can observe them, and then decide how they help you understand the text.

1. Read 1 Samuel 17:1–27. First, what do the details about Goliath's armor contribute to the passage? Second, notice the precise wording of David's questions in verse 26. What insight does it shed on later developments?

2. Read Luke 15:11–32. What do the details of the father's behavior in verses 20 and 22–24 contribute to the parable and to our concept of God? Look (beyond what we observed above) at the wording of the interchange between the father and the older son in verses 28–32. What does this contribute to your appreciation of the father?

3. Challenge exercise: Is there any clue in Genesis 4:1–7 as to why God accepted the sacrifice of Abel, but not that of Cain?

Notes

[1] Classes in the biblical languages prove this again and again. As students labor to get the sense of every word in a verse of Greek or Hebrew, they are forced to slow down and notice everything. They often remark, "This statement is amazing. Why do none of the translations express what we have seen?" Then we look up the way our English Bibles render the verse and find that they *do* express the newly dis-

covered nuance. The students have simply been reading the English so fast, so carelessly, that they have never noticed it.

[2] For a list of church fathers taking this view, see the *Ante-Nicene Fathers*, ed. Alexander Roberts and James Donaldson, 10 vols. (Grand Rapids: Eerdmans, 1985–87), 3:375, note 15.

[3] Strikingly, the umbrella simply disappears (it is not dropped, stolen, or otherwise lost) after it plays its role in the beach scene.

[4] Leland Ryken, *Words of Delight* (Grand Rapids: Baker, 1987), 75ff.; Robert Alter, *The Art of Biblical Narrative* (New York: Basic Books, 1981), 114–30, esp. 126; Meir Sternberg, *Poetics of Biblical Narrative: Ideological Literature and the Drama of Reading* (Bloomington: Indiana University Press, 1985), 331–37, passim. For an example of the use of detail to aid interpretation, see Bruce Waltke, "Cain and His Offering," *Westminster Theological Journal* 48 (Fall 1986): 363–72.

[5] Derek Kidner, *Genesis: An Introduction and Commentary* (Downers Grove, Ill.: InterVarsity Press, 1967), 156. Hair also plays a minor role in the stories in Daniel and Luke.

[6] Johannes Lindblom, *Prophecy in Ancient Israel* (Philadelphia: Muhlenberg Press, 1962), 66–67. For the same account of the facts, but a very different view of the story, see John Gray, *I and II Kings: A Commentary*, 2d ed. (Philadelphia: Westminster Press, 1964), 480.

[7] William L. Reed, "Baldness," in *The Interpreters Dictionary of the Bible*, ed. George Arthur Buttrick (Nashville: Abingdon, 1962) 1:343–44.

[8] The Old Testament forbids shaving the head, at least for priests (Lev. 21:5) and for mourners (Deut. 14:1), but not for prophets.

[9] My translation. All three verbs are in the imperfect tense in the Greek, the tense used for continued or attempted action in the past (among other things). The NASB and RSV, as usual, come closer to a literal translation. The NIV, as it often does, exchanges precision for readability.

[10] Robert Alter, *The World of Biblical Literature* (New York: Basic Books, 1992), 149–51.

[11] Donald Carson describes this danger, which he calls "distanciation," in *Exegetical Fallacies* (Grand Rapids: Baker, 1984), 19–22, 129–30, 136–37.

[12] Anthony Thistleton, *The Two Horizons: New Testament Hermeneutics and Philosophical Description* (Grand Rapids: Eerdmans, 1980), 305–6, 371–72; Ludwig Wittgenstein, *Philosophical Investigations*, trans. G. E. M. Anscombe (Oxford: Basil Blackwell, 1958), sec. 129, 109; Wittgenstein, *Remarks on the Foundations of Mathematics* (Oxford: Basil Blackwell, 1964), 1, sec. 141 (p. 43e).

[13] Ludwig Wittgenstein, *Philosophical Investigations*, sec. 129 (p. 50e), 66 (p. 31e); Wittgenstein, *Remarks on the Foundations of Mathematics*, 1, sec. 141 (p. 43e).

[14] Hans-Georg Gadamer, *Truth and Method*, trans. Garrett Barden and John Cumming, 2d ed. (New York: Seabury Press, 1965), 236–45.

[15] Ibid., 263–66.

[16] Jane Tompkins, "Indians: Textualism, Morality, and the Problem of History," *Critical Inquiry* 13 (1986): 111–13.

[17] Gadamer, *Truth and Method*, 272–73.

3

The Literary Context

What's in a Context?

Certain Christians opposed radio in its early days. They believed it was Satanic, and they found a text to prove their case: "Satan is the prince of the power of the air." This kind of abuse of the Bible evokes an easy laugh today. After all, every experienced Christian teacher knows the slogan, "A text without a context is a pretext." Yet we often make similar mistakes and take biblical statements out of context in subtler ways. Why? Practically, it takes time and effort to study the context of a passage.

While we know that context is important, we may not know how to study it effectively. Besides, "context" means different things to different people.

Two Types of Context

We must distinguish its two basic types, historical and literary contexts, as the following scene illustrates.

Imagine for a moment that you are walking through your church building in the middle of the week. Your feet make the only sound in the empty building, but as you turn a corner you begin to hear an animated conversation. Actually, it is only half of a discussion—

someone is on the phone. You catch a word or two, and then hear your name. Realizing that you are the topic of conversation, you move, almost against your will, toward the voice. As the conversation grows louder, you decide the speaker is a fellow choir member. You hear him say, "You don't know John the way I do. He can't be the one. It's contrary to his nature. He simply is not capable of it. It has to be someone else." The conversation begins to wind down and you tiptoe away, wondering, *Who was on the other end of the line? What were they talking about? What was the other person saying? What does my "friend" from the choir think of me?* Naturally, everything depends on the context of his remarks. But a little thought shows there were several contexts.

The comments of the other party to the conversation are central. Was he accusing you of starting a vicious rumor? If so, the choir member thinks highly of you and was defending you. But if the other party was proposing that you fill a leadership position, then your "friend" was belittling you. If the conversation were transcribed, the words before and after the speech you heard would be the *literary context* of the discussion. The literary context consists of the sentences and paragraphs before and after the text you are studying. (I use the phrase "literary context" because the Bible is a body of written work, or literature.)

But suppose the other half of the conversation is irretrievably lost. Even without the verbal or literary context, the social, moral, ecclesiastical, auditory, and visual contexts would help you decide whether the person you overheard supported you or not. Is your relationship with the choir member close or distant, warm or cool? Have you worked together successfully in the choir or not? Is that person prone to gossip or to defending others? Is he hushed and secretive or loud and free, unconcerned about who might hear? Finally, what is his posture? Is he hunched over the phone, eyes down or darting to and fro? Or does he stand erect, moving about freely and gesturing broadly?

All these factors put the conversation in context and let you draw certain conclusions. We will call such relational, moral, and ecclesiastical factors the *historical context*. In the Bible, historical contexts include such matters as the identity of the author and his readers, and the time, topic, and reasons for writing. We can also try to discover if the author and his audience had a history or if the audience had any extraordinary needs or challenges.

Definitions

Literary context is the words, sentences, paragraphs, or chapters that surround and relate to a text.[1] The study of literary context (1) describes how a paragraph or some other unit fits into a larger section of the text, even the whole work. It (2) gains access to literary context by reading the original document attentively. The study of literary context can go on, even if we know nothing about the writer and his times, and nothing about the original readers and their concerns. (3) To exaggerate slightly, literary context allows us to ignore the author and the audience and to study the words of the text by themselves.

Historical context is the culture, customs, languages, beliefs, and history of the author and his original audience. The study of historical context (1) describes how a portion of the Bible fits into its world. It (2) gains access to historical context through background study of the language, history, customs, and philosophy of the author and his audience. The student of historical context doubts that we can fully understand words on any page without some knowledge of the people who wrote and read them. (3) To exaggerate slightly, historical context allows readers to overcome the feeling that the text belongs to another time or culture and allows them to enter the world of the original speakers, writers, and readers.

How to Study Contexts

The methods for studying historical and literary contexts differ considerably, but both begin by finding the main themes and purposes of the book to be studied. If you plan to study or teach a series of lessons from one book of the Bible, your first step is to read your entire book to gain a view of the whole. What is the main theme? What are the main divisions? What issues come up repeatedly? Who is the author? What prompted him to write? Who is the intended audience? Are they believers or not, faithful or not, or Jewish, Gentile, or mixed? How much do they know? What are their needs and concerns?

You can answer many of these questions yourself by reading your book carefully, noting the author's statements of purpose. For example, Paul spends the first 16 verses of Romans leading up to his great theme, "The righteous will live by faith." New Testament writ-

ers often state their purpose at the beginning or the end of their letter or gospel. For example, John wrote his gospel to bring people to
faith and eternal life (John 20:31). He wrote his first letter to give genuine believers assurance of their faith and salvation (1 John 5:13).
Jude wrote to contend for the faith against false teachers (Jude 3).
Paul wrote Romans as he prepared to visit Rome on the way to
Spain. His letter is a gift, given to pave the way for a good reception
(Rom. 1:8–15; 15:23–24). Luke wrote to give his readers an orderly
and accurate account of the life of Christ, in order to strengthen
them in their faith (Luke 1:1–4).

If you cannot find a statement of purpose in a book, try to formulate one. For example, Paul wrote Galatians to refute false teachers who were perverting his gospel, and to reestablish the Galatians
in the gospel of grace and justification by faith alone. Old Testament
books rarely make explicit statements of purpose, but we can readily see that Genesis is about the beginnings of humanity and of the
covenant people, and that Exodus is about Israel's escape from Egypt
and the beginning of her national life. After you have examined the
book yourself, read an introduction that covers the same ground and
compare notes. If time is short, or if you are studying only one text
from a book rather than doing a series, you may want to go directly
to a reference work (see appendix E).

Literary and historical contexts overlap, influencing and inform-
ing each other. But after the initial survey of a book, the literary and
historical contexts part ways. The rest of this chapter will discuss literary context; the next chapter explains how to study historical context.

Literary Context

Think of literary context through two images, a ladder and a pond.
Picture the passage you are studying as a ladder, a ladder of ideas.
Just as we climb from the ground to a roof one step at a time, so biblical texts present their teachings one step at a time, in an orderly
way, as each idea leads to the next. Just as it would be absurd to try
to climb a ladder by leaping from the first to the seventh rung, then
down to the third and up to the eighth, so is it foolish to leap about
in the Bible, paying no attention to its "ladder" of ideas and events.

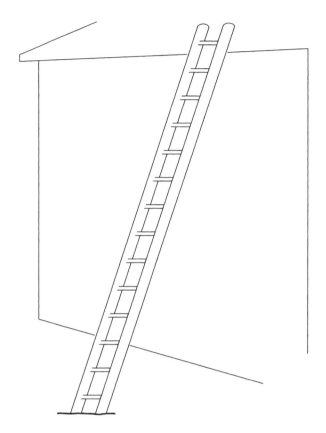

Your book is also like a pond. When someone throws a pebble into the pond, a series of rings surrounds the spot where the stone fell. The point of impact corresponds to the passage you are studying, and the radiating rings correspond to the rest of the book. The closer the circle is to the center (your text), the more it influences your passage.

To examine a literary context, therefore, you need to have provisional ideas about the book you are studying. With that loosely in hand, you can take the next steps.

▶ Principle 1: Interpret single verses in light of their immediate context.

For example, read Luke 17:5. Taken by itself, the apostles' request, "Increase our faith," seems commendable. But if we read Luke 17:1–10, we begin to have doubts. In verses 3–4, Jesus charges his disciples to forgive one another seven times in one day, if necessary. In this light, "Increase our faith" becomes ambiguous. They may be saying, "Give us more faith, so we can obey you," or they may mean, "We cannot obey you unless you give us more faith." Jesus' reply (vv. 6–10) shows that they are guilty of the second attitude. When Jesus says a mustard seed of faith can move mountains, he implies that they already have enough faith (v. 6). Next, Jesus tells a short parable about a servant doing his duty (vv. 7–10). The story implies that the act of forgiving one's brother is no extraordinary service—not a great act of faith, but simply a servant's duty (vv. 7–10).

Thus, the context demonstrates that the cry, "Increase our faith," far from being commendable, is rather an excuse for disobedience. The application shifts significantly once we understand the context. Although some texts encourage us to pray for faith, Luke 17:5 is not one of them. If anything, it warns us not to hide our disobedience behind pious words.

▶ Principle 2: Interpret paragraphs and episodes in light of the paragraphs or events around them.

Groups of paragraphs, even groups of chapters, can build on one another. For example, suppose you wish to study the topic of rewards and punishments. Matthew 19:28–30, which promises rewards and thrones to disciples, is on your list. What light can the context shed on the passage? The context begins with the story of the rich young ruler, who refused to sell his possessions and follow Jesus. Grieving, he left Jesus. Jesus then commented to his disciples, "It is easier for a camel to go through the eye of a needle than for a rich man to enter the kingdom of God" (v. 24). Peter replied, "We have left everything to follow you! What then will there be for us?"

(v. 27). Peter was saying that the disciples, unlike the ruler, had left everything to follow Jesus. Peter is thinking, "We have entered the kingdom, and the rich who refuse to do so will be punished—but what is our reward?"

Jesus answered Peter and described the disciples' generous rewards (19:28–29). But he also warned against a reward-hungry mentality. "Many who are first will be last, and many who are last will be first," he remarked cryptically (v. 30). What might this mean? Jesus explained himself in the next chapter, in the parable of the workers in the vineyard. In that parable, a landowner hires several groups of day laborers. He hires some for twelve hours, for a wage of one denarius. Others work nine hours, six hours, or one hour, with the master promising to pay each one what is right. At the end of the day, those who worked but one hour receive an entire denarius, and so those who toiled through the heat of the day begin to hope for more. But when they receive the same payment as the others, they begin to grumble. "Why do you complain?" the landowner asks. "Did I not pay you what we agreed? Why should you begrudge my generosity to others?" Jesus concludes by repeating, "So the last will be first, and the first will be last" (20:16). So Jesus warns Peter—and everyone else—that an undue interest in rewards can cause us to fix our eyes on that reward, take our heart away from the master, and so jeopardize the highest reward of all, joy in the Lord himself.

The context for Jesus' teachings on rewards shows, therefore, that while questions about rewards are natural (19:16–26), and God does reward his people (19:28–29), selfish interest in rewards can cause estrangement from God, who is our great reward. When the mother of James and John appears a little while later, asking for thrones for her sons (20:20–28), we see that the quest for rewards dies hard and has an ugly and ignorant side. By putting the teaching on rewards in this context, Matthew warns disciples not to seek rewards, but rather to follow Christ, seeking to serve, even at great cost (20:26–28).[2]

> ♦ **Principle 3: Try to determine why your text belongs precisely where it is, and nowhere else.**

When we ask why a passage is here, and nowhere else, we look into the effectiveness of its location. For example, Luke 15 begins,

"Now the tax collectors and 'sinners' were all gathering around to hear him [Jesus]. But the Pharisees and the teachers of the law muttered, 'This man welcomes sinners and eats with them.'" The Pharisees' grumbling prompted Jesus to tell three parables, each defending his habit of associating with sinners. If a shepherd has one hundred sheep and loses one, will he be content with ninety-nine? No, and just as a shepherd searches for even one lost sheep until he finds it, so Jesus searches for lost people until he finds them (15:3–7). Again, if a woman with ten coins loses one, is she content to have nine? No, and just as she searches for the lost coin until she finds it, so Jesus searches for lost people until he finds them (15:8–10). Finally, if a father has two sons and loses one (15:32), is he content to have one? No, and when the lost one returns, he runs to greet him, just as Jesus runs to greet lost Israelites who return to him. So the parable of the prodigal son is here to answer the Pharisees' complaint, and it stands at the end of the series because it is the climactic analogy.

Yet we can pursue the principle further. The three parables of lost things (a sheep, a coin, and a son) seem to be a winsome, reasonable, and complete defense of Jesus' association with sinners. Indeed, the second part of the final story (often ignored, as the ordinary name of the parable shows) appears to be superfluous. Why then is it here? Because Jesus does not just want to answer the Pharisees, but to engage them. So he creates a character, the older brother, who resembles them. Like the Pharisees, the older brother inflates his own righteousness, complains about the welcome given to a sinner, and is more distant from the Father than he realizes. As the older son must ultimately decide if he will welcome his sinning-but-restored brother and enter the party, so too the Pharisees must decide if they will welcome restored sinners and join the kingdom celebration. Jesus even leaves the final decision of the older brother in doubt, to keep the Pharisees involved by inviting them to finish the story for themselves.

It can sometimes be difficult to determine why a text has a particular location. For example, Proverbs has whole chapters where context means little. The same is true of certain prophetic oracles and some groups of Jesus' sayings. Historical narratives may be linked only by the sequence of events. But there is usually some link, and finding it greatly aids interpretation.

◆ **Principle 4: Look for thematic statements that introduce or interpret an entire section.**

Many passages open or close with a great truth that the rest of a section develops. A few examples follow; more appear in the exercises for this chapter.[3]

Genesis 1:1 says, "In the beginning God created the heavens and the earth." It introduces and summarizes the creation narratives of Genesis 1 and 2.

Judges 17:6 and 21:25 both say, "In those days Israel had no king; everyone did as he saw fit." They introduce and explain the terrible, lawless acts described in Judges 17–21.

1 Samuel 23:14 says, "Day after day Saul searched for him [David], but God did not give David into his hands." This summarizes most of 1 Samuel 20–27, recounting the time of David's flight from Saul.

In Matthew 5:20, Jesus tells his disciples, "Unless your righteousness surpasses that of the Pharisees and the teachers of the law, you will certainly not enter the kingdom of heaven." In Matthew 5:21 to 6:33, Jesus presents his standards for a righteousness that exceeds that of the scribes and the Pharisees.

In Galatians 1:11–12, Paul denies that the gospel he preaches was made or taught to him by man. Rather, he "received it by revelation from Jesus Christ." The rest of Galatians 1 and 2 describes what Paul was before he received the gospel and how the gospel changed him and his relations with the church.

James 1:26–27 says that true religion means keeping a tight reign on the tongue, looking after orphans and widows (the poor and helpless), and avoiding the pollution of the world. Chapters 2, 3, and 4 expand on each theme.

◆ **Principle 5: Look for repeated words or phrases.**

Repetition frequently indicates the theme for a section. Whole books sometimes repeat key words and phrases. For example, the word *holy* appears more in Leviticus than in any other book, and Leviticus is concerned with Israel's holiness. The books of Kings, always evaluating the faithfulness of Israel, compare southern kings to righteous "David, their father," and northern kings to wicked "Jeroboam, son of Nebat." Matthew, Mark, and Luke stress Jesus' reign and kingship by mentioning "the kingdom" about one hundred times. John stresses Jesus' identity by recounting many "I am" sayings. The terms for righteousness and justification appear frequently in Romans and Galatians. Careful readers of Philippians notice how often Paul uses the words "joy" and "rejoice," even though he remains imprisoned.

A section may also have its own refrain. As Genesis 1 and 2 recount God's creation of the world, we hear the refrain "And God saw that it was good" several times, until the creation of humanity, which is "very good." This shift hints that the creation of mankind is the climax of God's work. But then in 2:18, where God creates Adam before Eve, we read, "It is not good for the man to be alone." The phrase "not good" ought to leap from the page, prompting the reader to wonder how the creation now falls short and what may be coming next. The terms *kingdom* and *righteousness* appear over a dozen times in Matthew 5 and 6, and indeed the theme of the Sermon on the Mount is kingdom righteousness. Paul uses the term *wisdom* sixteen times in 1 Corinthians 1:17–3:19, in such phrases as "wisdom of God," "wisdom of men," and "wisdom of the world."[4] Thus, we decide to conduct our analysis of any smaller text within 1 Corinthians 1–3 within the context of Paul's broad discussion of wisdom.

Individual verses may also be linked by a repeated word or phrase. For example, James 1 opens with the statement, central to the whole book, "Consider it pure joy, my brothers, whenever you face trials of many kinds, because you know that the testing of your faith develops perseverance. Perseverance must finish its work so that you may be mature and complete, not lacking anything" (vv. 2–4). Verse 5 follows, "If any of you lacks wisdom, he should ask God, who gives generously." By repeating the term "lack," James suggests something like this: Trials develop mature believers, people who lack nothing. But to pass the trial, to become mature by it, you need (must not lack) one thing, wisdom. The next verses (6–8) begin to describe how one gains wisdom.

▶ **Principle 6: Locate your text in the purpose of its section and the whole book.**

Small biblical episodes may baffle us until we locate them in their larger unit. For example, we might wonder why 2 Samuel 9 tells the story of David's kindness to Mephibosheth (also discussed in the previous chapter). Is this really a significant part of David's rule, compared with all his military exploits and acts of faith? Yes it is, if we recognize that the whole of 2 Samuel 6–9 portrays David's reign at its apex. God dwells at the center of David's kingdom (chap. 6). The kingdom is God's gift and blessing, ruled ultimately by the Messiah (chap. 7), and its king enjoys victory over his enemies (chap. 8). The story of David's generous treatment of Mephibosheth then demonstrates the moral qualities of his kingdom. There is justice and mercy for the weak; the king is faithful to his word and his people. The story, sadly, also has links to the large section on David's decline (chaps. 11–20), for there we see that David rashly rescinds much of his favor to Mephibosheth (chaps. 16 and 19).

Context Illustrated

Context is so important for the interpretation and application of Scripture, that it is worthwhile to illustrate its principles at some length.

Suppose that a godly woman is married to an oafish fellow who never attends church. Mysteriously, he announces one Sunday morning that he will be attending services with the family. The pastor happens to be preaching on the family. This Sunday, after a month on the essence of marriage, he begins a series on the responsibilities of husbands and wives from Ephesians 5, taking wives first. After the service the husband rubs his hands together in glee. "Boy, am I glad I went to church today," he begins. "Did you hear what he said? 'Wives submit to your husbands.' I liked the way he explained it, too: 'as to the Lord.' You have to submit to me the way you submit to the Lord, and I know what that means—absolute obedience in everything! Sweetheart, I'm going to give you a chance to apply the sermon right away. There's a big football game coming on in about half an hour and I want to watch it all. I want my dinner on a tray by 12:45. Then close the door to the family room and keep the kids quiet. Get me a coke around the end of the first quarter, and when I call out 'Halftime!' I want everybody out of the bathroom."

The wife may well respond, however, that her hammer-headed husband has violated almost all of our principles (a fate he could have avoided had he read our book!). Eager to "claim" Ephesians 5:22, he has ignored verse 21, "Submit to one another out of reverence for Christ," and verses 25–29, "Husbands, love your wives . . . just as Christ does the church." So he violated principles 1 and 5: *Interpret single verses in light of their immediate context,* and *look for repeated words or phrases.*

His selfish use of Ephesians 5:22 also misses the broader context for the passage. All of Ephesians has an interest in Christian unity. Christ brings Jew and Gentile together by reconciling both to God through the Cross (2:11–22). The Lord has united all Christians by making them one body, by giving them one faith, one baptism, one Spirit (4:1–5). Diversity of gifts and roles leads to unity and maturity, not selfish advantage (4:11–16). This recalls principle 6: *Locate your text in the purpose of its section and the whole book.*

Unfortunately, most English translations obscure a crucial aspect of our context. The idea of mutual submission actually explicates 5:18, "Do not get drunk on wine, which leads to debauchery. Instead, be filled with the Spirit." "Be filled" is the central command, governing the entire section of 5:18–21. The verbs of verses 19–21, which the NIV renders "Speak to one another with psalms . . . sing and make music . . . always giving thanks to God . . . submit to one another," are all participles in the Greek. Grammatically, each verb depends on the main clause. The effect is that each one explains what Paul means by the command "Be filled with the Spirit." A slight rephrasing might go like this: "Be filled with the Holy Spirit, by speaking to one another in psalms . . . by singing and making melody in your hearts to the Lord, by giving thanks always . . . by submitting to one another in the fear of Christ, by wives' submitting to their husbands and by husbands' loving their wives." So, the statement "Wives, submit to your husbands" in 5:22, far from permitting husbands to lord it over their wives, actually describes the fullness of the Spirit, which comes in part through mutual submission.

If someone objects that these insight are hidden from those without knowledge of Greek, we must admit that mastery of Greek enriches one's Bible study. Nonetheless, one need not know Greek to see these points. First, the NASB translates these verses literally, so one can see all the points we made in the last paragraph. Further, by reading 5:21–6:9 as a unit, we readily notice that the whole section develops 5:21, "Submit to one another out of reverence for Christ." While the precise meaning of that statement is controverted, it certainly rules out all selfish uses of authority. This reminds us of principles 2 and 4: *Interpret paragraphs and episodes in light of the paragraphs or events around them,* and *look for thematic statements that introduce or interpret an entire section.*

Conclusion

This chapter describes the first in the series of skills summarized by the acronym CAPTOR: Context, Analysis, Problems, Themes, Obligations, and Reflections. The study of literary context illumines a text by examining the words, sentences, paragraphs, and chapters that surround and explain a text. First, it studies the verses immediately before and after the text. Then it casts a wider net, to see how the text is embedded in a larger discussion and to determine what contribution the text makes to it. The study of literary context is the first and perhaps the most important method of all. Literary context is distinguished from the historical context, which we will consider in chapter 4.

Exercises

This chapter's exercises give the opportunity to practice all six principles of examining the literary context.

1. Interpret single verses in light of their immediate context.
   a. James 2:23
   b. 1 Samuel 15:26, 31
   c. Challenge exercise: 1 Samuel 10:7

2. Interpret paragraphs or chapters in light of those around them.
   a. Interpret teachings on vengeance in Romans 12:17–21 in light of 13:1–5.
   b. Read 1 Samuel 24–26 as a unit describing lessons David learned when he had the upper hand, even as a refugee.

3. Try to determine why your text belongs precisely where it is.
   a. How does Genesis 6:1–8 form a bridge from Genesis 5 to the flood narrative?
   b. Why does Romans 4:1–8 follow Romans 3? How does it advance the teaching begun in chapter 3?

    c. Challenge exercise: How is Matthew 13:1–17 a response to 12:22–45?

4. Look for thematic statements that introduce or interpret an entire section.
    a. How does Romans 1:18 introduce 1:18–3:20 on human sin? Try to find another verse that summarizes the section.
    b. How does Romans 12:1–2 introduce the life of obedience described in Romans 12–15?
    c. How does Romans 14:23 interpret 14:1–23?
    d. How does Judges 2:10–19 introduce Judges 3–16?

5. Look for repeated words or phrases.
    a. Why is "King of kings and Lord of lords" repeated in Revelation 17:14 and 19:16?
    b. What repeated words can you find in Matthew 5 and 6? In Matthew 24:36–25:46? How do they explain their sections?

6. Locate your text in the purpose of its book and section.
    a. How does the promise to Abraham (Gen. 12:1–3) shape the rest of Genesis?
    b. How does the promise to David (2 Sam. 7:8–29) introduce the rest of Samuel and Kings?
    c. Challenge exercise: How does Hebrews 1:1–4 introduce the whole book, and how does 12:1 apply it?

Notes

[1] Linguists sometimes call this the "cotext." The cotext is "the sentences, paragraphs and chapters surrounding the text and related to it." See Peter Cotterell and Max Turner, *Linguistics and Biblical Interpretation* (Downers Grove, Ill.: InterVarsity Press, 1989), 16. By calling the words around a text the "cotext," one can restrict the meaning of "context" to the social and historical setting of a passage. Although this is more precise usage, the present chapter follows current usage.

[2] The unit just studied covers 19:16–20:28, illustrating that chapter divisions often split up unified discussions; see appendix B, on choosing a text.

[3] For more on the topic of the repetition of a phrase at the beginning and end of a passage, see the discussion of inclusion in appendix B, on choosing a text.

[4] The prevalence of the word *wisdom* in this passage is the more striking if we realize that Paul uses the term sixteen times here, but only eleven more times in the rest of his writings.

4

The Historical Context

Getting the Big Picture

My best friend from seminary days now teaches at a seminary near San Diego. After he and his family had spent their first year there, he called me on the phone and began to extol the virtues of southern California. "The beach is less than an hour to the west; the mountains are two hours to the east. It's so dry you never feel hot in the summer, and in the winter it rarely goes below 50 degrees at night. You can eat outside. You can play tennis or softball all year long."

I knew all that; why was he reminding me? Besides, although we call each other a couple of times a year, we always have some occasion, some business, that provides a pretext. His boasting was out of character, too. Then he changed gears: "Well, Dan, let me tell you what I am calling about. There's an opening here in the New Testament department and . . ."

Ah, now it all made sense! My friend's words had been clear enough, but I understood him only when he told me why he was calling. That put his words "in context." Just as the knowledge of a friend's situation, goals, and motives clarifies a conversation, so the knowledge of biblical contexts enhances our understanding of Scripture.

One major goal of Bible study is to discern the goals of the authors and determine the needs of the first readers. If we can do that, we go from peeking in windows of the Bible to touring its spacious rooms. When we study historical contexts, we discover the Bible's historical character. It sprang from the heart of an author and touched the souls of listeners—whether frightened or confident, stubborn or eager—who lived long ago.

The study of historical context (this chapter) and literary context (the previous chapter) have important things in common. Both let today's reader touch the mind of the author and the original audience of the Bible. Both begin by reading the entire book to be studied, searching for its purposes and themes. Yet, after this first step, their methods go in different directions.

Contrasting Methods of Studying Literary and Historical Contexts

Literary context	Historical context
• Studies the written text	• Studies the people and culture receiving a text
• Can ignore identity of author and audience	• Stresses identity of author and audience
• Can study words in themselves	• Stresses author's intent as he uses words
• Considers what any competent reader hears	• Considers what the original audience heard
• Is accessible to any attentive reader	• Is accessible to readers who know background
• Rewards intensive study of one text	• Rewards cumulative study of many texts

When we study historical contexts, we try to capture the big picture, the entire scene in and around a book. Who is the author and why is he writing? What is the need of the hour and what does he hope to accomplish by writing? Who is reading and why? How do the readers live and think day by day? A study of the historical context has three goals: (1) to retrieve, as best we can, the world of the Bible, (2) to discover the circumstances involved in the writing and the reading of particular books, and (3) to investigate the individuals and groups who play roles in the biblical drama.

The World of the Bible

The world of the Bible includes its politics, geography, agriculture, economics, social customs, methods of warfare, family structures, and gender roles. Just a little knowledge of daily life—how people ate and dressed, worked and slept—illumines hundreds of passages. Consider how an awareness of daily life clarifies these familiar gospel texts:

1. Why were the scribes and Pharisees upset to see Jesus eating with sinners (Luke 15:1–2; 19:1–7)? *Social custom* said that table fellowship signified intimacy, acceptance, and close friendship. *Religious custom* said that a holy man avoided all contact with ordinary, ignorant people, whom they disparagingly called "the people of the land," because such contact would defile him.[1] Their aversion was so strong that they even said, "Let a man not associate with the wicked, not even to bring him to the law."[2] As for food, the Mishnah says, "He that undertakes to be trustworthy [that is, a faithful tither] tithes 1) what he eats and 2) what he sells and 3) what he purchases, and 4) does not accept the hospitality of an Am-ha-aretz [people of the land]." A rabbi would not do that because he could not be sure that the host had tithed what he served.[3] Since the scribes and Pharisees took Jesus to be a rabbi, his willingness to dine with ignorant people seemed improper to them, and they opposed him.

2. In Jesus' parable about prayer in Luke 11:5–8, how could there be a "friend" who would refuse to rise and get some food for his neighbor who had unexpected midnight guests? Actually, the refusal was disgraceful, but it had a veneer of plausibility because Palestinian homes typically had but one room (*architecture*), in which the whole family worked, ate, and slept most of the year (in the summer they slept on the roof). Sometimes animals spent the night in the same room. To try to get bread at midnight, without lights (*technology*) and with children sprawled around him on mats (not raised beds) would have been like trying to cross a mine field.

3. Why did Jesus enter Jerusalem on a donkey instead of a horse (*animal husbandry*)? Horses were rare in Palestine, and were ordinarily used for war. By riding into the city on a donkey, Jesus indicated that he came in peace, not for military conflict.

4. Why did Jesus wash the disciples' feet at the Last Supper (John 13)? Palestinian roads were merely packed earth. A low servant cus-

tomarily washed everyone's feet before meals (*dining customs*). But Jesus and the Twelve had no servants, so one of them had to do it. Yet, since the disciples all wanted honorable positions in Jesus' kingdom (Matt. 20:20–28; Luke 22:24–30), none was willing. When Jesus arose and began to wash the disciples' feet, they were all stunned and ashamed—and ready to learn a lesson about service.

5. A little knowledge of Palestinian *clothing* explains or deepens several passages. Clothing was very expensive in biblical times because raw materials were scarce and their manufacture was labor intensive. A typical person owned less than ten garments in the New Testament era. So when Jesus said, "If someone wants to sue you and take your tunic, let him have your cloak as well" (Matt. 5:40), he required painful sacrifice; no one had five more jackets and ten sweaters in his closet. If you ever wondered why the soldiers at Jesus' crucifixion would want to gamble for the soiled garments of a convicted criminal, the cost of clothing is your answer. Executioners got the clothes of the dead as a kind of "perk," for even used garments were valuable.

All of these points would have been shared knowledge for the author and his original audience. Whenever we are ignorant of such basic customs, the Bible may baffle us. Knowledge of the historical context allows us to reenter the world of the Bible—its customs, language, and ways of thinking. Knowledge of that world even deepens our grasp of stories we think we know inside and out, such as Jesus' parable of the prodigal son (or "lost son").

Consider the younger son's request for his share of the inheritance. By asking for his inheritance while his father was still alive, he implies that he wishes his father were dead so he could have his inheritance. His spending spree wastes more than money—it squanders the family inheritance and future livelihood.[4] When the father ran to meet his returning son, threw his arms around him, and gave him a kiss, the audience might have snickered at the image of such undignified behavior. In tucking up his robes to run, the father would have exposed some of his undergarments. But the father cared more for his son than for propriety. When the father gave him the robe, ring, and sandals, the original hearers knew he was in the family again.

Ignorance of background sometimes leads contemporary Americans to sympathize with the older brother, which Jesus never intended. We read the parable, in part, as another example of younger children getting away with murder while older children do their duty. But Jesus' audience would have taken the older brother as a rude fellow who disrupted family order and honor. He refused to participate in his brother's welcome-home celebration, even though custom required him to lead the festivities.[5] His speech to his father was riddled with rudeness and self-pity: "Look! All these years I've been slaving for you and . . . you never gave me" a party (v. 29). If we put a hard eye on the older brother, we realize that the parable is at least as much about his self-righteous hardheartedness as it is about the sin of the prodigal. So, Jesus' parable has two aims. It invites sinners—like the tax collectors and those with whom he associated (15:1–2)—to come home, for the Father will welcome them. And it invites self-righteous—dutiful people like the Pharisees—to come in and join the party.

We have already illustrated the value of knowing about clothing, architecture, family life, technology, animal husbandry, as well as religious, social, and eating customs. It also helps to know about geography, economics, political history, and military customs.

For example, have you ever wondered why there are so many wars in the Old Testament? One reason is that Israel is located on the land bridge connecting Europe and Asia to Africa. When the Babylonians, Assyrians, and Egyptians went to war with each other and some other nations, they had to travel through Israel, and Israel got caught up in their campaigns. Have you noticed how many wars feature a siege or a standoff? Wars involved sieges because defensive armies would retreat to well-supplied fortresses built on hills. Jerusalem was built on a low mountain and possessed a modest water supply, making it nearly ideal for a defensive war. Invaders laid siege to Jerusalem, rather than attacking at once, to avoid fighting a literal "uphill battle."

This series of examples shows how valuable it is to know the times and customs of the Bible. They lead us to our first principle for historical context:

> ▶ **Principle 1: The more we know about the world of the Bible, the better we understand the Bible itself.**

This knowledge helps our study of every book, even if, as in the case of Joshua, Samuel, Kings, Chronicles, and Hebrews, no one knows who wrote them or when they were completed.

How to Learn About Antiquity

If you are convinced of the value of knowing about historical background, you may be wondering what to do next. Let me suggest several steps:

1. Increase your sensitivity to background information. As you listen to sermons, attend Bible studies, and read the Bible or other books, notice references to customs, geography, economics, means of travel, plant and animal life, and more.

2. If you are engaged in a serious study of one biblical book, read through it for hints about the daily world of the author and his readers. Jot down your observations and your questions.

3. Develop and use a Christian library. Consult your Bible dictionary or encyclopedia whenever you have the time to pursue a question. If you are responsible to teach through a book of the Bible and want to master its background, you must get a modern exegetical commentary. Anything published more than thirty years ago, and any recent work that ignores background, will let you down—at least at this point.

4. The basic Christian library will tell you most of what you want to know, but a vast, complicated literature winks at and whistles to the curious. Its information comes from archaeology and ancient writings. Archaeology studies ancient buildings, pots, water supplies, roads, and tools of all kinds. Ancient writings include sacred literature, wills, bills, letters, chronicles, memoirs, textbooks, plays, and inscriptions on buildings and tombs. See appendix E for suggestions for a home reference library.

The Local Situations of Biblical Authors and Audiences

If broad sensitivity to the nuances of the ancient culture is a silver coin, then knowledge of the conditions that moved the prophets and apostles to write individual books is the gold. Here we explore *why* authors said what they did when they did. What was the issue of the hour? Where did the mind of mankind cry for the mind of God? Where did the fires of spiritual battle burn brightest? Here we must ask, "What prompted Moses, Jeremiah, Paul, or Luke to write? What did they hope to accomplish?"

For example, about two years ago I decided to write an article on family planning. I had taught on the topic occasionally, casually, for several years. But in a short span of time I read a couple of severely misguided books and met several married couples who were disagreeing sharply on the issue, largely because they had read one of the misguided books. It seemed to me that someone needed to critique those books, and soon I was in the library and at the computer, and an article emerged. In a roughly similar way, many books of the Bible were written when the Holy Spirit used local crises to prompt his servants to write.

It is just as important, although harder, to locate a book's first readers and consider how it struck them. What were their needs, problems, and hopes? What events frightened or stirred them? Persecution lurks behind several New Testament books. Israel's ongoing lust for other gods stimulated much of the Old Testament. But what precise form did these temptations take, and what other issues troubled Israel or the church?

Relationships Between Authors and Readers

In a slightly different vein, it often helps to track the audience's relationship with the author. Were they old friends (Hebrews), strangers (Paul and the Romans), antagonists (Isaiah, Jeremiah, or Ezekiel and most Israelites)? We can reconstruct the relationship by examining how the author treats his readers. Does he expect them to share his beliefs or resist them? Does he expect his readers to greet his message by digging in their heels or by rejoicing?

There are perhaps three broad types of relationships of readers to authors in the Bible:

1. *Accepting.* Authors may expect their readers to accept their message without reservation. Their books never hint that their readers may question or reject what is written. In this category we think of Genesis, Judges, Ruth, Psalms, Proverbs, Matthew, Philippians, 1 and 2 Timothy, Titus, 1 Peter, and 1 John.

2. *Ambivalent.* The Lord himself describes the second type of audience when he tells Ezekiel, "With their mouths they express devotion, but their hearts are greedy for unjust gain. Indeed, to them you are nothing more than one who sings love songs with a beauti-

ful voice and plays an instrument well, for they hear your words but do not put them into practice" (Ezek. 33:31–32). Several other prophetic and historical books fit in the same category: they are respected, but ignored.

3. *Rejecting.* In a few books, such as Jeremiah, Amos, Galatians, and 2 Corinthians, prophets and apostles had to face bona fide opposition. False prophets of Judah accused Jeremiah of betraying his people. Many wanted to kill him, and they did toss him into a pit (Jer. 26, 37–38). When Amos prophesied against the corrupt northern kingdom of Israel, a false prophet in the northern king's pay greeted him, "Get out, you seer! Go back to the land of Judah. Earn your bread there and do your prophesying there" (Amos 7:12). The false prophet was implying that the king of Judah (in the south) might be willing to pay Amos to prophesy against the northern kingdom—as long as he did his work in the south!

> ▶ **Principle 2: To evaluate the relationship between a writer and his readers, look for pointed questions and objections, sharp rebukes, and terms of endearment.**

We know that there is tension when a writer has to defend his authority, answer challenging questions, or rebuke his readers sharply. But not all questions signify rebellion. Romans and James both answer objections, but they are more theological than personal. Paul and James knew their readers might hesitate to accept their message for spiritual or intellectual reasons. Their status as God's spokesmen was not at stake, but they knew they had to break through defenses. Some of their hearers were dullards who might sleepily nod in agreement and then awaken to do their own pleasures.

Similarly, sharp rebukes, by themselves, prove only that the readers are guilty of sin. In books such as Hebrews, Numbers, and parts of Isaiah and Ezekiel, the authors issue sharp rebukes, but they still count on their people to listen respectfully. In Jeremiah and Galatians, however, the man of God has to fight just to get a hearing. James has to issue rebukes, yet he often speaks affectionately to his readers. They are "my dear brothers" (James 1:16, 19; 2:5). John often addresses his readers as "dear friends," "dear children," and "my dear children." Similarly, Paul calls Timothy "my dear son" (2 Tim. 1:2).

Occasionally we can detect how much the author expects his readers to know. For example, Samuel and Kings assume their readers know the Old Testament law, for they often allude to it. For instance, the description of Solomon's reign in 1 Kings 1:28–11:8 invites comparison to the laws for Israel's kings in Deuteronomy 17. But Kings does not spell out the lesson that Solomon broke every rule. The author trusted his readers to see it for themselves.

Many say that Matthew wrote his gospel for Jews, Mark for Romans, and John for everyone. These assertions come from reading the Gospels and asking what target audience would be best served by each one. Matthew quotes Scripture frequently and rarely explains Jewish customs, which is fitting for a gospel intended for Jews. Mark rarely quotes Scripture, and he explains Jewish customs and words in terms familiar to Romans. John rarely quotes Scripture, but he scatters subtle allusions to Scripture and to Jewish customs throughout his gospel. This suggests that he wants to reach both simple Gentiles and sophisticated Jews.

The Third Dimension: Biblical Actors

So far, we have discussed the mind of authors and readers. This tells us most of what we need to know for the Epistles, the writing prophets, and the wisdom books. Our third principle pertains to historical writings.

▶ **Principle 3: In historical books we need to understand the cultures of the people who acted out the dramas of the Bible.**

For example, Abraham and Elijah did not write any part of the Bible, but to get the most out of Genesis or Kings, we need to walk a few miles in their shoes. Before Abraham came to Palestine, for instance, the Bible mentions that he lived in Ur and Haran. Ur was a very large, wealthy city in antiquity, complete with libraries and elegant two-story homes (besides a fully developed system of moon worship).[6] By contrast, in Palestine Abraham was a nomad, living in tents. The contrast helps us appreciate the sacrifice Abraham made when he followed God's call.

Many readers of the New Testament find it hard to believe that Herod slaughtered all the infants of Bethlehem aged two and under.

What king would murder dozens or hundreds of children in his own kingdom, just a few miles from the capital? But historians such as Josephus assure us, sadly, that such an action was entirely consistent with Herod's character. Herod murdered his own wife and several sons when he suspected them of plotting against him. He was a man of war and killed many. Indeed, at the end of his life he ordered that hundreds of Jewish leaders be slain on the day he died—to ensure that they would not plot against him, and so there would be sorrow in Israel on the day he died! Fortunately, Herod's successors ignored his decree, but it shows a callousness that is consistent with Herod's murder of Bethlehem's children.[7]

Learning About Biblical Actors

There are ways to discover the traits of the actors in biblical stories. First, read the entire book, jotting down the names of the characters and asking the six basic questions about them—Who, what, when, where, why, and how?—as you go along. Second, read a serious introduction to your book, looking for answers to the same questions.

Who? Who are the people and groups mentioned in the book? Do they have a history? Consider Jacob and Esau, David and Saul, the Israelites and the Philistines, Jesus and the Pharisees, Paul and the Judaizers. It is helpful to list all the major individuals and groups in a book, and better yet to list all the characters and groups who participate in an event (see the next chapter for details).

When? When did the events described take place, and when was the book written? What had God and his people done recently? Where did the event stand in the history of redemption? How much did the people know about the way of salvation? Remember what life was like in that epoch of biblical history. If the event is recorded in the Old Testament, are the people faithful or unfaithful, prosperous or oppressed? If the event is in the New Testament, does it come before or after the Resurrection?

Where? In what land and culture did the events occur? Most of the events in the Bible took place in Palestine, but the culture changed over the years. Abraham traveled through Palestine as a simple nomad when it was thinly populated. When Joshua conquered the same land more than five hundred years later, it supported an advanced but degraded agricultural life. Jerusalem was an isolated, rocky citadel when David captured it. Jesus' Jerusalem sprawled, and Greco-Roman influences infiltrated every corner of it. Of course, when the action moves to Babylon or Rome, to Philippi or Syrian Antioch, we want to know something of those lands.

What? and Why? What did the author want to teach to his people through the story he relates? And why did the characters act as they did? What did they know or not know? What is their history? These questions help us find the right perspective for a book and point us toward its main ideas.

Again, after you have read through your book yourself, looking for answers to the six basic questions, consult an article in a Bible dictionary or encyclopedia, or even a study Bible. If you have read carefully, they will confirm many of your ideas and add some points you missed. If time is short, you may simply read a reference work, but you will learn far more if you do your own digging first.

The study of historical context reminds us that the Bible was originally written for people whose world differed greatly from ours. It reminds us that everything the Bible says to us, it said first to them, so that the Word comes to us almost secondhand. The study of historical context grants us access to worlds of mysterious sayings, customs, and problems. It also prevents errors by reminding us that everything the Bible means today it first meant to someone else. So a text cannot mean today what it never meant to the original audience.[8] Applications can change, of course. "You shall not steal" now covers microwave ovens and computer software. But every principle we find in the Bible must be one they could have found first.

We now turn to some biblical teaching that shows just how valuable a knowledge of historical context can be.

Faith and Works in James and Galatians

Every young Christian learns that we are saved by faith, not works. As Paul says, "A man is not justified by observing the law, but by faith in Jesus Christ. . . . Clearly no one is justified before God by the law, because, 'The righteous will live by faith.' . . . A man is justified by faith apart from observing the law" (Gal. 2:16; 3:11; Rom. 3:28). Young Christians who have sound guides will soon learn that righteous deeds do have an important place in the redeemed life. But that simple truth will not prepare them for what they find James saying about faith and works.

> What good is it, my brothers, if a man claims to have faith but has no deeds? Faith cannot save him, can it?[9] . . . Was not our ancestor Abraham justified by works when he offered his son Isaac on the altar? You see that his faith worked together with his works, and his faith was completed by his works. . . . And the scripture was fulfilled that says, "Abraham believed God and it was credited to him as righteousness." . . . You see that a person is justified by what he does and not by faith alone . . . . Likewise even Rahab the prostitute was justified by works. . . . As the body without the spirit is dead, so faith without works is dead. (James 2:14–26, adapted from NIV)

This sounds quite different from Paul's doctrine of justification by faith! Why do James and Galatians differ so? Are they really teaching opposite things? A reconstruction of the historical context will resolve our problem.

Who? James, the brother of Jesus, wrote the book of James.[10] Although James doubted Jesus before his resurrection, he believed afterward and eventually became a principal leader of the church in and around Jerusalem (Acts 15:13–21; 21:17ff.; Gal. 2:6–13). As a leader, James manifested zeal for the law and for the salvation of the Jews (Acts 15; 21; James 2). The apostle Paul, the great missionary to the Gentiles, wrote Romans and Galatians.

To Whom? When? and Where? James addressed his letter to "the twelve tribes scattered among the nations." The phrase "twelve tribes" suggests that James wrote for Jews. Five quotations from the Old Testament and numerous additional allusions to it confirm the impression. Yet James also wrote for Christians, as we can see from his references to Christ and his teachings. The illustrations James uses fit life in Palestine, and so we know his primary audience lived in Palestine. For example, the patient farmer of James 5:7 waits for early and late rains, a weather phenomenon limited to the eastern end of the Mediterranean.[11] The letter also mentions poverty repeatedly (1:9–11, 27; 2:1–5, 14–16; 4:1–4, 13–5:6), and historians know that poverty was widespread in Palestine, especially among Christians, in the first century. James also describes the poor as day laborers (5:3–4), as they were in Palestine, rather than slaves, which many were in the rest of the Roman empire.

Paul wrote Galatians to a group of gentile Christians living in the Roman province of Galatia in Asia Minor. Paul had evangelized them on his first missionary journey, and they responded enthusiastically to the gospel of grace (4:13–15). Later, however, some Jewish "Christians" (known as Judaizers) visited the same churches, insisting that Paul's gentile converts follow certain Old Testament rites, such as circumcision. The Judaizers declared that Paul had no right to be an apostle. Further, they said, he had removed some of God's legal requirements in order to make his gospel more attractive to the Gentiles (Paul answers the charge at 1:10).

What? and Why? James and Paul both wanted to teach their churches about the proper relationship between faith and works. But their readers needed to learn different things about faith and works because they had fallen into opposing errors. Paul's Galatian friends needed to know that no one can do anything to earn God's favor or salvation. If they followed Jewish rituals in order to add their good works to Christ's atonement, they were no longer trusting him alone. They jeopardized their joy, their freedom, and even their salvation. When false teachers say that Christians must add their good works to the work of Christ if they want to be saved, Paul says, "A man is justified by faith alone."

James wrote for Jewish Christians. For centuries the Jews tended to know more than they practiced. They took pride in their knowledge of orthodox doctrine. Sometimes they acted as if knowledge alone were enough, as if *knowing* the right thing excused them from *doing* it. (See Matt. 2:1–12 and 23:2—the scribes told Herod and the Magi where the Christ had to be born but never joined the pilgrimage to see him.) This is James's central concern. He says, "Do not merely listen to the word, and so deceive yourselves. Do what it says. . . . Who is wise and understanding among you? Let him show it by his good life, by deeds done in the humility that comes from wisdom. . . . Anyone, then, who knows the good he ought to do and doesn't do it, sins" (1:22; 3:13; 4:17).

James's readers seemed to think that if they confessed orthodox doctrine, they would be justified. James replied that even demons possess orthodox doctrine—and shudder (2:18). By itself, knowledge of doctrine never saves. If a Jew thinks he is a Christian simply because he believes the right doctrines, James says that that sort of faith must be completed by works. Only works can prove that that kind of faith is alive. The book of James, then, is for people who believe they are justified because they have been baptized, catechized, and sanitized from all major sins. That faith is dead, James says, unless it is completed by works.

How? Later chapters will detail the methods authors use to communicate effectively. For now, it is enough to observe the tone of a book, and see how the writer makes contact with his readers. In Galatians, Paul draws partly on shared memories of the warm relationship he once had with the Galatians and the joy the Galatians had when first saved. James tries to shake up his listeners. He asks them provocative questions: "What good is it, my brothers, if someone says he has faith, but has no works? Faith cannot save him, can it?" No, faith cannot save someone like that, James implies.[12] Such remarks probably stunned James's early readers as much as they do us, and prompted them to examine themselves, to see if their faith could save them.

After we allow for the differences between the situations addressed by Paul and James, we conclude that they both took precisely the same position on the relation between faith and works.

The following chart summarizes the major options: (The arrow means "produce(s).")

• Good works → salvation.	• Not even the Judaizers believed that works alone merit salvation.
• Faith + good works → salvation.	• The Judaizers said faith + legal works bring salvation.
• Faith → salvation + good works.	• Both James and Paul say that works must follow salvation.
• Faith → salvation (no works).	• No apostle taught that good works have no place.

Some books offer bigger targets than others. In Romans, for example, we know that the author is the apostle Paul. In chapters 1 and 15 he tells us exactly why he is writing. Isaiah and Jeremiah tell us precisely when they served as prophets, and what those times were like. But no one knows the author or date of some books. In books that treat universal themes (such as Genesis, Psalms, Proverbs, and Romans), the particular circumstances of writing fade in importance. The historical context matters most for books that respond to a special need, such as Habakkuk, Nehemiah, 1 and 2 Corinthians, and Hebrews.

Conclusion

This chapter has attempted to show how the mastery of historical contexts solves interpretive problems and enriches innumerable passages. The gathering of historical background information is a lifelong task. The difficulty of pursuing background studies is that it takes far more time than an ordinary person can devote to it for one lesson. But the beauty is that you only have to do extended background reading once for each book you study. No one has the time to do all that research for one talk or sermon. But if one study bears fruit for four months, surely we can muster the energy. Furthermore, every time you study the background for a topic and teach it to others, you will keep part of that study for a lifetime.

The idea of laboring for a lifetime to acquire a skill reminds me of the summer I graduated from high school and worked on a maintenance crew for a milk processing company. The company's three-pound boxes of cheese sold well enough for them to make their own boxes. One day the box maker was sick, and since I had a slight reputation for nursing balky machines, the boss nominated me box maker for a day. I mastered the repetitive procedure by 10 A.M. and spent the rest of the day alternately pitying the regular box maker and giving thanks that I was going to college soon.

One can learn the essentials for menial and boring tasks, like box making, in hours. But life's noblest tasks are never accomplished in "five easy lessons." From musicianship to leadership, mastery is cumulative, never ending. Learning the historical setting of the Bible is one of the nobler tasks. Getting started is one of the harder steps, but the more you learn, the easier it is to learn even more. If you are beginning serious biblical studies, acquire a Bible dictionary or encyclopedia, be patient, research one issue each week, and keep on reading the Bible, always attending to its basic themes and central passages. Excellence develops slowly, but it rewards handsomely.

Exercises

1. *Whole books.* Read through one of the books we discussed most in this chapter, Galatians and James, and add what you can as you answer these questions:
   a. Who wrote the book? Describe his character and interests. Who received it? What was their relationship to the author?
   b. What are the main themes of the book?
   c. When was it written? Forget the date; get a feel for the spirit of the time. Describe the readers' land and culture.
   d. What did Paul or James hope to accomplish by writing?

2. *Broad historical context.* Read an article on some aspect of life in Bible times—perhaps clothing, war, money, food, Rome, or slavery. Apply what you read to some passages you have read recently.

3. *History within a book:*
   a. Read Matthew 16:1–4. How does the prior history of Jesus and the Pharisees shed light on Jesus' refusal to give the Pharisees a sign? (See Matt. 9 and 12.)
   b. Read 1 Samuel 17:1–11, 25–26, 32–41. List all the members of the audience for David's battle with Goliath. What was on the minds of each group as they watched David approach Goliath?

Notes

[1] See *Mishnah: A New Translation,* trans. and ed. Jacob Neusner (New Haven: Yale University Press, 1988), passim. See, for example, 1050–53 (Tohorot 7:1–8:3). The Mishnah is a compilation of the beliefs and customs of Jewish rabbis. The traditions recorded in it are older, but it was probably compiled over one hundred years after the New Testament was completed.

[2] From a commentary on Exodus, cited by I. H. Marshall, *Commentary on Luke* (Grand Rapids: Eerdmans, 1978), 599.

³ Mishnah, 37 (Demai 2.2).

⁴ The Greek of 15:12–13 reads, in part, that the Father "divided his *life* between them," and that the son "squandered his *existence* in dissolute living."

⁵ Kenneth Bailey, *Poet and Peasant* and *Through Peasants' Eyes,* combined ed. (Grand Rapids: Eerdmans, 1976), 1:194ff.

⁶ This is the kind of information that every good Bible dictionary or encyclopedia—such as those listed in appendix E—will have.

⁷ For more on Herod, see Josephus, *Antiquities,* and Josephus, *Wars of the Jews,* available in several editions. See also Bo Reicke, *The New Testament Era* (Philadelphia: Fortress, 1968). For more on the value of understanding biblical actors, see chap. 5 and appendix D.

⁸ Gordon Fee and Douglas Stuart, *How to Read the Bible for All Its Worth* (Grand Rapids: Zondervan, 1982), 27.

⁹ Most translations phrase this question "Such faith cannot save him, can it?" However, the word "such" is not in the Greek. James's wording puts the issue as starkly as possible.

¹⁰ This is the consensus of modern evangelical scholarship. See the leading evangelical introductions: Donald Guthrie, *New Testament Introduction* (Downers Grove, Ill.: InterVarsity Press, 1991), 723–33; D. A. Carson, Douglas J. Moo, and Leon Morris, *An Introduction to the New Testament* (Grand Rapids: Zondervan, 1992), 410–13.

¹¹ Peter Davids, *The Epistle of James* (Grand Rapids: Eerdmans, 1982), 171–72, 183.

¹² In asking the question "Can faith save him?" James uses a Greek form that requires the answer to be "No, it cannot." Even without knowing Greek, the reader sees James's conviction that faith without works cannot save.

5

Analyzing Narratives

A Likely Story

"Once upon a time there were four little Rabbits, and their names were Flopsy, Mopsy, Cottontail, and Peter. They lived with their Mother in a sand-bank, underneath the root of a very big fir tree. . . ."

"There was once a fisherman who lived with his wife in a poor little hut by the sea. . . ."

"Once upon a time there lived a very rich king whose name was Midas. . . ."

"These are the voyages of the Starship Enterprise. . . ."

Lines like these tell us to sit back and relax; a story is coming. When a story starts with the words "Once upon a time," we know that a certain kind of story is coming. The moment we hear that Peter is a naughty rabbit, every child knows or can guess that he is going to get into trouble and then get out of it, after learning a lesson. In fact, Peter does disobey his mother. He goes to Mr. McGregor's garden, where he munches lettuces and beans until he nearly collides with Mr. McGregor, who chases and almost catches him. After long, frightened wanderings, Peter sees the gate, dashes for it, and makes his escape. Exhausted, Peter goes to bed with nothing but chamomile tea, while his good sisters enjoy bread, milk, and blackberries.

Simple as they are, the adventures of Peter Rabbit follow the most common structure for drama, from Mark Twain to Shakespeare, from *Star Trek* to the Bible. In that structure, readers meet a hero (Peter) in settings (Mr. McGregor's garden) that bring adventure (munching stolen food), followed by tension that reaches a climax (the chase) and a resolution (escape from the garden). Finally, we read some comment on the story that helps us interpret it after it unwinds. In Peter's story, the little rabbit limps home and goes to bed without supper, which suggests that rebellion does not pay.

Broadly speaking, biblical truth comes in two basic literary forms, *narrative* and *discourse*. Narratives are stories or dramas. About one third of the Bible is narrative. With few exceptions, such as Jesus' parables, biblical narratives are historical. They tell what happened in space and time to the people who appear in the story. Narrative is the most common literary form or "genre" in the Bible, with more pages than law, prophecy, letters, or visions. In this book, we will collect all the other genres of the Bible under the term *discourse*. Discourse includes laws, letters, prophecies, proverbs, psalms, speeches, prayers, and visions. Within the CAPTOR format (Context, Analysis, Problems, Themes, Obligations, Reflection), we now move to the first part of analysis. Chapter 6 presents methods of analyzing biblical discourse. This chapter describes methods of analyzing narratives.

In an important sense, the Bible is one long narrative. It tells the story of the Creation, the Fall, and the redemption of the world. Shortly after the sin of Eve and Adam, the Bible begins to narrate God's plan to restore humanity to himself. Every part of the Bible fits somewhere within that narrative. Within the overall story, at a middle level, there are substories of the various biblical periods. There is a unity to the narrative of the patriarchs, the Exodus, the kings, the Exile and return, and Jesus and the apostles. At the lowest level, we have individual narratives, such as the story of Samson and Delilah or the account of Solomon's request for wisdom. We usually study the Bible at this level, yet we must always locate individual narratives in the context of their era and of God's wider plan.[1]

But what, precisely, is narrative? Narrative is history, and yet it does more than report what happened. It conveys moral lessons, but it is more than a morality tale. Biblical narratives describe the redemptive acts of God. They all lead to the climactic work of Christ in his life, death, and resurrection. The authors of biblical narratives present God's perspective on these redemptive events.

Biblical authors use various methods to engage readers and enable them to see events as God does. They repeat crucial ideas. They preview the future, so readers will know where events are leading. They review the past, so readers can see connections between events. They present characters with whom we can identify. They leave some things unexplained, so the reader will get involved in the task of interpretation. In these ways (and more), the author uses the story to teach his readers about God, humanity, and the relations between them.

Types of Narrative

All narratives report events and tell stories, but they can follow one of several patterns. In this chapter we will distinguish the three most common types of narrative. We study the types of narrative to make it easier to discover the main point of each passage.

1. *Reports* are brief records of things such as battles (for example, David's defeat of the Ammonites, 2 Samuel 10), building projects (for example, Solomon's temple and palace, 1 Kings 6–9), dreams, or the reign of a minor king. Reports present facts or simple events. They typically lack lively characters or dramatic tension. Although they may not tell us a great deal by themselves, reports do often develop or allude to important themes that recur in larger texts.

> ◆ Principle 1: To discover the point of a report, compare it to other reports or examine several reports together.

When we collect and compare reports, themes begin to emerge. For example, when we compare the report of the building of Solomon's house to the report of the building of God's house, and observe that the king invested more time and money on his own house, it tells us something about his priorities. When Acts reports the steady growth of the church on six separate occasions, we realize that the church is indeed spreading to the ends of the earth, even as Jesus said it would (Acts 1:8).

2. *Speech stories* primarily report what someone said in a historical setting.

▶ Principle 2: In speech stories, the main event is the speech, not the story surrounding it.

What is said matters most. Speech stories include reports of Moses' speeches to Pharaoh (Ex. 5–10), Solomon's speech and prayer at the dedication of the temple (1 Kings 8), and the sermons of Peter and Paul (Acts 2; 13; 17). In speech stories, there are characters in a setting and perhaps limited action, but the speech is the main action. To interpret speech stories, ask why the speaker gave his speech. What were the issues of the hour and what did he say about them? What did the speaker want his hearers to think or do?[2]

Speech stories (sometimes called "pronouncement" stories) occur rather often in the Gospels. There may be a brief miracle, encounter, or conflict, followed by a climactic saying that presents an important point. For example, in Matthew 8, a Roman centurion asks Jesus to heal his servant. Jesus offers to go and heal the man. The centurion, perhaps aware that Jesus would violate Jewish standards if he entered the house, says, "Lord, I do not deserve to have you come under my roof. But just say the word, and my servant will be healed" (v. 8). This striking confession causes Jesus to marvel, "I have not found anyone in Israel with such great faith. I say to you that many will come from the east and the west, and will take their places at the feast with Abraham, Isaac and Jacob in the kingdom of heaven. But the subjects of the kingdom will be thrown outside, into the darkness, where there will be weeping and gnashing of teeth" (vv. 10–12). Because Jesus' statements about the faith of the centurion and the faithlessness of Israel are longer than the miracle itself, and seem more important, we call the passage a pronouncement story.

The calling of Matthew (Levi) is similar (Matt. 9:9–13, with Mark 2:13–17). As Matthew himself describes it, the call of Levi the tax collector lacks character development or tension: Jesus summons Levi to follow him, and he responds right away, without apparent difficulty. He then invites "sinners" to meet Jesus at a dinner. When the Pharisees protest, Jesus replies, "It is not the healthy who need a doctor, but the sick. But go and learn what this means: 'I desire mercy, not sacrifice.' For I have not come to call the righteous, but sinners." Of course, the calling of Matthew is important, but the gospel subordinates the call of Matthew to the comment that Jesus made about his mission.

In speech or pronouncement stories, therefore, we focus on speech, even if we are actually reading a narrative. The main point of the speech most often comes at the beginning or the end. If it is long enough, we can interpret the speech itself according to the principles set forth in the next chapter. In the rest of this chapter, we will attend to the principles for interpreting true dramas.

3. *Dramas,* the longest and most complex type of narrative in the Bible, are the focus of this chapter. We recognize dramas by the presence of one or more vivid characters, including a hero, and movement from tension (some problem in the life of the hero or the people he encounters) to resolution.[3]

Before we go any further, let me emphasize that my use of the words *story* and *drama* in no way implies that they are *mere* stories or dramas. Apart from obvious fiction, such as parables, biblical dramas are true accounts describing actual events. Some critics regard biblical narratives as self-contained stories that do not refer to the external world. What actually happened is irrelevant, they say, as long we are willing to enter the imaginative world of the Bible and allow it to stir our faith. But the Bible constantly assumes that Adam, Abraham, Moses, and David, to name a few, were real people, whose actions shaped history. In the New Testament, Paul says that everything rides on the historicity of the accounts of Jesus: "If Christ has not been raised, our preaching is useless and so is your faith" (1 Cor. 15:14; cf. 15:17).

Studies in archaeology, history, and linguistics support the reliability of biblical narrative, and we rightly seek such confirmations, for our faith rests on the certainty that God actually accomplished his plan of redemption in history. Biblical dramas do not, therefore, follow the patterns of literary dramas because someone "massaged" the stories to make them fit. Rather, God has structured human nature and creation so that certain elements are present in all stories worth telling. If biblical dramas have the same structure as fiction, it is because art imitates life, not because the Bible imitates art.

Aspects of Biblical Drama

Almost all dramatic stories, including many short ones, have certain phases. First, we meet the characters in their setting. The main characters pulse with life and face struggles so close to our own that we could hardly forget them, even if we tried. The action may begin slowly, but before long troubles develop. These build to a climax, followed by a resolution. Next, the story unwinds to a peaceful conclusion. Then, either the narrator or a character in the story typically says or does something that interprets the event and its consequences. If we analyze a biblical story that spans less than one chapter, few of these stages will be developed at length.

The pattern sometimes varies. One climax may lead swiftly to another problem and a second climax, as in some of Jesus' conflicts with the Jewish leaders or in his trial (Matt. 12; Luke 22–23). Sometimes one comment explains several stories that span several chapters. For example, the statement "Day after day Saul searched for him, but God did not give David into his hands" (1 Sam. 23:14) interprets most of 1 Samuel 21–23. Sometimes the author interprets a series of events before they happen. This is especially true of Jesus' predictions of his death (Luke 9:44, 51; Matt. 20:25–28).

The climax and the final comments of a drama usually join to present the main point. We will chiefly explore how this applies to individual events, such as the miracles of Jesus. But it also applies to whole books, such as Ruth and Esther, and to stories that span several chapters, such as the Joseph narrative (Gen. 37–45), the escape from Egypt (Ex. 1–20), the life of Samson (Judg. 13–16), and David's years before his coronation (1 Sam. 17–31). Here are the chief elements in biblical dramas:

1. Setting the Stage

The setting establishes the mood of a story and tells where it takes place in space and time.

Time. Does the action occur in one episode or over a period of time? During the day or the night? For example, Nicodemus visited Jesus at night; Peter walked on the water during a storm at night; Jesus' interrogations and trial took place at night. How does the idea of darkness change the way we read these three narratives? On the other hand, what do we learn about Abraham when we read that he set out early in the morning to offer his only son Isaac to the Lord (Gen. 22:3)?

Spatial Setting. Does a story occur inside or outside? In holy space (temple, synagogue) or common space? Are the main figures at home or on enemy or pagan territory? Is the hero safe or threatened, free or restricted, isolated or crowded? In the Gospels we slowly learn that the temple and the synagogue, which should be holy and safe, are actually dangerous and profane; mountains are more likely to be truly holy places (consider the Sermon on the Mount and the Transfiguration).[4]

Sometimes the spatial setting is absolutely essential to a story. David's combat with Goliath depends on its spatial setting. First, the armies of Israel and Philistia meet near Socoh, near the border between Israel and Philistia, but a mere fifteen miles from David's home town, Bethlehem, in the center of Israel. Second, the armies of Philistia and Israel face off on two hilltops, with a valley between them. Day after day (time!) each army waits for the other to attack, while they defend the high ground. Goliath offers himself in solo combat against a hero from Israel, drawing on military custom to end the standoff—and to open a highway to the heart of Israel.

Social Setting. Time and place may combine to form special social situations, such as meals. Social settings are most likely to contribute to the meaning of dramas when several similar scenes occur in one book. For example, numerous episodes surround meals in the gospel of Luke. By providing food for hungry crowds, Jesus shows that the kingdom has arrived, because the hungry are filled (Luke 9:10–16; cf. 6:21). While Jesus often reveals himself to his followers at meals with them (9:10–16; 22:14–38; 24:30–32), meals that take place in the homes of Pharisees are fraught with conflict (7:36–50; 11:37–54; 14:1–24).[5]

2. Understanding the Characters

After you establish the place, time, and social setting of a story, list all the characters in it. Remember that God is at least a background character in every biblical drama. Characters may be individuals or groups, new or familiar. If your story has Pharisees or Philistines, demoniacs, disciples, or some other familiar group, draw on what you know about them from other parts of the Bible. Here are some suggestions for understanding the people in biblical dramas:

Look for at least one believer, one unbeliever, and one undecided individual or group. Of course, there will probably be more or less than three characters. But the basic trio represents the typical reactions of people through the ages to God's work in the biblical drama: belief, unbelief, and uncertainty.

Expect the Bible to show or tell the traits of each character.[6] The Bible sometimes tells its readers that Moses was humble (Num. 12:3) or that Joseph was just (Matt. 1:19). But such explicit evaluations are rare. The Bible prefers to show a character's traits through his or her speech and actions.

Compare the thoughts, words, and deeds of a character. Coherence between words and deeds builds confidence in a character; variance signifies trouble. For example, in the years when Saul pursued David, David twice spared Saul when he could have killed him. Saul wept and proclaimed David's innocence. So when Saul resumed the hunt, he seemed weak as well as evil. On the other hand, when John the Baptist calls the Pharisees a brood of vipers, and they then plot against Jesus, we recognize them as vipers indeed.

Be prepared to revise your estimate of a character. Our opinion of Samson and Judas sinks as time passes. Other characters, such as Joseph, Moses, and Peter, grow as their story unfolds. Some, such as Jacob and Paul, are made new. When the text shows rather than tells, we have to decide what to make of each character. When they take a turn for better or for worse, we may need to reread their stories and revise our estimate.

Rely on dialogue. Dialogue plays a huge role in biblical narratives, especially by revealing character. Character emerges in both the content and the manner of speech. Are speakers gentle or rude, condescending or respectful, sincere or manipulative, confused or insightful? Do they twist God's words (Gen. 3) or declare divine truth?

3. Conflict

Shortly after we meet the characters, a problem or conflict arises. The conflict often has phases in which the problem becomes more complex. A biblical drama usually has at least one of three types of focal points: a test, a quest, or a choice.

In a *test*, events try or probe the mental, moral, or spiritual character of the story's hero. David's combat with Goliath tests his fitness to be king (1 Sam. 17). The temptation and trials of Jesus test him (Matt. 4; 26–27, and parallels).

In a *quest*, the main character pursues a goal, which he usually obtains despite obstacles in the path. Abraham's life is largely a quest for the blessings that God has promised him, especially the promise of an heir (Gen. 12–22). In the Gospels, a sinful woman and Zacchaeus both go on a quest to see Jesus (Luke 7:36–50 and 19:1–10).

In a *choice*, the main character or characters must decide between two courses of action. David had to choose whether to avenge himself on Saul on two occasions (1 Sam. 24; 26).

As we will see shortly, the same event may provide a test for one person in the drama and a choice for another. But one of the three focal points will dominate the main story.

4. Crisis and Climax

The conflict becomes more severe as obstacles mount up or a great test looms. Be prepared for surprises or reversals. Expect dialogue to move a story forward as much as other events do. The climax is the moment of greatest tension, the moment when the original witnesses were holding their breath. The climax occurs when the first-time reader is asking, "What is going to happen next? Who is going to succeed and who will fail?" In the story of David and Goliath, the crisis and climax occur when David marches out to meet the giant.

Locating and appreciating the crisis can be difficult for people who have heard the great stories of the Bible numerous times. The suspense is long gone because they know precisely what happens and when. Seasoned readers should occasionally try to imagine that they are hearing the story for the first time—to suspend their knowledge, and let the story wash over them again.

5. Resolution

Here we find out what happened, which brings us to our third principle for analyzing narratives.

> ♦ **Principle 3: When you find the crisis and resolution of a drama, you usually find the main point as well.**

The Lord resolves David's crisis by giving him victory. This proves the main point, that God gives the victory to his anointed one, that the battle is the Lord's (1 Sam. 17:45). The sinful woman also fulfills her quest; she meets Jesus, and he forgives her sins (Luke 7:36–50).

This demonstrates Jesus' power to forgive sins and his willingness to receive sinners.

6. Following Action

A following action or saying commonly interprets a biblical drama. It may indicate the main lesson or show how the event fits into redemptive history. Witnesses to an event may make comments that interpret it. The Lord himself may speak, or the narrator may speak for him. A following episode can help explain the significance of a drama.

To illustrate, when we read about the time when Jesus raised up the only son of the widow of Nain (Luke 7:11–17), we may be unsure of Luke's main point. Is the lesson that Jesus has resurrection power? That he is compassionate? That he is the Christ? The account teaches all three lessons. But the crowd especially comments on who Jesus is—a great prophet, whose miracle signifies that God has visited his people. Of course, the crowd has discerned part of the truth, but Jesus is more than a great prophet. The next passage declares the greater truth about Jesus: he is the coming one, the Messiah. Since both the following dialogue and the next passage focus on Jesus' identity, we assume that that is the main point of the story. The other ideas, about Jesus' compassion and power, serve the greater one. They show that Jesus is more than a great prophet: he is the compassionate Messiah, who comes with resurrection power.

Charting Your Story

There are two good ways to follow a story. First, you can paraphrase it, scene by scene, summarizing each one as the plot advances toward its climax and resolution. Second, you can list the events of each scene more briefly on a visual chart. You can chart dramas using the simple pattern on page 70. Each number represents one of the phases of a drama.

Here is a hint for recognizing a new scene within a drama: a scene ordinarily has just two characters or groups. Scenes change when a drama continues in a new location or when a small change of characters occurs. But do not be alarmed if you cannot clearly tell where each phase begins; the phases of a drama may overlap.

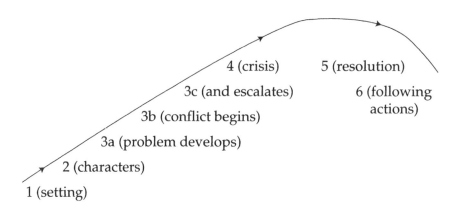

An Illustration: A Paralytic Healed (Luke 5:17–26)

Jesus was teaching and healing people in a house in Galilee (cf. Mark 2). Pharisees and scribes joined the crowd that swelled beyond the capacity of the house. Some friends of a paralytic carried him to Jesus to be healed. Determined to get him to Jesus, but blocked by the crowd, they decided to lower him through the roof. They tore a hole in the roof, tied ropes to the stretcher, and lowered the paralytic through the hole. The people below, we imagine, heard the pounding, felt the debris falling on them, and watched in wonder as the hole grew before them. All eyes and ears converged on the paralytic, until Jesus, seeing the faith of the man and his friends, declared, "Friend, your sins are forgiven" (Luke 5:20).

Setting the Stage. The paralytic was carried to Jesus at a time when "the power of the Lord was present for him to heal the sick" (v. 17). The setting, in a crowded house, is vital to this story. The crowd causes a striking development—a man is lowered through the roof—and heightens the drama (v. 19). A house is usually an intimate and protected space, but a crowded one, stuffed with Pharisees and teachers from Jerusalem, is another matter (vv. 17, 19). And we wonder what the owner thought of everything that was happening in and to his home.

Characters. This story features Jesus, the disciples, crowds, scribes and Pharisees, an owner (presumably), the paralytic and his friends, and "the power of the Lord" (v. 17). Within this group we have believers, unbelievers, and uncommitted spectators. Luke never says that the Pharisees were hostile to Jesus. Rather, his report of their internal reaction, "Who is this fellow who speaks blasphemy?" (v. 21), shows us their hostility. Luke first *shows* us the faith of the paralytic and his friends, and then he *tells* us that Jesus saw their faith.

Conflict. The drama begins when a large crowd thwarts the quest of a paralytic and his friends to reach Jesus for a healing. The crowded room is an obstacle that they swiftly dispatch, by removing part of the roof. When they lower him through the roof, the end of their quest is in view. For Jesus, the same event is a test. This is not a simple test of his power to heal. By forgiving the man's sins before he does anything, Jesus raises the stakes; he says he can forgive sins, but can he prove it? The Pharisees perceive the statement "Your sins are forgiven" as a claim to deity. Why should Jesus forgive a man he never met before? The statement implies that somehow the paralytic sinned against him. But that is impossible if Jesus is an ordinary man, for the paralytic had no opportunity to sin against him. On the other hand, God is offended by every sin, and has the right to forgive all sins as well.

So when Jesus forgives the man, he claims deity. The Pharisees grasp all this and grumble, thinking, *This fellow is blaspheming.* So, is Jesus a blasphemer or does he have the rights and powers he claims? Everything hangs on what happens next.

Crisis and Climax. Dialogue carries the story to a deeper crisis. Jesus, knowing the Pharisees' thoughts, incites a crisis, a showdown: "'Why are you thinking these things in your hearts? Which is easier: to say, 'Your sins are forgiven,' or to say, 'Get up and walk'? But that you may know that the Son of Man has authority on earth to forgive sins. . . .' He said to the paralyzed man, 'I tell you, get up, take your mat and go home'" (vv. 22–24).

In effect, Jesus tells the Pharisees, "I have forgiven this man, I do claim to be God, and I will prove both by healing him now." When Jesus commanded the paralytic to rise in front of everyone, the room was probably so quiet you could hear the slightest creak of the man's stretcher. What would happen next? Would the man rise or not? Did Jesus have the power to forgive sins or not? Is Jesus the Lord or a blasphemer?

Resolution. "Immediately he stood up in front of them, took what he had been lying on and went home praising God" (v. 25). Here, as the crisis finds resolution, we find the main point of the passage: Jesus does have the right and the power to forgive sins; he is the Lord, just as he says!

This episode involves both a quest and a test. The paralytic and his friends persist in their poignant quest, tearing up the roof when they have to. But in the climax we see that the test of Jesus is the heart of this passage. Who is he? What is the extent of his power?

Following Action. We know that the principal issue is Jesus' authority to forgive sins, because it comes up three times near the climax of the story (5:20, 21, 24). The healing proves the main point of the drama: Jesus can forgive sins, so he must be God. It may seem strange that no one at the scene grasps the lesson. The crowds praise God (so far so good) and say, "We have seen remarkable things today" (not so good). The careful Christian reader certainly knows this is a flawed response. But even an earnest seeker may recognize that the events call for a stronger confession. So he enters the story, asking himself, "What should the Jews have said and done? How should I respond today?"

Two More Hints. Charting the action is effective, but the nature of biblical drama requires us to watch for a few more things when interpreting a story. *First, look for repeated words or ideas.* In this account, we notice the repeated phrase "forgive sins," and that is indeed the main issue in the passage. *Second, remember that biblical narratives provide very few details.* Physical descriptions, internal dialogue, and disclosure of motives are given very sparingly. This means that most details make a difference (see chap. 2). On the other hand, the Bible sometimes leaves out details we wish we knew. The interpreter then has to enter the story and fill in the gaps imaginatively.

This reminds us that, even after we have taken all the right steps, we rarely have the entire lesson in our hand, crisp and neat like a new dollar bill. Instead, we have to scratch our heads and meditate a bit before the main point of a narrative rolls off our tongues. We might say that biblical dramas tell the truth and nothing but the truth, but the whole truth comes in whispers, not shouts—that is, by implicit rather than explicit clues.[7]

How Biblical Dramas Apply Today

So far, we have taken steps to discover what narratives meant when they were first written. But what do they mean or how do they apply today? After we have taken all the steps above, we can ask two kinds of questions that lead to current applications. First, what does the drama show us about the life that God blesses or judges? Is there activity here that we should imitate or avoid? How might we do so today? Second, what does this passage reveal about God and his ways with mankind?

The Life That God Blesses

Narratives have few commands that we can apply directly to ourselves. Even when the Lord himself issues a command, it is usually impossible or unnecessary to do that precise thing today. God commanded Adam and Eve not to eat from a certain tree, but now that Eden and the tree are gone, what are we to do? So, even though many biblical narratives have commands, few apply to us in a direct, literal way. Instead of looking for direct commands, we should ask what our narrative reveals about the life that God blesses or judges.

To do this, we need to read the story from the inside, as if we were there. First, look at your list of the actors in your drama. Try to see the story through the eyes of one of them. Look for the three chief types of character: believers, unbelievers, and undecided observers. As we noted earlier, few stories have precisely three characters. There may be two believers and no fence-sitters, and so on. Still, these three types offer every reader—believer, unbeliever, or undecided—someone with whom he or she can identify. They become a mirror, showing readers how that kind of person responded to events.

For example, list everyone who witnessed David's match with Goliath (1 Sam. 17).[8] Given all that we know about them, what might each group be feeling as the combatants approached each other? What thoughts swirled in the minds of Saul, David's brothers, and Israel's army? In the minds of Goliath and the Philistines? What did David think? What did God think? Or play the part of Zacchaeus or the people of Jericho when Jesus announced that he would dine with that notorious sinner (Luke 19). Can you see why the people

grumbled? Can you see why Zacchaeus promised quadruple resti-
tution to all he had defrauded?

Of course, we cannot simply shun unbelievers' ways and imitate
believers. That would hardly work when we read about the twelve
disciples! Actually, whenever we meet the human hero of a narrative, we tend both to identify with him and to evaluate him. That is,
we both see ourselves in him and keep our distance. We aspire to
his fidelity but admit that we fall short. We disapprove of his failures, yet we may admit that we fail in similar ways. And, of course,
we recognize that some of his actions have no parallel in our lives.
But despite limitations, the characters of a drama show us how we
should respond to God.

Just as we cannot obey every command that we read in narrative,
so we cannot directly imitate every righteous act we encounter. For
example, we dare not imitate Jesus as he called disciples to himself,
mastered nature, or read minds. We must remember Christ's unique-
ness every time we consider imitating one of his actions. On the other
hand, the apostle Paul says we ought to be like Jesus in kindness,
compassion, forgiveness, love, and humility (Eph. 4:32; 5:2, 25; Rom.
15:7; Phil. 2:5–8). Indeed, it is the Christian's destiny to be trans-
formed into the likeness of the Son (Rom. 8:29; 2 Cor. 3:18; Eph.
4:13). So, while we cannot be crucified for sin, we can refrain from
insulting those who mistreat us (1 Peter 2:18–23). Therefore, even if
we cannot imitate the precise deeds of Jesus, we can imitate his
Spirit as he performed those deeds. As John Murray says, "To aspire
to be like God in one sense is the essence of virtue, to aspire to be
like him in another sense is iniquity. To preserve this line of distinc-
tion is indispensable to all right thinking on truth and the right."[9]

God's Ways with Men

God is the leading character in every biblical drama. Nothing just
happens in the Bible; events happen because God orders them. If,
when we read the Bible, we see only who did what to whom, and
how the hero passed his tests and escaped his crises, we will miss
the overall thrust of biblical narrative. The Bible is not about the exploits of men and women, but rather the mighty acts of God.

It follows, then, that biblical history constantly displays the way
God acts toward his creatures, especially humans. God does not
treat all people the same way at all times; he does not even treat the

same person the same way at all times. Nonetheless, God always acts according to his unchanging character and plans. If you know who God is, if you know what he has said about his justice, mercy, holiness, wisdom, and truth, page after page overflows with examples of how those attributes played out in his past dealings with men. Since he does not change, we then see how he will treat people today.

Conclusion

This chapter has shown that biblical narratives are similar in form to narratives all over the world. We can analyze reports, speech stories, and dramas; we can inspect the characters and chart action. The content and purpose of biblical dramas, however, are quite different from other stories. Biblical narratives convey lessons about life under the blessings and curses of the covenant. More important still, they describe the redemptive acts of God—his acts on behalf of his people, and his covenant loyalty to them.[10] They are stories—and so very much more.

Exercises

1. Outline a nonbiblical story using the steps described above. Use a book, a newspaper article, a movie, or a personal adventure. What did you learn from the exercise?

2. Analyze the drama in Genesis 22 using the same steps that we used for Luke 5:17–26.

3. Analyze Acts 10 as a speech story.

Notes

[1] Gordon Fee and Douglas Stuart, *How to Read the Bible for All It's Worth* (Grand Rapids: Zondervan, 1982), 74–75.

[2] William Klein, Craig Blomberg, and Robert Hubbard, *Introduction to Biblical Interpretation* (Waco: Word, 1993), 270–71.

[3] The best guides to biblical narrative are: Robert Alter, *The Art of Biblical Narrative* (New York: Basic Books, 1981); Leland Ryken, *Words of Delight* (Grand Rapids:

Baker, 1987); Meir Sternberg, *Poetics of Biblical Narrative: Ideological Literature and the Drama of Reading* (Bloomington: Indiana University Press, 1985). See also Mark Allen Powell, *What Is Narrative Criticism?* (Minneapolis: Fortress, 1990).

[4] Elizabeth Struthers Malbon, *Narrative Space and Mythic Meaning in Mark* (San Francisco: Harper & Row, 1986), 84–89, 131–37; Powell, *What Is Narrative Criticism?* 76–77.

[5] See Robert Tannehill, *The Narrative Unity of Luke-Acts: A Literary Interpretation* (Philadelphia: Fortress, 1986), 1:170–71, 217–19, 289–92. Some books, such as Luke, place a series of episodes in remarkably similar settings; scholars call these type-scenes (see Tannehill, 1:170–72).

[6] Powell, *What Is Narrative Criticism?* 52–53.

[7] Sternberg, *Poetics of Biblical Narrative*, 230–63; Robert Fowler, *Let the Reader Understand* (Minneapolis: Fortress, 1991), 127–94. As Fowler and Sternberg both point out, the clues sometimes bring more puzzlement than certainty, at least in the short run.

[8] They were: Saul, David's brothers, Israel's army, the Philistine army, David and Goliath, and the Lord.

[9] John Murray, *Principles of Conduct* (Grand Rapids: Eerdmans, 1957), 177. The prophets and the apostles also had positions, powers, and knowledge that were denied to us. We cannot dry up the skies, call fire from heaven, or establish standards for the church. Yet we can imitate their faith (Heb. 11). See also appendix D.

[10] See chap. 13 and S. G. De Graff, *Promise and Deliverance*, 4 vols. (St. Catherine's, Ont.: Paideia Press, 1977–81).

6

Analyzing Discourse

Do You Follow?

A few years ago, I collected a file of surprising editorials, opinion pieces that defied conventional wisdom. The first several items, written when Mikhail Gorbachev still led the communist Soviet Union, argued that we should give financial aid to a nuclear power whose weapons were still pointed at us. Next, a hunter attacked the National Rifle Association for undermining the true interests of hunters.[1] Later, a liberal columnist announced that he was going to start sending small contributions to conservative political groups.[2] Finally, a political analyst wrote to praise low voter turnout.

The columns were not all equally serious, but they all needed to convince an audience that would resist their odd ideas. For example, Charles Krauthammer reasoned that low voter turnout shows that the disastrous social project of the twentieth century, the attempt to redeem society through grand political schemes, has failed. Low turnout means that we do not care so much about politics any more. We know that history cannot be changed for the better by politics. Democrats and Republicans now debate small matters of management. Low voter turnout means that people see politics as a marginal part of their lives, and that is healthy. Low turnout is "a leading indicator of contentment." It shows that people have rightly decided that "that government is best that governs least."[3]

Whether or not you agree with these columnists is beside the point. They demonstrate that when you want to persuade someone of an idea, you must bring reasons with you. Biblical authors, from Moses and Hosea to Peter and Paul, knew this. They often stood in the same position as modern columnists who advance novel ideas. "Take up your cross and follow me" is a command, but Jesus deigns to give reasons for obeying him. The prophets and apostles wanted to convince their audience, but that audience included skeptics. To win over those who resisted, they supported their teaching with rational evidences and emotional appeals.

Some teachers love the old saying, "The Bible teaches it, I believe it, and that settles it." But they forget that seekers, doubters, and unbelievers slouch in the pews and chairs of all growing churches. Unsure of their convictions, these people do not share our passion for the Bible. The simple authority of the Bible does not "settle it" for them. They want to know why the Bible says something, not just what it says. They want proof for assertions and reasons for commands.

God does often accommodate human weakness by granting reasons why we should believe and obey. Unless we likewise explain those reasons to the skeptics seated in our churches, we may lose them. Because almost every tenet of the faith may be questioned today, teachers must first understand the biblical concepts, and then grasp the reasoning God has revealed along with them.

Of course, sometimes faith must operate in the absence of reasons, or even contrary to what seems reasonable (see Gen. 22). Sometimes "blind" obedience bespeaks a supreme loyalty to God (2 Cor. 5:7; Heb. 11:1). Ordinarily, however, Scripture discloses some reasons for its assertions and commands. And ordinarily pious men and women seek to understand them and communicate them to others.

Careful analysis also strengthens the mature believer. It unlocks difficult texts and illumines clear ones. When we grasp the argumentation for an idea, when we feel its emotional power for ourselves, we own it more. We can explain it, defend it, and infer additional truths from it. So, even if we already accept what the Bible teaches on its own authority, discourse analysis is beneficial.

What Is Discourse Analysis?

Discourse analysis is the study of the way authors put sentences and paragraphs together to make their points.[4] A discourse can be a letter, a sermon, a public address, a conversation, or even a poem, a song, or a prayer, as long as it makes assertions. Biblical discourses include Moses' sermons on the law in Deuteronomy, the Sermon on the Mount, Peter's sermon at Pentecost, and the letters of the New Testament. Discourse analysis discovers the main ideas of sections of the Bible and explores the way biblical authors present and defend their ideas through logic and rhetoric. The goal of this chapter is to explain how to discover the main points of biblical discourses.

In analyzing a discourse, it helps to begin with at least a rough idea of the theme before the detailed analysis begins. Fortunately, good authors scatter clues that help readers find their main topics and ideas:

1. *Location.* The main idea frequently occurs in the first or the last sentence of a section or a paragraph, or in both.

2. *Restatement.* Authors restate, repeat, or return to the main concept. For example, James says three times in James 2:14–26, in slightly different ways, that faith without works is dead.[5]

3. *Direct address.* Authors may address their hearers before stating a main idea. Biblical writers have used such addresses as "Hear, O Israel," "Brothers," and "Dear friends."

4. *Introductory formulas.* To draw attention to their chief points, authors introduce them with phrases like "I want you to know" or "I write these things to you so that."

5. *Concluding formulas.* Look for words that summarize a discussion, such as *therefore, thus,* or *so.*

People learn discourse analysis only by studying examples and doing it themselves. Your first passage is Matthew 18:15–20, printed out below. I have italicized the words that mark a transition between one thought and the next. Read the text carefully, trying to observe how the teaching proceeds. First, using the principles above, try to find the main idea. Then notice the connections between concepts that develop it. Jot your observations down on a sheet of paper.

> [15]*If* your brother sins against you, go and show him his fault, just between the two of you. *If* he listens to you, you have won your brother over. [16]*But if* he will not listen, take one or two others along, *so that* "every matter may be established by the testimony of two or three witnesses." [17]*If* he refuses to listen to them, tell it to the church; *and if* he refuses to listen even to the church, treat him as you would a pagan or a tax

collector. [18]*I tell you* the truth, whatever you bind on earth will be bound in heaven, *and* whatever you loose on earth will be loosed in heaven. [19]*Again, I tell you* that if two of you on earth agree about anything you ask for, it will be done for you by my Father in heaven. [20]*For where* two or three come together in my name, *there* am I with them.

The general topic, which appears in the first sentence and re-peatedly afterwards, is what to do if your brother sins against you. Jesus presents a series of steps to be taken, one after the other, if one brother sins against another. We immediately notice five occurrences of "if" in the first section (vv. 15–17), indicating five conditional clauses ("then" is implied in the next clause all five times). Specifi-cally, the offended person must (1) go (2) to reprove his brother (3) alone and (4) to win the brother. When someone takes these steps, the sinning brother may either repent or resist. *If* the rebuke fails, *then* he must enlist the aid of the church to verify the offense and strengthen the correction (vv. 16–18). *If* the offender refuses to repent, *then* he must be put out of the church.

Matthew does not specify the connection between verses 15–17 and verses 18–20. It is implicit, so we have to figure it out ourselves. Fortunately, it is clear that verses 18–20 are commenting on the process of discipline described in verses 15–17. Jesus assures the apostles and later Christians that when they undertake the solemn task of resolving conflicts, heaven stands behind their decisions. The Father will be with them, hearing their prayers and granting his presence. At first glance, the words "if two of you on earth agree about anything" might suggest that we are reading general truths about prayer. But the context looks back to the offenses just men-tioned. That is, where two or three gather to resolve any matter, any affair, any offense, God will be there with them and hear their plea for help.[6]

Peter's response reminds us that dealing with sin involves more than following a procedure; there is also a human element.

[21]*Then* Peter came to Jesus and asked, "Lord, how many times shall I forgive my brother when he sins against me? Up to seven times?" [22]Jesus *answered,* "I tell you, not seven times, but seventy-seven times. [23]*Therefore* the kingdom of heaven is like a king who wanted to settle accounts with his servants. . . . "

"Then" explicitly connects Peter's question to the preceding verse, although, technically, it only says that he asked a question next. But we may assume that he is taking up the question of resolving offenses. We can expand his question in verse 21 this way: "I understand that if my brother sins against me, I must confront him. I also know what to do if he refuses to listen. But what if the first step works? What if he listens? I presume I have to forgive him. But what if he offends me repeatedly? How many times do I have to forgive him? Is seven enough?" No, Jesus replies (18:22), you must forgive him again and again.[7] This is a difficult teaching; "therefore" (18:23) Jesus tells a story to motivate his disciples to forgive. Because some of the logical steps in these verse are implicit, we cannot prove that we have discovered the logic of the passage. Yet our analysis has a very high degree of probability if we merely assume that Matthew reports a real event with an economy of words.

General Principles for Discourse Analysis

The preceding introduction modeled two major principles for discourse analysis.

▶ **Principle 1: Look for words and phrases that explicitly connect one idea to another.**

Some of the most common connecting words appeared in the passage above: *and, but, if, then, therefore, for, so that.* Each word connected one sentence or clause to another. In English, other common connecting words are *because, so, since, when, just as, in order that, while, after,* and many more. Significantly, these terms connect phrases within sentences, not just whole sentences.

▶ **Principle 2: Look for implicit and understated connections.**

We noticed that the connection between verses 17 and 18 is implicit; no term told us how to correlate the two paragraphs. The connection between verses 20 and 21 is understated. That is, although we read that Peter "then" asked a question, it did not merely happen next; Peter was responding to Jesus. Sometimes authors spell out their reasoning; often they do not. Many portions of the Bible, upon close reading, have implicit logic. To get the most from the Bible, therefore, we must find the logical steps that remain half-buried, like blankets on a wind-swept beach.

Perhaps you have noticed that discourse analysis draws on familiar skills. Like the study of literary contexts, discourse analysis asks how a series of sentences fits together. Both ponder how one thought leads to another. They consider why the author put this thought or event here, and nowhere else. Like dramatic analysis (see chap. 5), it builds to a peak, such as Peter's question. Nevertheless, there are differences. The climax of a discourse analysis is its central truth, rather than the climactic event, and we come to it by following thoughts, rather than by tracking events. Narratives resemble roller coasters more than dissertations; there are reasons for the dips and curls, but the ride itself is essential. While a discourse may have moments of flash and emotion, it appeals mostly to the mind.

Analyzing Paragraphs and Larger Sections

To capture the message of the Bible, we need to study paragraphs more than single words or even sentences.[8] That is, discourse analysis works on paragraphs, whole chapters, and even larger segments of books, as well as sentences.[9] Analysis of large paragraphs and larger sections can be extremely rewarding, as we see next, in analyzing Galatians.

From the start, recall the historical context of the book. The apostle Paul wrote Galatians to a group of churches he founded in the Roman province of Galatia during his first missionary journey. They seemed secure until a group of Jews (called Judaizers) visited them, teaching two errors: (1) They said that Gentiles had to obey Jewish ceremonial laws regarding circumcision, food, and holy days in order to be saved. Essentially, Gentiles had to live like Jews to be Christians. (2) They claimed that Paul's gospel lacked authority, since he was no apostle. The Judaizers persuaded many Galatians and confused more. When word of the Judaizers' disruptions reached Paul, he responded with the letter called Galatians.

It is possible to see the whole book as a simple discourse. First, Paul declares that he is an apostle, commissioned by Jesus and accepted by the other apostles, who approve his gospel, as an equal

(1:1–2:14). Because he is an apostle, Paul's message has authority (1:6–10). Second, Paul's gospel says, "A man is not justified by observing the law, but by faith in Jesus Christ" (2:15–21). Paul then demonstrates (3:1–18) and expands (3:19–4:31) his message. Third, even though Christians are not required to obey the law in order to be saved, they must prove their faith by acts of service and love and by manifesting the fruit of the Spirit (5:1–6:10). With the big picture established, we can begin a discourse analysis of Galatians 3.

Thinking in Paragraphs: An Analysis of Galatians 3

As you begin, remember that Paul wrote Galatians 3 to prove the veracity of the gospel presented in 2:15–21. As you read, try to form at least a provisional idea of the main point of each paragraph in Galatians 3, and see how it develops the theme. While the paragraph divisions in our Bibles have been devised by translators, they are usually reliable. So, we will follow the chapter divisions of the *New International Version*. Look for the theme of these paragraphs: 3:1–5, 6–9, 10–14, 15–18, 19–25 (three short paragraphs that are closely related). Jot down your ideas as you go; resist looking at our answers until you have finished. After you have finished, compare your analysis to the one provided below.

Paragraph 1 (3:1–5): Your experience verifies Paul's gospel. By asking a series of rhetorical questions, Paul challenges the Galatians to remember that their experience agrees with his gospel. How did they receive the Holy Spirit? How did they begin their new life? How did God work miracles among them? Because of their faith or because of their obedience? Five consecutive rhetorical questions sting and rouse emotion, showing the Galatians that their errors bring Paul to grief and dismay, not merely disapproval. Jesus, the author of Hebrews, and James also used a series of rhetorical questions to show shock and pain over people's errors (see Mark 8:14–21; Heb. 3:16–18; James 2:5–7). And, by posing questions, they expected the reader to join in the judgment. To put it another way, Paul's language, "O foolish Galatians! Who has bewitched you?" (3:1), would have been insulting if it had not been so evident that he had agonized over them and now believed that they knew better.

Paragraph 2 (3:6–9): Abraham's experience verifies Paul's gospel. Just as the Galatians' experience proves they are justified and enjoy the benefits of salvation by faith, so does Abraham's experience.[10] Scripture says that Abraham "believed God, and it was credited to him as righteousness." We are children of Abraham, Paul asserts, blessed with him. This paragraph advances the same idea as the first one, but the basis for argument is now Israel's experience. The emotional atmosphere also changes from anguish to confidence, as Paul tells the Galatians that they are Abraham's children, blessed with him.[11]

Paragraph 3 (3:10–14): The law verifies Paul's gospel. The law also agrees with Paul's gospel. The law curses all who do not continue to do everything written in it (v. 10). But no one can be so perfectly obedient (v. 11). Therefore, the righteous will live by faith (v. 11), not works. Christ became accursed for us, not to make it possible for us to try harder to obey the law, but to redeem us and bless us (vv. 13–14). Rhetorically, we notice that Paul shifts from the indefinite pronouns "all . . . all who . . . no one" in discussing the curse (vv. 10–11), to the warmer, more encouraging personal pronouns when discussing redemption: "Christ redeemed *us* . . . so that . . . *we* might receive the promise of the Spirit" (vv. 13–14).

Paragraph 4 (3:15–18): God's covenant with Abraham verifies Paul's gospel. God promised to give land, heirs, and blessing to Abraham and his line 430 years before God delivered the law to Israel. If he promised in a covenant to give the inheritance freely, he cannot legally set that covenant aside and add new terms later on (vv. 16–17). To illustrate, suppose I tell my children unconditionally, "I am taking you all out for ice cream tonight." I would be an unjust father if after supper I announced, "If anyone still wants to get some ice cream, come and get your list of chores." Today we have the saying, "You cannot change the rules in the middle of the game." Paul said, in effect, "God did not change the 'rules' for covenants in the middle of redemptive history." God bestowed the first, most basic covenant blessings by grace, not law, and his subsequent blessings adhere to that pattern.

Paragraphs 5–7 (3:19–25): The purpose of the law verifies Paul's gospel. Paul anticipates an objection: if keeping the law plays no part in receiving salvation, then what was its purpose? The law was added because of transgressions, answers Paul, to show mankind its sinfulness, and so to lead us to Christ (vv. 18, 22–24).

Additional Principles of Paragraph Analysis

Our survey of Galatians 3 illustrates the chief principles for paragraph analysis.

> ▶ **Principle 1: Locate the main thought of each paragraph.**

Once you have the theme of your paragraphs, look for terms that show the connection between them. Galatians 3 has connecting terms (and here I translate directly from the Greek) such as "just as" (3:6), "for" (3:10), "brothers, I speak like a man" (3:15), and "what, therefore" (3:19). This then is

> ▶ **Principle 2: Determine the relations between paragraphs.**

But Galatians 3 has an emotional as well as a logical aspect. Paul chides the Galatians at the beginning of the chapter (3:1–6). But he soon encourages them by including them among the objects of God's saving love (3:7–14). Thus,

> ▶ **Principle 3: Observe signs of the emotional atmosphere.**

Another principle, already mentioned in the chapter on context, applies here too.

> ▶ **Principle 4: Some propositions function two ways at once, ending a line of thought in one sentence or paragraph, and simultaneously leading into the next.**

By a "proposition" I mean any expression in which a verb or predicate affirms or denies something about its subject. Propositions may be as short as a fragment of a sentence.

Close Analysis of a Single Paragraph

For the beginner, discourse analysis is most fruitful in the study of paragraphs. Still, there are times when authors, like travelers preparing for a long trip, pack meaning in tightly enough to reward more intensive study. Because the tools for analysis may be new to you, we will first practice them on a familiar text, Romans 12:1–2. The following translation is rather literal, to bring out the sense of certain Greek words. The explicit transitions in thought have been marked again. Try to find the implicit ones as you read.

> *Therefore,* I urge you, brothers, by the mercies of God, to present your bodies as sacrifices that are living, holy, and well pleasing to God, *which* is your reasonable service. *And* do not be conformed to this world, *but* be transformed by the renewing of your mind, *that* you may prove what the will of God is, that it is good and pleasing and perfect.

Paul's main idea is the command "Present your bodies . . . to God." Of the five chief clues that authors use to indicate their main idea, four appear here. "Present your bodies" is (1) the first proposition in the paragraph, and it is set apart by (2) the direct address "brothers," (3) the introductory formula "I urge you," and (4) the concluding term "therefore."

"Therefore" shows that Paul sees the commandment as the conclusion of some things he said earlier. Does it refer to the doxology in chapter 11? To all that Paul said about God's saving plan for the Jews? To the entire description of God's salvation from 1:17 onward? The answer seems to be yes all three times. The phrase "by the mercies of God" states the means or basis of Paul's urging. The plural "mercies" hints that the reader might search all of Romans to find many reasons for offering himself to God.[12]

The phrases "living, holy, and well pleasing to God" and "which is your reasonable service" both modify or specify the nature of the sacrifice. At a minimum, "living" means that the reader should present himself all through life, not just once; "holy" means that we should consecrate ourselves to God; "well pleasing to God" means that we offer ourselves on his terms—to please him, not ourselves. To discover the full meaning of the terms, one must look up the individual words and study the sacrificial ritual and other customs of the day. "Your reasonable service" evaluates the sacrifice.

"And" (v. 2) seems simply to add another command. But, upon reflection, it introduces two subordinate commands that support the main one, "Present your bodies . . . to God." Both tell the Romans how to offer their bodies. Negatively, they must resist the world's pressures to conform to it. "But" establishes a contrast; positively, they must transform themselves by the renewing of their minds.

"That" means "in order that," and introduces the purpose (and possibly also the result) of obedience to Paul's commands. If the Romans resist the world, renew their minds, and generally offer themselves to God, they will have an opportunity to put God's will to the test and find that it is indeed good, pleasing, and perfect.

Our examination of Romans 12 has followed the principles for analysis stated earlier. As before, the first step was to identify the theme of the paragraph and state it as a simple "kernel" sentence. "Present your bodies to God" is the theme of the paragraph, and every following word supports it, presenting reasons, methods, and the result. Finding the kernel sentence enabled us to follow the apostle's thought as he developed it. That done, we located terms that explicitly signified relationships between ideas or propositions. Next we searched for implicit and understated connections.

Analyzing Hebrew Poetry

So far in this chapter, we have discussed the analysis of the prose found in letters and speeches, but we must also say a word about biblical poetry, since it is found throughout the prophetic books, Psalms, the wisdom books, and even the Gospels. Biblical poetry involves parallelism—the stating of similar ideas in a two- or three-line stanza divided by a short pause. For example:

> Blessed is the man who fears the LORD,
>> who finds great delight in his commands. (Ps. 112:1)

In parallelism, the second line looks back on the first, completing it, commenting on it, restating it, expanding it, or intensifying it:[13]

> Hear my prayer, O God;
>> listen to the words of my mouth. (Ps. 54:2—restatement)

> Be strong and take heart,
>> all you who hope in the LORD. (Ps. 31:24—completion)

> The ox knows his master,
>> the donkey his owner's manger,

but Israel does not know,
    my people do not understand. (Isa. 1:3—intensification)

The first two examples require no comment, but the text from Isaiah shows that parallelism can be more complex. Isaiah's first term of comparison, an ox, is not especially praiseworthy, but oxen do work hard and obey well. Even a donkey, an animal famed for its recalcitrance, at least knows where to be fed. But Israel does not know or obey even that much.

Many parallel lines resemble the example from Isaiah. They have the form "A, and, as a matter of fact, B" or "Not only A, but even B." This sense that the second line adds to or intensifies the first line creates a sharpness, and perhaps a touch of mystery, to many texts. Proverbs 26:9 (translated literally) has both.

A thorn goes up into the hand of a drunkard,
    and a proverb into the mouth of a fool.

The proverb clearly intends a comparison between the two lines, but its precise nature is unstated and hence presents a minor mystery. The idea is probably that no one should be impressed by a proverb in a fool's mouth, for it entered there just as randomly as a thorn enters the hand of a drunk who thrashes through the bushes.[14]

The idea with biblical poetry is not to classify it, but to see how pairs of lines work together. James Kugel and other recent analysts critique the once-standard idea that there are three types or forms of poetic parallelism: synonymous, antithetic, and synthetic. The three categories are too rigid, according to Kugel. He says that in biblical parallelism the second line always adds something to the first, but that the addition takes dozens of slightly different forms. "Biblical parallelism is of one sort, 'A, and what's more, B,' or a hundred sorts; but it is not three [sorts]."[15]

The New Testament also uses parallelism. The principles for interpretation are similar to those for the Old Testament. Here is one example, where restatement dominates.[16]

Ask, and it will be given you;
seek, and you will find;
knock, and it will be opened to you.
For every one who asks receives,

and he who seeks finds,
and to him who knocks it will be opened. (Matt. 7:7–8 RSV)

Relations Between Propositions:
A Simple English-Based Model

To develop any powerful and rewarding skill, is to pay a price. In the movie *A League of Their Own,* which presents life in the women's baseball league of the 1940s, the star catcher of the team decides to quit just before the league championship. "It just got too hard," she explains. The manager ignites, "It's *supposed* to be hard. If it wasn't hard, *everyone* would do it. The 'hard' is what makes it great." The manager got it exactly right, both for baseball and for Bible exposition. If you want to rise above mediocrity and reach excellence, this is the time to count the cost. It is hard to teach the Bible faithfully and accurately. Precisely for that reason, not many do it. The following pages are for those who are ready to expend the effort.

Until now, we have examined the relations between propositions inductively, observing them between paragraphs and sentences, but not labeling them. Now we turn to a more systematic discussion of the relations between propositions. A short English-based list of the most common relations follows. (Longer, more technical descriptions of the relations between propositions appear in appendix C. One applies to all languages; the second, to New Testament Greek.)

This list offers a little more precision than we can obtain by circling key words. First, it describes the most common relationships between ideas. This is especially helpful when we have only implicit markers. Second, many terms that mark logical relationships have two or more meanings. When trying to decide which sense of a word is intended, we need to know all the options. For example, "then" can denote sequence (one action followed another) or causation (one action caused another). Our simple system will divide possible relations into three groups: addition and subtraction, cause and effect, clarification and explanation.

Addition and Subtraction

Addition takes place when we read a simple sequence of events, things, or ideas, as in the sentence "We had dinner, and then walked along the beach." The acronym BAT covers the principal possibilities: *but, and, then.*

1. *But* statements contrast two propositions. They subtract or take away something from another statement, as in, "Kevin made the game-winning shot, but Jim's pass set him up." Words like *yet, on the contrary, on the other hand,* and *however* also express contrast.

2. *And* statements add ideas. Similar to *and* are *also, furthermore, moreover,* and *in addition.* Commas frequently function like the word *and.* For example, "The fruit of the Spirit is love, joy, peace, . . . gentleness and self-control" (Gal. 5:22–23).

3. *Then* propositions describe sequences of events. "Then" words include *before, after, then,* and *next.* We describe simultaneous events with words like *during, while,* and *meanwhile.*

Cause and Effect

Cause-and-effect relations exist when one statement gives the reasons, results, means, conditions, or conclusions to be drawn from another, as in the sentence "We were full from a large dinner, so we took a walk on the beach." The acronym this time is PRICE: purpose, reasoning, if-then, concession, effect.

1. *Purpose* statements describe actions taken in order to obtain specific results. They tell why an action takes place. Some purpose words are *so that, in order to,* and, in some sentences, *to* by itself.

2. *Reasoning* statements draw conclusions from prior assertions or state the basis for conclusions that have already been stated. Some reasoning words are *therefore, thus, so, since, then, consequently, for, for this reason, because,* and certain combinations that include these words and others.

3. *If-then* statements express possibility. Some if-then statements describe what is actually possible. Others explain that because of certain conditions, something is now impossible. If-then statements usually begin with *if,* but *then* is usually assumed rather than expressed.

4. *Concession* statements concede that one thing is true even though we have reason to expect another, as in "We had a wonderful picnic, even though it rained." Some common words introducing concessions are *although, even though, nevertheless, in spite of, yet,* and *nonetheless.*

5. *Effect* statements come in pairs. One proposition describes what happened or what is true and the second explains how or why it came about. For example, "Since it rained so hard, we had to cancel

the softball game." Words expressing effect include *since, because, then,* and *consequently.* Remember, however, that two statements may follow each other without having any causal connection. They may simply be two facts or reports of events that occurred together without one causing the other.

Clarification and Explanation

Ideas relate to one another in many other ways; we will mention a few here and leave others for appendix C.

1. *Introductions.* The Bible uses formulas such as *I urge you, I want you to know, truly I say to you, thus says the Lord,* and *the Scripture says* to prepare readers for important statements that follow.

2. *Summaries and restatements* remind the reader of what has gone before, often before starting a new topic.

3. *Illustrations* use events, stories, or figures of speech to make an abstract idea more concrete, or to add an emotional component to a passage.

This discussion has introduced some specific ways in which propositions relate to each other. Do not expect to learn all these categories at once; the goal is to raise your awareness of the way the Bible works. If you read the Bible more closely and notice some of the words and phrases listed, you will begin to detect others. Then (sequence and result!) you will find yourself perceiving ever more of the flow of argument. Appendix C explains these concepts in more detail.

Conclusion

This chapter has completed the second part of the CAPTOR outline. We have studied two sides of both Context and Analysis; the work on Problems, Themes, Obligations, and Reflection remains.

Discourse analysis may be the most difficult aspect of this book. Fortunately, one need not master all the concepts presented here in order to profit from the discussion. If you have become sensitive to the issues, if you are willing to slow down and look hard at the flow of thought, you have taken a large step forward.

Discourse analysis is more like playing baseball than it is like making boxes. You cannot master it before lunch, or even before supper. People become accomplished only through practice and a de-

sire to convey the results to others. Yet, like so many other demanding skills, it has a rich payoff. If God has called you to it, to
work hard in the Word is to love God with your mind. Through it,
your teaching can acquire a fire, a confidence, and a fidelity to God's
Word that you have never known before.

Exercises

Remember, discourse analysis is most important when a key text is
difficult to follow. It takes time, so don't use it on every text. If you
can follow the author's logic easily, devote most of your time to
other research.

1. Analyze the group of paragraphs in Matthew 6:19–24, which
   has three subsections: verses 19–21, 22–23, and 24. What is the
   theme of the whole unit? What is the theme of each subsection,
   and how do they relate to one another?

2. Analyze the propositions in these single paragraphs:
   a. Galatians 3:6–9. First, mark the terms that indicate the flow
      of thought. Then look for other, less obvious clues as to the
      shape of the discourse.
   b. Matthew 6:19–21. This short section has several explicit
      markers of thought, but some of them, such as "where,"
      function unusually. Other connections are implicit.
   c. The Old Testament generally has far fewer explicit markers,
      but you can try Psalm 25.

3. Analyze these large sections (this exercise takes longer):
   a. What is the theme of 1 Samuel 24–26? How does each chap-
      ter develop or modify the larger theme?
   b. What is the main point of Romans 1–3? What are the main
      sections? How do they build upon each other?

Notes

¹ Robert Hughes, "The NRA in a Hunter's Sights," *Time* (April 3, 1989), 86.
² Michael Kinsley, "The Check Is in the Mail," *Time* (April 9, 1990), 98.
³ Charles Krauthammer, "In Praise of Low Voter Turnout" *Time* (May 21, 1990), 88.
⁴ Discourse analysis is actually a very sophisticated discipline with several sub-
fields. For a sophisticated introduction, consult Peter Cotterell and Max Turner, *Lin-*

guistics and Biblical Interpretation (Downers Grove, Ill.: InterVarsity Press, 1989), 188–292; John Beekman and John Callow, *Translating the Word of God* (Grand Rapids: Zondervan, 1974), 212–342; Robert E. Longacre, *The Grammar of Discourse* (New York: Plenum Press, 1983). Rhetorical analysis has some affinities to discourse analysis. For an introduction, see Burton Mack, *Rhetoric and the New Testament* (Philadelphia: Augsburg, 1990), and George A. Kennedy, *New Testament Interpretation Through Rhetorical Criticism* (Chapel Hill, N.C.: University of North Carolina Press, 1984). The definition of discourse analysis given here is deliberately broader than that given in some technical works.

⁵ Typically, each statement is a little different: "Faith by itself, if it is not accompanied by action, is dead. . . . Faith without deeds is useless. . . . Faith without deeds is dead" (James 2:17, 20, 26). Double statement of the main point is very common, and there are other triple statements.

⁶ The Greek supports this interpretation, in that the word translated "thing" in the English "anything" in 18:19 (*pragma*) typically means an "affair" or "matter" (Rom. 16:2), with possible wrongdoing (1 Thess. 4:6; 2 Cor. 7:11), or even a lawsuit in the air (1 Cor. 6:1). See the full documentation in Duncan M. Derrett, "'Where two or three are convened in my name . . .': a sad misunderstanding," *Expository Times* 91 (December 1979): 83–86.

⁷ In chap. 7 we will take up the numbers that Jesus used.

⁸ Gordon Fee, *New Testament Exegesis: A Handbook for Students and Pastors* (Philadelphia: Westminster Press, 1983), 34–35, 128–29.

⁹ It also works on smaller segments, such as clauses and phrases within sentences. That demanding task can be pursued through the sources listed in footnote 4.

¹⁰ The NIV does not have a word corresponding to the Greek term *kathos* ("just as"), which begins v. 6. The NIV adds the command "consider" to compensate and suggest vaguely that the reader needs to think about something. The NASB says "even so"; the RSV, "thus." This illustrates again the value of having several translations, of knowing which are more literal and which are more free, and of having a pastor who knows Greek.

¹¹ Incidentally, besides introducing 3:7–9, v. 6 also concludes 3:1–5, saying, "Just as Abraham believed God and it was reckoned to him as righteousness." The idea is this: God supplies the Spirit and works miracles among the Galatians by faith (3:1–5); even so he justified Abraham by faith (3:7–9). In earlier chapters of this book, we have also seen that Ephesians 5:21 and James 1:5 conclude one section and open another.

¹² "Mercies" could also be plural simply because the language of the verse evokes Hebrew patterns, and the Hebrew term for *mercy* is plural.

¹³ See James Kugel, *The Idea of Biblical Poetry* (New Haven: Yale University Press, 1981), 1–58, esp. 1–12. For more on biblical poetry, see Robert Alter, *The Art of Biblical Poetry* (New York: Basic Books, 1985); David L. Peterson and Kent Harold Richards, *Interpreting Biblical Poetry* (Minneapolis: Fortress Press), 1992.

¹⁴ Kugel, *The Idea of Biblical Poetry*, 11. The next verse (26:10) explicitly raises the topic of random behavior, strengthening the probability of this interpretation.

¹⁵ Ibid., 58.

¹⁶ See Robert Stein, *The Method and Message of Jesus* (Philadelphia: Westminster Press, 1978), 27–32. Stein's categories basically follow the scheme that Kugel rejects, but he does demonstrate the frequency of parallelism in the teaching of Jesus.

7

Solving Problems

Middle-aged Hens and Other Problems

One day, when I was feeling especially appreciative of all that my wife had done for me, I decided to demonstrate my gratitude by cooking her a surprise gourmet dinner. I looked through her favorite cookbook, searching for something that would look and sound impressive, until the heading "Coq au Vin" caught my eye. The French title impressed me, and I saw only one or two ingredients that we didn't have. But what does it taste like? Conveniently, they supplied a description at the end of the recipe: "A wonderfully robust dish, full of friendly flavors in a rich dark sauce—and a good way to use a middle-aged hen."

That left me wondering—what is a friendly flavor? How can one tell if the frozen chicken in one's freezer is middle-aged, especially when it is no longer alive? To understand the recipe and then make an informed decision about it, I had to solve those two problems. (As you might guess, we ate out that night.)

For beginners, reading the Bible is like reading a book of recipes or even a manual on aircraft maintenance. From the beginning, they feel vaguely uncomfortable, out of their league. And if they encounter several puzzling phrases and concepts, they may be in danger of losing the message entirely. Not knowing how to proceed, they may want to give up. Sophisticated Christians encounter riddles, too. While mature readers will probably still get the main point, they may miss the precise thrust or some significant side point.

To study the Bible effectively, we must learn to recognize and solve the problems we encounter when reading texts. We recognize problems by reading slowly and carefully, taking time to pause over anything we do not understand. This chapter defines a problem as *any term, phrase, concept, custom, or teaching that eludes our understanding.* Many problems are solved by a thorough knowledge of the historical background.[1]

Kinds of Problems

We can distinguish three kinds of problems:

1. *Obvious problems.* These include places, names, words, or customs about which we know little or nothing. The names of unknown people or places, new or unusual terms or phrases, and references to half-forgotten events are all classic problems. For example, when Moses says, "Do not test the LORD your God as you did at Massah" (Deut. 6:16), you must know what happened at Massah to get the point. The third and fourth chapters of Ruth are full of problems for an uneducated reader. Why does Ruth gather grain in someone else's fields? Why is Boaz expected to be interested in marrying Ruth? Why does the person who buys Naomi's field acquire a wife in the deal? Why does Boaz discuss this matter with ten elders in the city gate?

2. *Teachers' problems.* Someone may know all the answers to the questions from Ruth. But teachers still need to determine if their group knows, too.

3. *Hidden problems.* Problems may also include terms or phrases that we have encountered before. We may have an opinion or a vague memory of the person, issue, term, or custom in view. But if we are reading slowly and honestly, we realize that we *know* very little about it. For example, we probably think we know what the term *desert* means. But if it refers to a place where there is no water, how could all Jerusalem and Judea go out to see John in the desert without perishing? The answer is that a biblical "desert" is an unpopulated area, not necessarily a waterless area.

The Most Fundamental Problem

To recognize and solve problems, we must be aware of our areas of ignorance. Putting it paradoxically, we need to know what we don't know. While we can never fully comprehend our limits (Would we need to know everything to do so?), to know the extent of our ignorance is itself a kind of wisdom. The key is to read slowly, considering each phrase and asking, "Do I know what this means? Or do I merely remember something I think I heard somewhere from someone a long time ago?" Unless we are reading several chapters of Scripture at once to get the big picture of a book, there is no need to hurry through a passage.

This does not imply that we flail about in a sea of ignorance so vast that radical skepticism is the best option. Generations of scholars have shed enough light on antiquity that we can reconstruct the essentials of ancient language and customs. Nor is the biblical message so difficult or convoluted that we constantly need to run to the experts. Although there is a place for teachers, the authors of the Bible assume that the covenant community can comprehend their message. To put it another way, when Peter himself says that Paul's letters contain "some things that are hard to understand" (2 Peter 3:16), we should emphasize the word "some." *Some* things are hard to understand, but it is almost impossible for an adult believer to misconstrue the main truths of the Bible.

We can compare the problems in biblical interpretation to riddles in detective work. When trying to solve a crime, investigators usually get to the point where they know who did it, even if their evidence is not legally airtight. Similarly, Christians can be confident that they have the main point, even without solving every problem in every verse. Newer Christians can work at basic questions. If older Christians keep studying, they will move on to more advanced areas. So, provided that we can recognize and solve the main problems, we can find the thrust of a passage. But how do we recognize problems?

Identifying Problems:
Three Sample Passages

We can start by reading a particularly rich passage and listing potential problems. Please list potential problems in the following text on a piece of paper as you read, using the categories of (1) obvious, (2) teachers', and (3) hidden problems, before reading the next paragraph of the book.

Acts 13:1–3

> In the church at Antioch there were prophets and teachers: Barnabas, Simeon called Niger, Lucius of Cyrene, Manaen (who had been brought up with Herod the tetrarch) and Saul. While they were worshiping the Lord and fasting, the Holy Spirit said, "Set apart for me Barnabas and Saul for the work to which I have called them." So after they had fasted and prayed, they placed their hands on them and sent them off.

Your list of *obvious problems* may include these questions of fact: Where is Antioch? What do we know about the church there? What do we know about the men Simeon, Lucius, and Manaen? Is "Saul" the same person as the apostle Paul, and, if so, why does he have two names? Obvious theological questions include: How did the Holy Spirit reveal that they should set apart Barnabas and Saul? Did they hear a voice with their ears? Did they hear something internally? Did some or all get a powerful impression?

Teachers may want to investigate fasting and prayer and the laying on of hands. Almost all adults have a superficial knowledge of these practices, but good teachers want to take their class deeper. How did they fast and pray? Did they drink liquids or not? Does one have to fast for a whole day for it to count, or can one fast for part of a day? If so, how is fasting different from missing a meal or having little food? What is the meaning of laying on hands? Is it formal, like ordination, or an act of fellowship? Is it sacramental? Did it impart real spiritual power for the mission, or was it simply an act of blessing and approving?[2]

Hidden problems begin as something we think we know. Then we see a feature of the text that makes us wonder if our confidence is well founded. In these verses, the prophets and teachers could be a hidden problem. The text is so casual about them, that we wonder what sort of prophets they were. Were they lesser prophets, like the men in the schools of the prophets with Samuel and Elijah? Are all prophets the same? Are all teachers the same? Can prophets and teachers be close to each other?

This is not the time to answer the questions we have just posed, valuable as that might be. The task at the moment is to recognize problems. So, on to another passage.

1 Samuel 17:1–10

> Now the Philistines gathered their forces for war and assembled at Socoh in Judah. They pitched camp at Ephes Dammim, between Socoh and Azekah. Saul and the Israelites assembled and camped in the Valley of Elah and drew up their battle line to meet the Philistines. The Philistines occupied one hill and the Israelites another, with the valley between them. A champion named Goliath, who was from Gath, came out of the Philistine camp. He was over nine feet tall. He had a bronze helmet on his head and wore a coat of scale armor of bronze weighing five thousand shekels; on his legs he wore bronze greaves, and a bronze javelin was slung on his back. His spear shaft was like a weaver's rod, and its iron point weighed six hundred shekels. His shield bearer went ahead of him. Goliath stood and shouted to the ranks of Israel, "Why do you come out and line up for battle? Am I not a Philistine, and are you not the servants of Saul? Choose a man and have him come down to me. If he is able to fight and kill me, we will become your subjects; but if I overcome him and kill him, you will become our subjects and serve us." Then the Philistine said, "This day I defy the ranks of Israel! Give me a man and let us fight each other."

This passage is full of *obvious* factual questions, but most people want to know about Goliath first. How big was he? (Nine feet, nine inches tall.) How much did his armor weigh? (The armor for his torso weighed 125 pounds.) How did he get so big? *Teachers* could ask if his size was related to demonic activity, and if he was related in any way—spiritually, not genetically, of course—to the Nephilim who lived before the Flood. Was he a Satanic figure or just an enemy warrior? Did he know that the Israelites claimed to be the people of God? Did his taunts have an edge because he knew that the Israelites despised the Philistines?

Some find the military customs interesting. What did the battle lines look like? What lies behind the idea of two heroes fighting each other? Was that common, or did the Philistines only propose it here because they thought they had an advantage? Would the army of the loser really submit to the army of the winner simply because one man had defeated the other?

The larger military and political picture could be our set of *hidden* questions. Exactly who were the Philistines? How much of a challenge did they pose to the Israelites? Where were the cities mentioned in the chapter? Were they in Philistia, in Israel, or on the border? (They were several miles into Israel.) What were they like? Do any of them have special importance in the Bible? (No.) Did they have strategic value? (Yes.) If so, was this a little border skirmish or a major invasion that threatened Israel's integrity? (It was possibly a major invasion.)

The short parenthetical answers you have been reading all come from detective work with maps, dictionaries, and encyclopedias, all of which you will learn to use. To begin, read one more text, state its problems, solve some of them, and watch how the investigation brings the passage to life. Pause and list some problems from this passage before you read the next section of this chapter. Then you will see how useful it can be to be able to investigate matters yourself.

Matthew 18:21-35

> Then Peter came to Jesus and asked, "Lord, how many times shall I forgive my brother when he sins against me? Up to seven times?"
>
> Jesus answered, "I tell you, not seven times, but seventy-seven times.
>
> "Therefore, the kingdom of heaven is like a king who wanted to settle accounts with his servants. As he began the settlement, a man who owed him ten thousand talents was brought to him. Since he was not able to pay, the master ordered that he and his wife and his children and all that he had be sold to repay the debt.
>
> "The servant fell on his knees before him. 'Be patient with me,' he begged, 'and I will pay back everything.' The servant's master took pity on him, canceled the debt and let him go.
>
> "But when that servant went out, he found one of his fellow servants who owed him a hundred denarii. He grabbed

him and began to choke him. 'Pay back what you owe me!'
he demanded.

"His fellow servant fell to his knees and begged him, 'Be
patient with me, and I will pay you back.'

"But he refused. Instead, he went off and had the man
thrown into prison until he could pay the debt. When the
other servants saw what had happened, they were greatly
distressed and went and told their master everything that
had happened.

"Then the master called the servant in. 'You wicked servant,' he said, 'I canceled all that debt of yours because you
begged me to. Shouldn't you have had mercy on your fellow
servant just as I had on you?' In anger his master turned him
over to the jailers to be tortured, until he should pay back all
he owed.

"This is how my heavenly Father will treat each of you unless you forgive your brother from your heart."

There are dozens of *obvious* problems in this parable. Why does
Peter offer to forgive his brother precisely seven times? Why do
some versions say Jesus replied seventy-seven times, while others
say seventy times seven? (Answer: The Greek is ambiguous.) Does
it matter whether he meant seventy-seven or seventy times seven?
(Answer: Not much. We can forgive seven times through self-
discipline, but we either explode or forgiveness becomes a way of
life long before one counts to seventy-seven, let alone seventy times
seven.)

The fate and the behavior of the leading servant are also perplexing. He could be sold; that implies that he was more like a slave.
On the other hand, what kind of a servant is this, to handle so much
money and accumulate huge debts? How much money is involved
in the story? Why is the first servant so harsh toward his fellow servant? Why is he jailed and tortured at the end? Is Jesus creating a
fantastic story, or are we missing crucial customs of the day? *Teachers* will be interested in all of these problems, but they might also explore the symbolism of the parable. Who do the characters represent?
Why does Jesus create a merciful king and a harsh, mean-spirited
servant? The fate of the unforgiving servant prompts a *hidden* question—is this a parable of grace, or is it primarily about the sources
and consequences of an unforgiving spirit?

How to Solve Problems

So far, we have focused our attention on factual problems.

> ♦ **Principle 1: Readers can solve most factual problems by using Bible dictionaries and encyclopedias.**

Appendix E lists recommended books for a quality home library. Most Bible encyclopedias and dictionaries are user-friendly. If you cannot find an entry for your topic, consult the index. The information you seek about swords may be listed under "warfare"; lions may appear in an article on "Flora and Fauna" or "Plants and Animals of the Bible." Articles typically convey more information than you need. Many long articles list their contents at the beginning. Most work first in the Old Testament, and then move to the New. Skim the article until you find what you need, since only a few points will apply to your problem. Do not try to cram your encyclopedic knowledge into your lesson; select whatever is truly illuminating. Of course, encyclopedias will not cover every question, but good commentaries also explain many factual questions. If a theological statement baffles you, look up the relevant topic in a handbook of theology. If a character in a narrative does something surprising, try to reconstruct the reason for that action within the story (see chap. 5).

We can now put these principles to work on Matthew 18, commenting on just two of the more complex problems, the amounts of money and the nature of the servanthood. Before reading on, you may want to try your hand at them. If so, look up both "servant" and "slave" (or "slavery"), since the two were closely related. For money, you may find separate articles on the talent and the denarius, or they may appear under "money" or "weights and measures." But fasten your seat belts; there is turbulence ahead.

The Talent and the Denarius

Modern English uses the term *talent* to describe God-given skills and abilities. But in New Testament times a talent was usually a unit of money or a weight of valuable metals. Study Bibles and commentaries give varying estimates of the value of a talent, and so they differ greatly concerning the ten thousand talents of Matthew 18:21–35. Notes in Bibles variously suggest that ten thousand talents equals "millions of dollars," "millions and millions of dollars," or "about $10,000,000 in silver content but worth much more in buying power." Two versions of the Bible from around 1970 drop the term *talent* altogether and substitute "ten million dollars" in one case and "twenty million dollars" in another.

Commentators also read the sums differently. Daniel Patte casually asserts that the debt was "the equivalent of millions of dollars."[3] Leon Morris, after noting that one talent is "a large sum of money," calls the debt "a vast sum," but goes no further.[4] Josephus pegs the total tax yield of Palestine at 8,000 talents, with Judea yielding 600 talents per year, indicating the enormous size of the debt.[5] In fact, the numbers are so high that at least one critical commentator speculates that Matthew has inflated the numbers Jesus used in the original parable.[6] But Duncan Derrett believes that the numbers and the story make sense if the servant is a regional tax chief.[7] Or, perhaps, since the number ten thousand was the largest in common use in antiquity, we should round the debt off, call it "a billion dollars" or "a billion pounds," and leave it at that.[8] Pheme Perkins says "several billion," and suggests that the story appeals to popular imaginations about "fabulously wealthy kings of the east."[9] Craig Blomberg, citing Perkins, suggests that the number teetered on the border between reality and fantasy.[10]

The denarius poses a smaller, but genuine, riddle. Marginal notes in Bible translations may say a denarius is worth eighteen cents (KJV), twenty-five cents (Berkeley), or a few dollars (NIV). Commentators and reference works all agree that a denarius equals one day's wage for a laborer, roughly comparable to a minimum wage. Therefore, the debt of the second servant is one hundred days' wages—a much smaller sum than the debt of the first servant, yet still a substantial one.

These issues make a real difference in interpreting the parable. A debt of ten million dollars, though vast, is understandable and perhaps payable. A billion-dollar debt, on the other hand, is almost beyond imagination or repayment. Which better expresses the concept of our vast debt before God and his amazing mercy? Which number better expresses the debt of the second servant? Eighteen dollars or one hundred days' wages? At this point, one might say, "This is complex; even the experts are divided. Who am I to get into this fray?" But it is far better to resolve, "I need to look into this. Perhaps there are some basic facts that everyone is interpreting differently. Perhaps one or two basic misconceptions are causing all the trouble."

Here, then, are the basics. Both ancient and modern factors cause estimates of the talent and denarius to vary. First, a talent was a measure of weight, varying from fifty-eight to eighty pounds from place to place and time to time. Although a talent was ordinarily a weight of silver coins, it could also be a weight of gold or copper. Second, inflation complicates everything, as the value of precious metals and other money keeps changing. When a Bible's study notes set the value of a denarius at eighteen to twenty-five cents, we have to ask, "Eighteen cents in what era—Tudor England? Frontier America? The Depression? The year 2000?" Unfortunately, many study guides simply repeat values from the distant past while inflation marches on.

> ♦ **Principle 2: After gathering the raw data, teachers must formulate it so that it communicates with ordinary people.**

With money, the best way to assess and communicate the data about coins and metals is to think in terms of purchasing power. This is best measured—and best communicated—by the length of time it took to earn the coin. All agree that a common laborer earned one denarius in one day. So the wicked servant in the parable had some reason to be upset with his fellow servant. That debt of one hundred denarii equaled one hundred days' wages, not just a few dollars! On the other hand, that debt pales in comparison to the debt owed to the king, for it took a laborer nearly twenty years to earn one talent. If one talent equals twenty years' wages, then the servant's debt of ten thousand talents to the king totaled two hundred thousand years' wages![11] Setting a current monetary equivalent is difficult because ancient and modern economic standards and systems are so different. Still, to satisfy the curious, if we set a year's wages at ten thousand dollars, the value of the debt is two billion dollars—a number that is both vast and round, like ten thousand talents. The number *one billion* reinforces the story's main lesson: the servant should have forgiven, for he had been forgiven so very much more.

Slaves and Servants

The second problem concerns the servants in the passage. Since the first servant could be sold, he must have been a slave. But how could a slave acquire such a debt? Slavery was different in the ancient world. Slaves lacked freedom to come and go as they pleased, or to marry, and they had few legal rights. But they were not segregated by race, language, or clothing, as in America. They could receive pay, own property (even fellow slaves), and take almost any job. People became slaves by being captured in war, by falling too far into debt, or by birth. But a few people sold themselves into slavery to gain security or to get an education at their owners' expense. Certain high positions, such as city treasurer, had to be occupied by slaves. Some prominent people were slaves, and our unforgiving servant appears to have been one of them. So Jesus' story is sensible, even if it is somewhat extravagant—as parables often are.[12]

These two studies do not, by themselves, disclose the thrust of Matthew 18:21–35. But they are a vital step in the process of exegesis. Occasionally, an exposition is essentially an exercise in solving problems, as in the case of Elisha cursing the boys of Bethel (see chap. 2). Most of the time, however, problem solving is just one step in the process of interpreting the Bible—important, but limited in scope. Problem solving has a sister skill, the development of themes, which we will take up in the next chapter. They constitute a pair of powerful tools in the workshop of Bible study.

Summary

Problem solving is the third phase of our plan for exegesis (CAPTOR), following Context and Analysis, and preceding Themes, Obligations, and Reflection. Problem solving begins when we face the extent of our ignorance. We discover problems by reading slowly and constantly asking, "Do I know what this means?" There are three kinds of problems. Obvious problems are presented by places, names, words, and customs about which we know little or nothing. Teachers read for problems differently; they ask what their students may not understand. Hidden problems hide in the fields of old, vague half-knowledge. Problem solving often entails the investigation of somewhat familiar things. Ordinarily, we have to turn to reference works to solve our problems and so enhance our instruction.

Exercises

List as many problems as you can from the following passages. You may categorize them as obvious, hidden, or for teachers. Which ones seem most important for understanding the passage? Solve some for each passage.

1. List the problems in Matthew 10:1–16 by paragraph (vv. 1–4, 5–10, and 11–16). Which ones seem to be most important? Solve a few, using a Bible dictionary or encyclopedia. Suggestion for an easy problem: What does the reference to Sodom and Gomorrah mean? Here is a harder one: Why did Jesus forbid the disciples to go to the Gentiles?

2. For a rich Old Testament passage, see 1 Samuel 24 or Genesis 15:1–19. Even after looking up *covenant* and *sacrifice*, you still might need a commentary to fully understand Genesis 15.

3. For a New Testament text that has few obvious problems, try Romans 8:1–4 or 12:1–2.

Notes

[1] To detect problems, we need the skills of observation (chap. 2). To solve them, we often need to know the historical context of the passage (chap. 4).

[2] Check your ability to discover questions by comparing your questions to the contents of a reputable commentary. You will probably miss some important issues and the commentary will probably skip some of your good questions. A good semi-popular commentary on Acts is I. H. Marshall, *Acts* (Grand Rapids: Eerdmans, 1980). A respected scholarly commentary is F. F. Bruce, *The Acts of the Apostles: Greek Text with Introduction and Commentary,* 3d ed. (Grand Rapids: Eerdmans, 1990). You need not start collecting commentaries now. Borrow them occasionally until you can recognize a good one.

[3] Daniel Patte, *The Gospel According to Matthew: A Structural Commentary on Matthew's Faith* (Philadelphia: Fortress, 1987), 257.

[4] Leon Morris, *The Gospel According to Matthew* (Grand Rapids: Eerdmans, 1992), 473.

[5] Josephus, *Antiquities,* 17.318–20.

[6] W. D. Davies and Dale C. Allison, *The Gospel According to Matthew* (Edinburgh: T. & T. Clark, 1991), 2:795–98.

[7] Duncan Derrett, *Law in the New Testament* (London: Darton, Longman & Todd, 1970), 34–37. Joachim Jeremias believes that Matthew embellishes numbers but that the original audience could have thought of a regional satrap in charge of revenue. See Jeremias, *The Parables of Jesus*, 2d ed. (New York: Scribners, 1963), 28, 210.

[8] For dollars, see Morris, *Gospel According to Matthew*, 473, n. 71; for pounds, see David Hill, *The Gospel of Matthew* (London: Oliphants, 1972), 278.

[9] Pheme Perkins, *Hearing the Parables of Jesus* (New York: Paulist Press, 1981), 123–24.

[10] Craig Blomberg, *Interpreting the Parables* (Downers Grove, Ill.: InterVarsity Press, 1990), 241–42.

[11] E. M. Cook, "Weights and Measures," in *The International Standard Bible Encyclopedia*, ed. Geoffrey W. Bromiley, rev. ed. (Grand Rapids: Eerdmans, 1979–88), 4:1046–55; H. W. Perkin, "Money," in *The International Standard Bible Encyclopedia*, 3:402–09. *The International Standard Bible Encyclopedia* may be the best single source for the kind of information cited here. The value of a denarius, the weight of a talent, and similar factual material can be found in any good reference work or commentary.

[12] Many sources describe what slavery was like in the biblical era. See Wayne Meeks, *The First Urban Christians: The Social World of the Apostle Paul* (New Haven: Yale University Press, 1983), 20–22, 63–64; S. S. Bartchy, "Slavery," in *The International Standard Bible Encyclopedia*, 4:539–46.

8

Developing Themes

The Million-Dollar Question

The question "What would you do for a million dollars" was forced on my community in 1994. Advertisements promoting a state lottery flooded local media outlets. Smiling pitchmen shoved microphones into actors' and citizens' faces and asked, "What would you do for one million dollars?" A withered octogenarian offered to kiss a turtle, a young beauty vowed to shave her head, and so on. But the question lost its innocence when it moved from ad lines to headlines, as intelligence officers arrested Aldrich and Rosario Ames for betraying their nation to the former Soviet Union for two million dollars. Lottery blurbs and anxious news analysts stood juxtaposed: what will a man or a woman do for a million dollars? The allure of gambling and get-rich-quick schemes had become strong, and the time seemed ripe to study the themes of money and greed.

So far, we have considered principles for inductive Bible study. But Bible teachers often want to study a theme. The impulse may come from a recent event, from the shocks of daily life, or from the reading of Scripture. Wise teachers make use of every opportunity to address timely needs, and to do so with an interested audience.

1. *Hot topics in the culture.* Teachers rightly pluck some topical studies from the headlines. Current events will prompt interest in important issues, as the spy scandal shows.

2. *Personal questions.* Requests for topical studies also come from personal experience. A deserted spouse asks for a study of divorce and remarriage. An African-American requests a study on dignity. Any experience, from the birth of a child to the onset of disease, from unemployment to unexpected blessing, can prompt a thematic study.

3. *Hot topics in the church.* The church also has questions that require complete answers. A pastor resigns, or the time comes to nominate church officers. What are the qualifications for Christian leadership? A guest musician arrives ready to accompany himself . . . on an electric guitar. What does the Bible say about musical instruments and styles of worship?

4. *Seasonal topics.* Christmas and Easter provide excellent opportunities for messages on the person and work of Christ, studies that people might consider too heavy in other seasons.

5. *Questions prompted by Scripture.* Bible reading also stimulates questions. In Bible studies where every genuine question is fair, participants will break in, "You know, I've always wondered about that verse. Could we stop and talk about it for a minute?" People may want to know more about the theme of a passage, but more often something on its periphery catches their attention. Even familiar topics can generate questions, especially if conventional wisdom makes no sense of the text. Or the text may address a subject that the church has wrongly ignored.

Summary and Illustration of the Origins of Topical Studies

1. *Hot topics in the culture:* gambling, lotteries, strikes, gender wars, sexual ethics
2. *Personal questions:* birth and death, prosperity and tragedy, quests for love and dignity
3. *Hot topics in the church:* leadership qualifications, worship styles
4. *Seasonal topics:* Christmas, Easter, Thanksgiving, Mother's Day, Father's Day
5. *Questions prompted by Scripture:* women saved through child-bearing?

So, thematic studies begin either when someone brings a question to the Bible, or when the Bible prompts a question. They can start with a headline, a personal experience, a tempest in the church, or a riddle in the Bible. Wise teachers see the opportunities for helpful topical study several weeks in advance, and prepare for them.

Thematic studies are important because they prepare Christians to fight where the battle rages, to take a stand by addressing the controversies of the hour. On the other hand, we should proclaim the whole counsel of God, and not merely race from one debate to the next. We must be willing to take up every biblical theme, even if it seems irrelevant at the moment.

Introducing Themes and Word Studies

How then do we develop effective topical studies that remove confusion and meet the needs of the hour? Analysis begins with the question, "What does the Bible have to say about this topic?" The topic may be hypocrisy, divorce, angels, justice, suffering, or whatever.

> ♦ **Principle 1: Even when examining a theme that spans the entire Bible, it is wise to begin with one central text and then go to others.**

Example: Money

Since money is both a hot topic and a biblical topic, we will begin with it, using Matthew 6:19–24 as our central text.

> Do not store up for yourselves treasures on earth, where moth and rust destroy, and where thieves break in and steal. But store up for yourselves treasures in heaven, where moth and rust do not destroy, and where thieves do not break in and steal. For where your treasure is, there your heart will be also. . . . No one can serve two masters. Either he will hate the one and love the other, or he will be devoted to the one and despise the other. You cannot serve both God and Money [*or* Mammon].

Beginning with this passage, we want to discover what the whole Bible teaches about money.

▶ **Principle 2: In preparing thematic studies, it is vital to distinguish between the concept and the biblical term or terms that describe it.**

In the case of money, we must distinguish between the concept of money and the words used to describe it, such as *wealth, riches, Mammon,* and *money.* Of course, word studies and thematic studies are related. We talk about themes with words, and we use words to express concepts. Yet, word study is a narrower business. Thinking they were the same thing, someone might look up *money* in an English concordance and miss other important terms. Or a person could get caught up in dozens of irrelevant references to purchases and collections. He or she might learn that the term for money in Matthew 6 is "Mammon" (in some translations) (Greek: *mamonas*), and then find only four uses of that word in the New Testament. Thus someone might conclude that the Bible says little about the spiritual side of money.

What then is the difference between the word *money* and the concept of money? Strictly speaking, money is nothing more than the accepted means of payment or economic exchange, from gold coins to gold credit cards. But the concept of money in Matthew 6 is another matter. It encompasses money as treasure, as the object of our affections, as a source of power and prestige, and as the object of the insinuating question, "What would you do for a million dollars?" Thus, a study of the concept would involve searching for references to the love of money and money as a seductress, as Babylon (Rev. 18), as an alternate God. This concept only partially overlaps the term *money.* Therefore, a trek through the concordance would not suffice; we need other methods to locate texts describing the love of money or money as a false god.

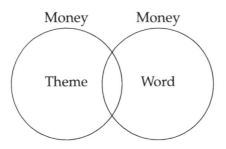

Money   Money

Theme   Word

How to Develop a Theme

▶ **Principle 3: The development of a theme has two phases, the survey of the data and the synthesis of the data.**

In the survey, we gather as much of the biblical witness as we can. In the synthesis, we attempt to summarize the biblical teaching and show its coherence. This process can be broken down into six steps, four of which focus on survey and two of which focus on synthesis. (But bear in mind that we unconsciously perform both tasks at all times.)

Step 1: Ask more questions. Jesus' pregnant pronouncements on treasures in Matthew prompt more specific questions. If we stay alert for answers, they will sharpen our focus. We might ask,

- In what sense does money, a mere tool of commerce, rival the Lord of the universe?
- Do I accept the dichotomy, "You cannot serve both God and Money"? After all, if I am on God's side, and he is on mine, is it not likely that he will bless me financially as well as spiritually?
- What does the rest of the Bible teach about money? Do other passages address money's tendency to become a god? Do they explain how it happens and how to break money's hold?
- What does God think of my possessions, my spending habits, my savings, my financial dreams?

Step 2: Brainstorm. Next, spend fifteen minutes alone with a blank slate. Jot down the most important things you already know about money. Recall anything, from recent reading to ancient memories. If the topic is money as a god, here are some ideas you might have:

- The rich young ruler refused to sell his possessions and give them to the poor when Jesus made that a condition for discipleship. On the other hand, Peter, James, John, and Andrew gave up their fishing boats and income when they followed Jesus. And Zacchaeus gave half of his possessions to the poor when Jesus came to his house.

- When God blessed a man in the Old Testament, he often became wealthy, as Abraham, Jacob, Joseph, Job, David, Solomon, Jehoshaphat, Josiah, and others attest. So money was not always viewed as a threat.
- Jesus told some people to give up everything to follow him, and he had nowhere to lay his own head. Yet he had wealthy followers, such as Joseph of Arimathea, who kept some property.
- Proverbs 30:8–9 regards wealth as a danger: "Give me neither poverty nor riches," it says, "but give me only my daily bread. Otherwise, I may have too much and disown you and say, 'Who is the Lord?' Or I may become poor and steal, and so dishonor the name of my God."
- First Timothy 6:9 also warns against the love of money: "People who want to get rich fall into temptation and a trap and into many foolish and harmful desires that plunge men into ruin and destruction. For the love of money is a root of all kinds of evil." Still, Paul commends contentment and the enjoyment of wealth.

If you noticed that the word *money* appears sparingly in the passages above, you can see why it is wise to brainstorm first. The mind makes connections that defy concordances and computer searches; if we were simply to look up the term *money*, we would miss them. Parenthetically, consider the time Jesus demonstrated his humble love by washing the disciples' feet. Because John never uses the words *love* or *humility*, a study of those words would never lead to John 13. Therefore, start by brainstorming.

Step 3: Use cross references to find related passages. Editors have designed cross references to lead readers from one text to others that treat the same topic or use the same words. At best, cross references point to texts with both verbal and conceptual similarities. Sometimes they mention contrasting passages, such as James 2 and Galatians 3. At worst, they lead to texts that share the same word, but not the same meaning. Chain-reference Bibles direct readers to dozens of passages on thousands of topics.

The cross references for Matthew 6:24 will include Luke 16:13, which is virtually identical to it. Thus, the reference to Luke 16:13 adds little in itself, but Luke 16:13 concludes a longer and very different discussion of money. Some Bible notes allude to Luke 14:26, on the need for disciples to give up their families. The Thompson Chain-Reference Bible notes for Matthew 6:24 refer to five series, labeled "Half-heartedness," "No Neutrality," "Double-mindedness," "Indecision," "Undivided Service," and "Worldliness." Of these, only the worldliness chain produces a helpful parallel (James 4:4). But the Thompson notes on 6:19–21 suggest dozens of illuminating verses on earthly and spiritual riches.[1] Some Bibles have better cross-reference systems than others. Avoid those that commonly recommend texts with only a superficial similarity to yours. Try out several before you settle on one.

Step 4: Scan a concordance. For a quick study, steps 1–3 may provide all you need. But for a complete analysis, you need to know how to use a concordance. Complete concordances, whether in books or software, allow you to locate every use of a term in any particular edition or translation of the Bible. (So there are Hebrew and Greek concordances, and concordances for various translations: NIV, RSV, NASB, KJV, etc.) Completeness is both the strength and the weakness of concordances. First, in supplying (so it seems) all the data, they often deliver too much data! Because they can dump more than you want to know, you have to know how to use a concordance effectively.

> ▶ **Principle 4: Read a concordance cautiously, intensively, selectively, broadly, and according to families of books.**

Read intensely. When a concordance leads to a promising parallel, read the verse in its context in the Bible, lest you take it out of context.

Read selectively. If your word is common, occurring dozens of times in the Bible, do not try to look up every passage. The word *money* appears over 130 times in the NIV. A quick scan of the entries shows that most them have little in common with Matthew 6:24. Therefore, skim through the concordance, searching for familiar and genuinely informative texts.

Read broadly. Search for more than your original word. To learn about money as a false god, investigate related words such as *riches* and *possessions.* Similarly, if you want to learn about persevering and perseverance, examine *enduring* and *endurance,* too, especially since *persevere* is not a common term.

Synonyms offer another advantage. If we can identify the related words that an author did not use, we may discover the precise meaning he sought. There is a gap between *announce* and *declare,* between *tenderness* and *compassion,* between *murder* and *slaughter,* between *power* and *authority,* between *compromise* and *negotiation.* Understanding the difference between related terms helps us discover an author's nuance. Therefore, since Hebrew, Aramaic, and Greek—the languages of Palestine in Jesus' day—all had other common terms for property and money, we justly ask why Jesus called it "treasure" and "Mammon." *Treasure* suggests not mere property, but something dear to the owner. *Mammon,* a relatively rare Aramaic term, meant possessions that have monetary value. But the term often had negative connotations, an association with dishonest gain. Some experts believe that Jesus chose the word *Mammon* because of its origin in the Aramaic verb *aman* or the Hebrew verb *amen.* Both convey the notion of trust, and could be used to describe a trustworthy statement or person. (The idea behind ending our prayers with "amen," incidentally, is that we declare that these petitions reliably convey our commitments and requests.) By adding an *m* to *amen,* the verb becomes a noun meaning "that in which one trusts"—a most clever name for money when it functions as God's rival! [2]

Know the families of books within the Bible. Selective reading means that you need not collect every verse on money. You may read only the occurrences of *money* in Matthew, or in the four Gospels, since you are apt to find the closest parallels there. This shortcut works throughout the Bible. First, look up all occurrences of your word in the book in which your main text appears. Second, examine the uses in the family of books most closely related to your text. To do this effectively, you need to know the families within the Bible. Here is a common and useful grouping:

> The Books of Moses: Genesis to Deuteronomy
> The Historical Books: Joshua to Esther
> The Wisdom Books: Job to the Song of Songs
> The Prophetic Books: Isaiah to Malachi
> The Gospels: Matthew to John
> History: Acts
> Epistles: Romans to Jude
> Revelation

The relationships between the various books of the Bible are more complex than this simple list indicates, however. For example, Joshua continues motifs found from Genesis through Deuteronomy. Old Testament history divides logically into books apparently written before or during the exile (Joshua through Kings) and those written after the return (Chronicles through Esther). Paul's letters form a natural group within the New Testament epistles.

Some books belong in more than one family. The four Gospels go together, but the gospel of John also belongs in a family with John's letters and Revelation. Luke and Acts form a pair because Luke wrote both. Matthew, Mark, and Luke paint very similar portraits of the life of Christ. Ezekiel, Daniel, Zechariah, and Revelation have some very similar visions, symbols, and themes. The same prophet wrote both Jeremiah and Lamentations. Within Paul's letters, 1 and 2 Timothy and Titus belong together, since he wrote all three for individual Christian leaders. A Bible handbook or dictionary can direct you to other useful categories.

Beware of the concordance. Word studies can be counterproductive if they become so time-consuming that they exclude other studies. The basic units of meaning in the Bible and all language are the sentence and the paragraph, not the individual word. We can forget that in the middle of a long word study. Some teachers become too enthusiastic about word studies and bury their audience under an avalanche of information about one word.

Overly enthusiastic word studies sometimes fall into an error known as illegitimate totality transfer, that is, a tendency to pour several possible meanings of a word into one use of it.[3]

To illustrate, imagine that you are learning English and come upon the word *post* in the sentence "The ambassador was reluctant to take up his new post in Albania." Opening your dictionary, you learn that a post (to create a partial list) can be (1) a piece of wood or metal fixed in an upright position, (2) the metal stem of a pierced earring, (3) the place where a soldier is stationed, (4) an office, duty, or position to which a person is appointed, or (5) a position in a basketball team's offense. Now we know it would be absurd to think that the ambassador was reluctant to go to Albania because he would be forced to wear earrings and hold wooden staves while playing basketball with enlisted men. Yet people do that very thing when they say the Greek word *parakaleo* means "to comfort, encourage, exhort, and call alongside." We do something similar when we find an entire theology of discipleship in one use of the term *follow.*

Shun the temptation to read several meanings of a word into one instance of it. Among the possible meanings, determine the one that best suits your sentence in its context, and disregard the rest.

Step 5: For in-depth study, read an article in a Bible dictionary or encyclopedia. Page for page and dollar for dollar, nothing is more valuable to the serious student than a Bible dictionary or encyclopedia. In longer articles on subjects such as law, sin, incarnation, and redemption, experts condense months of research, even the essence of whole books, into a few thousand words. Shorter articles gather essential information into just a few hundred words. Most articles suggest further reading. Every respectable encyclopedia will have at least one article on money and wealth.

Step 6: As a final step, consult a handbook of systematic or biblical theology. Your previous steps should have produced a large amount of information. It will not always be easy to see how the varied teaching of Scripture coheres. For example, we find somewhat different teaching about divorce in Nehemiah and Matthew. The descriptions of the state in Romans 13 and Revelation contrast starkly. There is tension between Jesus' custom of associating with tax collectors and sinners, and the command for the people of God to come out and be separate from sinners. There is no quick formula for resolving these questions. More than anything, we need to fill our minds with biblical principles and use them to test all things.

If necessary, we can turn to systematic theology here. It allows us to reap the written harvest of a mind that has been filled with biblical thoughts. The better systematic theologies present the essential elements of biblical truth in a topical manner. Some will present the history of Christian thought or debate on a topic before presenting their conclusions. Others begin with a statement in a creed, or a crucial Bible text, and proceed from there. Others stress the development of themes, from Genesis to Revelation. This allows you to watch biblical concepts develop, whether incrementally, by the addition of harmonious truths, or dialectically, as ideas stand in tension.[4] Whatever method they choose, the best theologies show how ideas develop. Systematic theologies may not have a special section on money, but a search of indexes will probably show some mention of money or wealth, perhaps under the headings of creation or discipleship.

♦ Principle 5: Know the times.

While the truth never changes, perversions of it shift constantly. Rival ideas and alternative lifestyles spring up like weeds. To know how to refute and prevent error, effective teachers listen to their culture. Of course, our culture hardly hides its view of money. Whether we live in a wealthy suburb, where professionals strive for more wealth, or in a struggling small town or inner city, where there never seems to be enough, everyone seems to believe that money solves most problems.

That is precisely what Jesus had in mind when he warned his disciples not to store up treasures on earth—when he declared, "You cannot serve both God and Money." In our society, the god Money simply offers to solve our problems. Money is a modest deity, by no means the kind of goddess that demands exclusive loyalty. It is satisfied with incense and a few holy days—there is no need to get down on our knees! Money is a polytheistic god; it only wants a spot in the pantheon—a pantheon that has room for a few other deities, such as status, power, pleasure, ease, reputation, and conviviality. In our culture, Money will even allow its worshipers to be "Christians."

Whether the possible origins of the term *Mammon* discussed above have any validity or not, people often speak as if Money, like other gods, is a deity they can trust.[5] What is a common name for our investments? Securities! What do we call our national retirement plan? Social security! We even name investment funds "trust funds" and "securities," as if we should trust them, and as if they can make us secure. Insurance and savings plans often aim for the same thing. Disciples know that only the Lord can grant us security, yet we sometimes seek it in both God and Mammon. Our society makes Money a god in other ways. We give it a divine name: the Almighty Dollar. We hold Money in awe and fall silent before it. What is the quietest store at the mall? The jewelry store! What is the quietest spot in the museum? The gem room! Like a god, Money also attempts to bend everything to its values. It reduces everything to buying and selling, value and profit—even people. It says people can be bought and sold. Obviously, slaves have a price. But, as the saying goes, everyone has his price. Like a god, Money also tries to judge the world. "How much is he worth?" Money asks, meaning, "How much money, how many assets, does he have?" But the language suggests that a person's worth and his net assets are closely connected.

So a look at the culture confirms Jesus' wisdom. Money was a rival to God in his day, and it still is now. The clearer the view of the problem is in our culture, the easier it will be to apply our study of money to it effectively.

Reading with Your Eyes Open

So far, we have discussed methods for topics we bring to the Bible. But themes come up as we read through Scripture, too. When I read through the gospel of Luke with my children, they asked at least one theme question every night: How did the demons know who Jesus was? Why did Jesus ask his disciples to leave everything to follow him? How could Jesus read people's thoughts? Why didn't Jesus' own people believe in him? Children can spot themes without trying, but adults are forced to curb the boundless curiosity of youth, if they want to get their work done. Eventually, they can even forget how to ask questions. So, how can we train ourselves to notice worthy themes? Here are some suggestions:

1. *Some themes recur in almost every passage.* Every text says something about the nature of God and mankind. All address our fallen condition and God's remedy. So, always seek answers to the question, "What does this passage teach about God, mankind, and redemption?"

2. *Themes often begin with a problem.* In the previous chapter, we listed problems in Acts 13:1–3 that called for factual answers: Where is Antioch? What is the city like? But soon we wonder why the church at Antioch became the first to send missionaries to the Gentiles. How did the church get started? Who were the prophets mentioned in verse 1? Do their names reveal anything about the congregation? The answers to these questions lead into the theme of church growth and evangelism. Again, the question "How did the Holy Spirit tell everyone to set Barnabas and Saul apart?" can lead to the theme, "How does God communicate with mankind?" The text also mentions fasting, prayer, and the laying on of hands—all

of which are worthy topics. The last question could lead to a study of ordination—a rare term, but a significant concept.

3. *Some themes emerge only when we read large blocks of Scripture.* If we read through Genesis in one week, for example, we are primed for certain themes. We notice that the Lord relates to his people, from Adam to Joseph, through covenants and promises that he makes to them and their descendants. We also see that the Lord providentially guarantees his promises despite threats on all sides: two patriarchs are childless for a long time, a third initially scorns the covenant, a fourth is sold into slavery.

4. *Some themes emerge through rereading.* In Luke one can overlook Jesus' custom of associating with outcasts because it comes up only occasionally and lacks a special vocabulary. Yet, in his first sermon, Jesus declared that he had come to preach the Good News to the poor and oppressed (4:18). He soon did that very thing by ministering to lepers, to the demon possessed, to women with unclean diseases (Luke 5:12–16; 8:26–39, 40–56). Jesus publicly reached out to moral outcasts. A tax collector became one of the Twelve, and he invited himself to the house of a chief tax collector, Zacchaeus, whom he made a model of repentance and salvation (5:27–32; 19:1–10). He chided the Pharisees for failing to invite the poor, the crippled, the blind, and the lame to their parties (14:12–14), and then he told a story about a godlike king who invited people like that, from all over the country, to his banquet (14:15–24). Jesus did not own a home, so he could not follow his advice and throw parties for outcasts, but he did the next-best thing, by going to their parties and dining with them (15:1–2; 19:5–7).[6] Beyond spending time with these people, Jesus blessed them. Even on the cross, for example, he reached out to an absolute outcast, the thief executed beside him, and blessed him (23:40–43).

These points suggest that God's love of outsiders lies near the heart of the gospel.[7] If so, why do pulpits and lecterns neglect it? Perhaps exclusiveness is to adults as disrespect is to teenagers—almost invisible to those who commit it. We cannot see that we shun people from other social strata, because we think it praiseworthy to greet our friends, praiseworthy to welcome visitors who look just like us. Or perhaps the reason is that the welcome of outcasts embellishes the fringe of a text, but never holds the center.

How can we escape our culpable neglect? First, if we actually practiced what little we do know, we would leap ahead in awareness. Second, the church's teachers should recognize that the theme of welcoming outcasts sweeps through the Bible. We ought to know that God welcomes sinners, and that we should too.

Conclusion

Following Context, Analysis, and Problems, this chapter presented the fourth part of the CAPTOR plan, Themes. Only Obligations and Reflection now remain to be treated. Until now, we have read one text closely. In this chapter we stressed the skill of reading for a broad array of theological connections. Good teachers will develop themes if the subject is important in their culture or the Christian community, or if it arises repeatedly in the Bible. To be good at this, you need to loosen up a bit. The tools for thematic study include cross references, concordances, Bible encyclopedias, dictionaries, and theologies, but you will not generate a good thematic study merely by scrutinizing key words or consulting sources. You must know the Scriptures, know people, know the times, and take a few risks to bring them together creatively.

Exercises

1. List themes worth developing from some passages we have studied, such as Matthew 18:21–35, 1 Samuel 17; Romans 12:1–2.

2. Study a topic of interest that seems to have no special "home" text. For example,

    a. What should one do if an employer commands something that is "gray" ethically—neither immoral nor illegal, but far from ideal?

    b. What does the whole Bible teach about the environment? About the process of aging?

Notes

[1] *The Thompson Chain-Reference Bible, New International Version* (Grand Rapids: Zondervan, 1983), 990.

[2] Colin Brown, *"mamonas,"* in *Dictionary of New Testament Theology,* ed. Colin Brown (Grand Rapids: Zondervan, 1967–71), 2:837.

[3] James Barr, *The Semantics of Biblical Literature* (Oxford: Oxford University Press, 1961), 218ff.; Moisés Silva, *Biblical Words and Their Meaning* (Grand Rapids: Zondervan, 1983), 22–32.

[4] Sometimes called "biblical theology," this method especially examines the way biblical truth unfolds in the different eras of redemptive history. The landmark work by an evangelical in the field is Geerhardus Vos, *Biblical Theology: Old and New Testaments* (Grand Rapids: Eerdmans, 1948).

[5] This paragraph is indebted to Jacques Ellul, *Money and Power* (Downers Grove, Ill.: InterVarsity Press, 1984), 9–33, 73–93.

[6] In biblical times, sharing a meal with someone indicated a far closer degree of friendship or intimacy than it does today.

[7] Conversely, self-righteousness, the defining trait of Israel's religious insiders, banishes one from the kingdom. See Mark Alan Powell, "Religious Leaders in Luke: A Literary-Critical Study," *Journal of Biblical Literature* 109 (Spring 1990): 93–110, esp. 95–99; Jack Dean Kingsbury, *Conflict in Luke: Jesus, Authorities, and Disciples* (Minneapolis: Fortress, 1991), 23, 82–83.

9

The Challenge of Application

Ducks Need Not Apply?

On a balmy Sunday morning in the land of ducks, all the ducks awoke, preened their feathers, and waddled to church. When they had found their respective pews and squatted down, their duck minister waddled arduously to the pulpit. Opening the duck Bible, he turned to the place where it spoke of God's great gift to ducks—wings. "With wings," the duck preacher orated, "you ducks can fly. You can mount up like eagles and soar to the heavens. You can know freedom from the confinement of pens and fences. You must give thanks to God for so great a gift as wings." All the ducks in the congregation heartily agreed, shouting, "Amen." Then they all waddled home.[1]

The parable of the ducks illustrates some of the challenges in applying Scripture. The duck pastor was too cognitive, appealing only to the mind of the ducks. He urged them to thank God for wings, not to use them. Or perhaps his own shortcomings—he too waddled into church—blinded him to the proper application. It would be embarrassing for a flightless duck to urge others to fly, embarrassing to watch them do what he could not or would not do. So the duck pastor made it easy for his congregation to neglect application.

Actually, there are probably more knots and puzzles in application than in any other aspect of biblical interpretation. Liberals and conservatives, Protestants and Catholics, faithful Bible professors and agnostic literature professors all agree that the valid interpretation of texts depends on the skills described in the preceding chapters. They agree, in large measure, on the procedures of exegesis.[2] But differences emerge when we try to establish our moral and spiritual obligations.[3]

First, who applies Scripture? God, the reader, or the teacher? Second, how does application take place? Can we leave it to the Spirit's inner testimony? Or does it come through intensive labor and soul-searching? If we come to Scripture with an open heart, will correct applications well up from within? Third, what is the chief goal of application? Greater human happiness? Correct ethical decisions? The formation of character? Fellowship with God?

Some critics deny that ancient texts can have absolute moral authority in modern society. They insist that a work "composed in an ancient time and an ancient culture has its meaning in that time and that culture, and in our time or culture may have a different meaning, or indeed may have no meaning at all."[4] James Gustafson says that the Bible informs our ideals, moral judgments, motives, and goals, but that there are too many factors in moral assessment, and too many divergent themes in Scripture itself, for any one biblical fact to determine a moral decision.[5] Critics have especially doubted that the historical passages of the Bible can have moral authority. They ask whether we can be sure the reported events actually occurred. If not, how can they have moral authority?[6] Besides, how can ancient history guide modern behavior?

The critics rightly say that cultures change and that decision making is complex. But change and complexity in no way undermine the authority of Scripture. They only show that we need to be thorough when applying Scripture to new situations. The fundamentals of righteous conduct may never change, but the assaults on it do. When confusion proliferates and the tangles of sin grow thick, they do not dissolve with the slash of a solitary proof text. Without compromising one iota on biblical authority, we can say that moral discernment is no simple matter.

Simplistic zeal presses on one side, and thorny questions press on the other, but evangelical scholars have given little theoretical attention to the task of applying the Bible.[7] Yet the need certainly exists, for far too frequently Christian teachers avoid the hard issues while repeating stale, subjective, vague, and irrelevant applications.

Let us therefore examine two invalid approaches to application, answer them, and propose a positive program.

Three Views of Application

View 1. Let It Flow

View 1 regards application as easy; it flows from our personal spirituality. On this view, application depends on the private spiritual life of teachers and preachers, on one side, and of their Christian listeners, on the other. Application is a subjective, personal affair. Teachers and preachers prepare to apply texts by meditating on them as they study them. As they probe the Scriptures, a truth about fear or self-control, for example, resonates deep within. They think, "Yes, that is true; I need to challenge my fears; I need to control my appetites." Thus they apply the passage to themselves, only half-aware of what they are doing. For some pastors, most application at least starts with this subjective experience. Later they ask, "Am I the only one dealing with this, or is it universal?" As one pastor put it, "In all my sermons, I preach to myself; the congregation overhears."[8]

Taken to its extreme conclusion, the "personal spirituality" view regards theoretical reflection on application as superfluous. If the speaker faithfully hears the text, he will know what to say. If a preacher keeps his congregation in mind as he prepares his sermon, "what he knows about them will suggest unexpected ideas and associations."[9] From the speaker's standpoint, therefore, application occurs without special effort. To use methods of application is to reject one's spiritual life for a fastidious preoccupation with methodology. On this view, application is better caught than taught. Students and novices learn it by watching wise preachers speak from the heart. As they are drawn to the pastors who fearlessly proclaim that which they have obviously learned in the school of life, the school of the soul, they learn to do the same.

This view contains both commendable and questionable ideas. True, a slavish devotion to methods eviscerates our spontaneous delight in God's Word. True, we should leave a place for God's voice in biblical interpretation; surely teachers need not take eight steps before they hear the Master. Too much method can squeeze God out of the study.

But let's not be naive. Those who quietly meditate on the Word hear other voices, not just the Lord's whispers, and some of them are not so trustworthy. Recent experiences will weigh heavily on those who meditate without structure. What books are they reading? What societal ills have they noticed? What troubled persons have stepped into their offices? What songs have they been singing? And what if these recent experiences have little to do with the text?

Further, we dare not neglect the role of the corrupted human heart in the process of application. What are the teacher's frustrated desires and dreams? Who has offended him and in what way? What would he like his hearers to do for him? Some leaders can find, in many a text, evidence that their goals and their programs are precisely God's will for themselves or their church. In short, free meditation has few safeguards against the infections of a deceitful heart.

View 2. Let God Do It

According to view 2, because application is problematic, it is best left to God. Application that actually produces decisions for God is the work of sovereign grace. We are too blind to our own compromises, too dedicated to our own agenda, and too ignorant of the real needs of others to apply the Word of God successfully. It is difficult for men "to be faithful to the text and also true to life in this present age." We must, therefore, leave application to God, for true application is, as Karl Barth put it, the result of a "direct encounter between man and God."[10]

Some leave application to God for another reason. They are afraid that if we take it upon ourselves to decide how to behave, we will enter a vortex that will suck us down into the abyss of legalism. Say one word about observance of the Lord's Day, for example, and pharisaism will soon be knocking at the door. Any attempt to prescribe behavior, they imagine, will soon center on works and nullify the gospel. Others contend that the Bible presents principles for life, not laws. Precise application betrays the spirit of Christian living, and trades the believer's freedom for fussy little rules.

A few adherents of the biblical theology movement avoid application for another reason. With its healthy emphasis on God's covenant and his sovereign redemptive work in history, it opposes the moralistic use of the Bible. According to this school, the teacher's goal in telling the story of Abraham or Solomon is not to show us what sins to avoid and what good deeds to emulate. Teachers should not offer moral lessons about what God rewards and punishes, for Scripture is God's self-revelation, given to move people to faith. God is the "prime agent" in every story. The Bible is God's self-revelation, given so that he and his people will "exchange the deepest love of their hearts." Therefore, "God must be made central" to every story. If, however, we speak of Mary's or John's love for Jesus, or Judas's hatred, we must not focus on Mary or Judas, but on "the One who awakened such love . . . [and] arouse[d] such great hatred." To stress the role of Mary and Judas as examples of love to be imitated or sin to be avoided is, according to this school, to stray from the gospel into a man-centered religion.[11]

Here again, we must weigh merits and demerits. The "leave it to God" view rightly points to the inherent capacity of the Word to touch our lives and to remain perpetually contemporary, far beyond our efforts to make it relevant. This view also knows a preacher's limits. Eloquent speakers can persuade people to change their behavior, give money, or sign up for a program. But no speaker, working alone, can change the human heart (2 Cor. 4:1–7). The triune God applies Scripture.

I saw this not long ago when someone approached me and said, "I cannot forget something you said in a sermon a few weeks ago. . . . I have been thinking about it constantly." The visitor paused, hesitant from emotion.

"Yes, and what is it? What did I say?" I asked, trying to help. But his reply astonished me: "You said we tend to hope someone notices when we do something noble, and hope that we will somehow be repaid for it. And I suddenly realized that I do that almost all the time. I am always hoping I will be repaid for my good deeds."

I was pleased that my visitor was dealing with an important issue, but also puzzled, for I remembered saying no such thing—at least not in that lecture. The visitor, sensing my perplexity, persisted, describing my remarks in much more detail, adding that he recalled it quite vividly.

At length, it came to me. Yes, in a moment, in a minor, tangential point, in an unplanned aside, I said it. God had prepared our listener, and so it took only a few words to reach him. Application is indeed the work of God.

Still, we must work at application. First, we must do something to stop the common perception that the Bible is irrelevant in modern times. Even Christians fail to see what the Bible has to do with their financial struggles and emotional decay at home, or with the temptations and the pressures to compromise at work. It stands mute, it seems, before the issues of the day—questions raised by constant change, the global economy, medical technology, and chronic poverty.

Second, pastors and teachers become complacent; they fall into ruts and stay there. Week by week they urge people to pray, trust God, observe the law, read the Bible, evangelize, and "show their commitment by getting involved." They fall back on clichés and avoid the real struggles, the hard questions of the day. They are, as John Stott says, too comfortable in the biblical world and too uneasy with the contemporary world. They contribute to the apparent irrelevance of Scripture by creating bridges that end in midair, never connecting the ancient and the modern worlds.[12]

View 3. Let's Work at It

View 3 recognizes that sound application is difficult, and therefore it deserves our best attention.[13] The previous two sections have shown that if application is a gift of God, it is like the gift of daily bread. We pray for bread and wait upon God for it, but we also have to toil for it. Without his provision, hearts "receive" sermons the way flames "receive" paper. The Lord makes words reach their targets and go far beyond them. Nonetheless, our laziness and passivity will destroy strong applications, for several reasons.

1. *To excel in application, one needs training in exegesis—the skills this book presents.* Pastors and scholars also need competency in biblical languages and extensive knowledge of the ancient world. Like most skills, these are largely amoral and open to all.[14] Trained agnostics are intellectually capable of comprehending the Bible—until they come to application.

2. *To excel in application, one needs character.* Selflessness releases an empathy that sees the struggles, addressed in the text, for all people.

Love says what must be said, tenderly yet plainly. Fearlessness watches our culture, so that we may address it as it really is, not as it is imagined in Christian ghettoes. Boldness risks the criticism and rejection that follow all who speak plainly about real issues. Patience listens quietly to the story of people just like us and people utterly unlike us, whether young or old, rich or poor, simple or wise, smooth or broken, so we can tell the biblical story to them. Meekness applies every text to itself first, driving out smug directions on how others should live. Integrity provides consistency between the word proclaimed and the word lived, lest, for example, fine sermons on self-control be shattered by the preacher's well-known temper tantrums.

Further, moral flaws impede interpretation. We do not wholly understand some things unless we know how to apply them.[15] A handyman does not "understand" his guide to household repairs if he has every tool but still cannot fix his faucet. A judge does not understand law and precedent if she cannot apply them to new cases. Likewise, teachers foolishly claim to understand faithfulness if they break their promises every time they become inconvenient. Teachers can address topics they have not experienced. The single person's explanation of marital love may be shallow, but it is not corrupted by a lack of experience. The same is true of many situations (unemployment, cancer, etc.) that teachers may need to address. But the failure to exercise a Christian virtue, when a test provides the opportunity to use it, is another matter. The person who consistently fails to be honest or pure or generous knows next to nothing about the discernment and endurance necessary for those virtues.

3. *To excel in application, one must be ready for all kinds of reluctant listeners.* Some are lazy. Preachers dare not simply impart information to them, John Calvin said, but must apply and threaten, for "if we leave it to men's choice to follow what is taught them, they will never move one foot." By itself, doctrine can "profit nothing at all," unless it is accompanied by exhortations.[16] Others are skeptics; they demand application or they will stop listening.

Some Christians come to church looking chiefly for mental stimulation. They view their teachers as spiritual entertainers. They forget that the goal of biblical exposition is Christian living, not merely Christian thinking. They forget that faith without works is vain. Likewise, instruction that does not produce love, mercy, service, and Christian community is vain and ultimately lifeless.

4. *To excel in application, one must be ready for eager listeners—people who want to be godly, but face perplexing questions.* Like the penitent soldiers who stood before John the Baptist, wondering how to prove their repentance, the faithful do come to their teacher wondering what to do. They want to know how to love their adolescents, how to respond to pressures to compromise at work, and much, much more.

5. *To excel in application, one must combine the seemingly opposed faculties of discipline and imagination.* Discipline takes one step at a time, persevering in the study of a familiar text, so that none of it is lost. It works through the several phases of application. It states the principles of godly living and suggests ways to accomplish them.

Imagination jumps around, connecting ideas in unexpected ways, bringing fresh insights to the process of application. Through imagination, the teacher locates answers to questions that never explicitly arise in the Bible. It finds obscure connections between biblical and modern cultures. It sniffs out the ways in which people will object to the truth. It knows they will bow to the truth, and then evade it. It anticipates the obstacles to obedience and lays plans to go around them. It offers specific suggestions to goodhearted people who want to do what is right, but cannot see the next step.

Take the topic of service, for example. At one level, every disciple understands what it means to serve. But people are so loaded with bad habits, bad examples, and pure selfishness, that we dare not assume that they know how to serve. Imagination sees through the man who believes in service but acts like a sloth at home and a visitor at church. It completes the task of application by suggesting what service should mean to him, in detail, in concrete incidents. It says something like this:

> Men, if you want to serve at home, get up and help clear the table after the next meal instead of looking for a way out. If coats sprawl on the floor, if the milk is sunning itself, if towels molder in heaps, put them away, instead of yelling at your wife and children to do something about it. Clean the car before someone's dress is ruined. When the chore is done, let it be your secret. At church, don't avoid unpleasant tasks by claiming, "It's not my gift." As a diagnostic test, when was the last time you took a turn in the nursery? More broadly,

ask yourself, "Am I doing something for someone for which I can gain nothing—no pay, no favors, no praise?"

To recapitulate, the first principle of application is this:

▶ **Principle 1: Application is both a necessary and a difficult phase of teaching, one that cannot simply be "left to God."**

Compelling application depends on exegetical skill, character, and preparation for all kinds of listeners. The next section illustrates the challenge of application in two common situations. In the first, the application is clear, but few Christians practice it. In the second, we ponder a question that is common, but alien to the biblical world.

Two Illustrations of Application

Case 1: A Simple Text

In Matthew 18:15, Jesus opens a section on reconciliation by saying, "If your brother sins against you, go and show him his fault, just between the two of you."[17] Nothing, so it seems, could be simpler than applying this text.[18] Yet, judging by Christian behavior, we realize that understanding the text is one thing and heeding it is another. Christians often act as if Jesus said, "If your brother sins against you, go withdraw, sulk, complain, and gossip."

Pastors often endure conversations that go like this:

OFFENDED PARTY: "My so-called friend has taken advantage of me again, and I don't know what to do about it. I am at my wit's end."

PASTOR: "What did he say when you talked to him about it?"

OFFENDED: "Oh, I didn't talk to him about it. I didn't think there was any point to that."

PASTOR: "But Jesus said the first thing you should do is talk to the person who offended you. If you haven't spoken to him, we should not even be talking now."

OFFENDED: "Oh, but I could never talk to him."

PASTOR: "Why not?"

(The answers vary—the offender is touchy, illogical, mean, intimidating, vengeful, and so on.)

How can we explain such conversations? The root of the problem is not rebellion, but fear. Fear of rejection, fear of an ugly scene, and fear of a counterattack overcome the desire to obey. A wise teacher should motivate his students and address obstacles to obedience. To motivate, a teacher can observe that true friends care enough to risk hurting the feelings of those we love. Further, if someone is a friend, we can probably think of a way to win him over.

The chief obstacle to obey Jesus' words in Matthew 18:15, surely, is that the one who points out sin rarely receives a warm welcome. Pastors can address this by noting an implicit obligation in verse 15. When someone comes to rebuke our sin, we should listen carefully and thankfully. We should be thankful, because his presence shows that he cares enough about us to take this painful step. Again, we should be thankful because we have nothing to lose from a sincere rebuke. If someone accuses us erroneously—a genuine possibility—we lose nothing vital and may grow through self-examination. If we are correctly rebuked, we have an opportunity to shed sin. Thus, Scripture says, "Rebuke a wise man and he will love you" (Prov. 9:8).[19] Even a malicious rebuke does limited harm. After all, we know the truth, as does the Lord, and he will vindicate the just.

Like many applications, and many truths of every sort, these points are obvious, once they are stated. Yet, because of our frailty and the complexity of life, what should be evident often eludes us. For that reason, wise teachers will gladly teach basic doctrine and basic ethics. They "dare to be boring." They will repeat old, familiar truths—in fresh ways, of course—as frequently as the situation calls for it.

> ◗ Principle 2: Sound application often consists in restating truths and removing common obstacles to obedience.

Case 2: An Obscure Question

Our second case takes up a question the Bible never addresses: How should a believer pray before entering an athletic contest? Christians often ask this, but teachers rarely address it, for several reasons. It contains an embarrassing whiff of self-interest. We suspect that we care about sports more than we should. We do not know where to turn for an answer. Sensible arguments have roughly equal weight on either side of the question. No, we may not pray for victory. To pray for victory is self-centered, because my victory is necessarily someone else's loss. Yes, we may pray for our victory, because our heavenly Father wants us to take our cares to him, and we do care about sports. Here is a method for handling obscure questions: (1) State the question as precisely as possible. (2) State the obvious or certain parts of an answer. Use them as the anchors or parameters for the rest of your reflection. (3) Draw on as many Bible texts as possible. (4) If an authoritative answer is impossible, don't force it.

Whatever the obstacles, the question is real and deserves an answer. How should believers pray about sports? Obviously, we can pray that no one gets hurt or that no one loses his temper. Then what? May we pray that we win? An apostolic prayer (Phil. 1:9–11) holds some clues.

> And this is my prayer: that your love may abound more and more in knowledge and depth of insight, so that you may be able to discern what is best and may be pure and blameless until the day of Christ, filled with the fruit of righteousness that comes through Jesus Christ—to the glory and praise of God.

This text, we notice, lacks any petition for material benefits, whether health or prosperity, good jobs or happy homes. Rather, Paul asks for broad spiritual virtues—love, knowledge, insight, discernment, blamelessness. The rest of the book shows that the Philippians did have concrete needs, but Paul declined to pray for concrete, particular needs.[20] Perhaps he reasoned, "If God grants them the great things—love, discernment, and purity—the smaller troubles will take care of themselves."

The biblical focus on spiritual benefits seems to rule out the simpleminded petition, "Dear Lord, let us win." I suspect that "Dear Lord, let us play our best" also has a selfish element, as it virtually prays for a win—or at worst a gallant defeat. May we therefore pray that we try our hardest? That seems better, for giving one's all is a virtue. Yet it fails to do full justice to Paul's central petitions, for love, discernment, purity, and blamelessness.

How then do we show discernment and love in an athletic contest? Purity and blamelessness require that we play according to the rules, even if—and this can be excruciating—our opponent is cheating. Whatever the sport, love banishes "trash talk"—abusive language—and "cheap shots"—blows intended to injure or provoke an opponent. We need discernment to distinguish between exploiting a weakness in order to defeat our opponents, and exploiting a weakness in order to humiliate them.

Meditation on these qualities leads us to wonder if other Christian virtues particularly apply to the sporting contest. Self-control and honesty come to mind. Yet we err if we simply list Christian character traits and pray that the athlete will produce them all. To ask that Christian football players be kind and gentle (Gal. 5:22–23) is, to say the least, incomplete. It neglects the nature of football, and ultimately avoids the question at hand. The impulse for virtue must, therefore, be redirected.

Ultimately, the goal in a sporting match is to conduct ourselves in a manner worthy of our calling while having fun and getting exercise. If our teammates and rivals do not share our faith, we especially want to avoid anything that compromises our confession of Christ. Negatively, we can pray that we avoid acts that would let observers conclude that Christian convictions have no effect on Christian conduct.

Positively, we may pray that our play will, however dimly, represent God's character. God is faithful; therefore, we should be faithful to our team, by showing up ready to play with the concentration that banishes sloppy play. God is mighty; therefore, we may pray that we will play mightily. Paul's charge in 1 Corinthians 16:13 seems to apply: "Stand firm in the faith; be men of courage; be strong." The Christian has every right to pray that he will play like a man—like the Adamic man in his original grandeur, like a man of God feeling the firstfruits of restoration. To play like a man is to play with an intensity and strength that disproves the notion that Christians are wimps who turn to religion as a crutch because they are weak. Thus, we can pray that we will run fast and hit hard; we can pray for authoritative rebounds, ringing doubles, clean blocks, whistling fastballs, and blistering overhead smashes.

The prayer for virtue and strength finally gets us back to victory, not as an end in itself, but as a consequence of the virtue and strength we justly seek. The realization that victory is not our ultimate goal should liberate us to play without fear, and hence more freely. So, should we pray to win or not? Each one will have to answer that for himself or herself. But we can all pray that we will manifest the divine virtues that tend to produce victory in any contest—athletic or otherwise—whether we win or not.

Conclusion

Having assembled the CAPTOR data from studies in Context, Analysis, Problems, and Themes, in this chapter and the next we begin to bring our research to bear on life, on our ethical Obligations. These case studies have shown that application is not so easy that it can be left to the listener, nor so problematic that it must be left to God. Rather, it is a challenge that demands sustained effort. We have blind spots, and sin dulls our judgment. It is difficult, but vital, to draw lines between biblical truth and the specific questions of an honest life. In the next chapter, we will attempt to show how to do just that.

Exercises

1. List the basic obligations set forth in Galatians 6:2–5, a clear text. List the ways in which people resist obeying the command to bear one another's burdens. Answer some of them.

2. Here is a highly debated question that the Bible never addresses directly: Should a woman remain in the home, in a marriage, with an abusive husband? Marshall your resources and draw a defensible conclusion.

Notes

[1] This story is sometimes ascribed to Søren Kierkegaard, who told many parables, but apparently not this one, according to the indexes of his works and some experts I have consulted.

[2] They do not entirely agree. Conservative Christians believe all parts of Scripture are true and agree with one another, and they ordinarily try to show this in their expositions. Critics may or may not believe a passage to be true and coherent. Further, some schools of exegesis (deconstruction, some types of reader-response theory, and some feminist hermeneutics) practice what is called a "hermeneutic of suspicion." These schools may deny that (a) biblical authors were capable of presenting a recoverable message or that (b) the apparent meaning of biblical texts is their real meaning.

[3] A confession: I speak of "obligations" in order to get the O in the acronym CAPTOR. But "application" is the more common term for the skills described in this chapter.

[4] James Barr, *The Bible in the Modern World* (New York: Harper & Row, 1973), 39–44. The statement is Barr's description of "cultural relativism," a view he generally rejects, although he finds it "stimulating and fruitful."

[5] James Gustafson, "The Place of Scripture in Christian Ethics," *Interpretation* 24 (October 1970): 444–55, esp. 450–51. In this sophisticated article, Gustafson is quite interested in biblical authority, but he consciously refrains from granting it supreme moral authority.

[6] Philosophers such as Lessing have argued that historical events cannot prove moral truths. Moral truths are universal. All rational people can see the necessity for basic moral truths. They can see that there must be a ban on murder, lying, and treachery, for example, or human society would be impossible. At best, historical reports illustrate moral truths. But only reason can establish moral truth. See Gotthold Lessing, "On the Proof of the Spirit and of Power," in *Lessing's Theological Writings*, trans. and ed. Henry Chadwick (Stanford: Stanford University Press, 1957), 51–56.

[7] As I. H. Marshall put it, "Discussions on biblical hermeneutics have given us a fair amount of guidance on how to elucidate what the text said—its original meaning and significance for its original readers. They have not done a lot to help us to take the passage from what the text said to what it says" to readers today ("New Occasions Teach New Duties? 2. The Use of the New Testament in Christian Ethics," *Expository Times* 105 [February 1994]: 136). In their hermeneutics text, Klein, Blomberg, and Hubbard remark that skill in application is more caught than taught, and then add wryly, "But sound application often seems hard to find, let alone catch." William Klein, Craig Blomberg, and Robert Hubbard, *Introduction to Biblical Interpretation* (Waco: Word, 1993), 403.

[8] The quotations in this section come from a series of interviews with pastors in 1994 and 1995. Most of the pastors I interviewed articulated some form of this position, although they sometimes combined it with elements of the other views. Books on interpretation do not explicitly advocate this view, although one can detect it between the lines.

[9] Karl Barth, *Prayer and Preaching*, trans. B. E. Hooke and Sara F. Terrien (London: SCM Press, 1964), 107.

[10] Ibid., 66, 108–9.

[11] S. G. De Graff, *Promise and Deliverance*, 4 vols. (St. Catherine's, Ont.: Paideia Press, 1977–81), 1:17–23.

[12] John Stott, *Between Two Worlds: The Art of Preaching in the Twentieth Century* (Grand Rapids: Eerdmans, 1982), 137–41.

[13] Three semipopular books that represent this view are Jay Adams, *Truth Applied: Application in Preaching* (Grand Rapids: Zondervan, 1990); Jack Kuhatschek, *Taking the Guesswork out of Applying the Bible* (Downers Grove, Ill.: InterVarsity Press, 1990); Dave Veerman, *How to Apply the Bible* (Wheaton, Ill.: Tyndale, 1993).

[14] They are amoral in the sense that one need not be a good person to be a good actress, violinist, poet, carpenter, or exegete. Morals are not wholly irrelevant, of course. Moral faults such as laziness, dishonesty, or alcoholism impair the use of all skills.

[15] This paragraph depends broadly on Hans-Georg Gadamer, *Truth and Method*, trans. Garrett Barden and John Cumming, 2d ed. (New York: Seabury Press, 1965), 277–305.

[16] John Calvin, *Sermons on Epistles to Timothy and Titus* (1579; reprint, Edinburgh: Banner of Truth, 1983), 947.

[17] See the discussion of this passage in chap. 6.

[18] I sometimes dream of reading a passage like this and preaching a one-minute sermon on it. The outline would go like this: "You heard what the text said, and you know you aren't doing it. God will forgive you for your failure, but you should still start obeying now." In fact, I did it once in a casual setting, with the knowledge and approval of those who invited me. The pastor missed my intent, however, and delivered a full-throated, ten-minute "closing prayer" that covered the entire text.

[19] See also Prov. 3:11; 15:31; 17:10; 19:25; 25:12; 27:5; Eccl. 7:5.

[20] This is common in Paul's prayers: e.g., Eph. 1:15–21; 3:14–19. See W. B. Hunter, "Prayer," in *Dictionary of Paul and His Letters*, ed. Gerald Hawthorne, Ralph Martin, and Daniel Reid (Downers Grove, Ill.: InterVarsity Press, 1993), 733–34.

10

The Practice of Application

Applications in the Cards

We had eaten all we wanted at the Peking lunch buffet, shoved our plates aside, and settled in for business—a discussion of the challenge of applying the Bible. My friend had just preached on 1 Corinthians 10:14–33, Paul's teaching on meat offered to idols. "Paul's message," he declared, "is perfectly clear, but perfectly irrelevant at a literal level today. Paul has three points," he continued. "First, the Corinthians cannot eat meat at an idol's feast, because they will be enmeshed in something bigger than a dinner (vv. 18–22). But, second, in private they can eat whatever they want, because the meat really belongs to the Lord, not to an idol (vv. 23–26). Yet, third, if a pagan invites some of them to dinner and says, 'This meat has been offered to an idol,' the Corinthians should not eat, because the pagan will think they are violating their conscience (vv. 27–28)." The problem, we agreed, is that contemporary Christians never face the situation Paul addressed. After all, how many North American Christians have ever sat down to a dinner served with this warning: "Before we begin, you might like to know that this roast was offered to an idol this morning."

"So how did you apply the passage to your congregation?" I inquired.

"I applied it to cards and gambling," he replied. "Like meat, cards are neither morally good nor evil in themselves. So, in private, you can use them. Still, I told them, don't play cards at the riverboat casino. You get entangled in something that is bigger than cards, something far beyond your control. Like an idol feast, gambling partakes of a godless system that involves more than what appears on the surface."

I thought my friend had made a solid application, but I also wondered, "How did you come to connect meat to gambling? What made you confident it was correct?" His energetic smile drained into a pensive frown. "I don't know," he responded. "It just came to me. Cards and gambling are issues in my church, and the teaching on meat seemed to apply."

Our discussion illustrates several key issues in applying the Bible. It shows that even the best teachers could use a method for application. If we rely on flashes of insight, on ideas that come to us, what will we do when creativity dries up? And if we don't know where our applications come from, how can we confirm that they are sound?

The story also shows that application often begins by facing the issues of life and bringing them to Scripture. Is it an accident that my friend applied 1 Corinthians to gambling just as riverboat gambling was an issue in our state elections? Application often begins when we recognize our need for divine guidance and take our needs to the Scriptures, expecting answers. We are much better at applying the Bible when we read it with questions in mind. For example, when we are ill or abused, we find more guidance for sufferers. Or, if we have become more conscious of sin in our lives, passages about penitence, mercy, and forgiveness leap off the page.

Speaking more broadly, the key is to look in every text for a remedy to some aspect of our fallen human condition.[1] Application should always show how God heals some part of our sin and brokenness. I do not mean that we should always look for instruction about the way of salvation; relatively few verses provide that. But all Scripture says something about God's salvation and our new life. Our task, in applying the Bible, is to search the whole Bible to find answers to questions that arise through the whole of life.

The goal of this chapter is to present a method for rich, varied, and sound application, in several steps. First, we will see in more detail why application is difficult, requiring a method. Second, we will see that we can find application in all kinds of Scriptures, not just the ethical portions. Third, we will present a method for building bridges from ancient biblical precepts to the contemporary culture. After looking at some illustrative studies, we will consider the role of the will in application. More detailed ideas for applying particular genres of Scripture, such as narratives and wisdom literature, appear in appendix D.

Application: Hard Enough to Require a Method

If you read the Bible devotionally, you can usually find something edifying, something that meets a current need, in your daily reading. But if you want to teach others with precision and depth, if you want to do more than remind yourself of familiar truths, you need a method. You cannot rely on intuition and prayer alone, for the following reasons:[2]

1. The Bible is neither a casebook for personal decisions nor a detailed guide to daily conduct. It does not tell us, directly, whom to marry or what our calling in life should be. It will not dictate answers to complex ethical questions, such as What should I do when I suspect, but cannot prove, that a coworker is deceiving a customer?

2. The Bible does not explicitly address some contemporary issues. For example, how should I use the communications media? How fast should I drive when everyone around me is speeding? How does the command to love my neighbor apply to competition in business? Is my competitor my enemy? If so, how do I love my enemy, if his gain is my loss?

3. The Bible is not a text of moral philosophy. It does not provide a list of first principles and postulates. It does not outline a theoretical system for moral analysis or present a multistep plan for making moral judgments.

4. We wonder how much the Bible is meant for everyone and how much it applies only to believers. In the Old Testament, how much is strictly for Israel? How should we take commands to individuals such as Abraham or Peter? Should we expect pagans, who lack certain motives and spiritual capacities, to observe commandments about selfless love, when we ourselves struggle to keep them?

5. How can we apply Scriptures that lack commandments? What do narratives, promises, and songs require? For instance, should

we search narratives for examples of godly and godless living—examples to follow or avoid? Should we view apostolic missionary methods as models for our mission work?

6. How can we tell whether a biblical injunction is limiting the damage of a corrupt social structure or approving that social structure? Jesus says that Moses permitted a hardhearted nation to operate with loose divorce regulations. But God's ideal for marriage is much higher (Matt. 19:3–12; 5:33–42). We view the Bible's toleration of polygamy and slavery in the same way. Are other social institutions similar?

7. Reading the Bible is like entering a conversation with someone from another culture—someone with a unique history, language, and set of customs. Human nature is constant enough that communication is possible, yet the strain to communicate proves that there is a distance between cultures.

8. The Bible is the story of salvation, not a handbook of moral living. The evangelists wrote that we might believe that Jesus is the Christ and have life in his name (John 20:31). Yes, Jesus commanded the apostles to "Go and make disciples of all nations . . . teaching them to obey everything I have commanded you" (Matt. 28:19–20). Yet the gospel never starts by describing what God's people ought to do for him. It starts by describing what God did for us when we could not do a thing for ourselves.

So, then, our desire to apply the Bible faces obstacles. Above all, the Bible is the history of salvation, not a handbook of ethics or church leadership. Further, cultures change constantly, creating apparent gaps between biblical commands and contemporary issues. Biblical statements about meat, idols, oxen, feasts, and priests seem irrelevant on one hand. On the other, we sometimes search the Bible in vain for answers to questions raised by a technological society—questions about medical ethics, the media, and much more.

We must therefore have a strategy for finding our duties. Some approaches are clearly wrong. If someone tells us they have found a verse in Ezekiel that settles the question of genetic engineering or interplanetary travel, we ought to be wary. Yet, since Scripture does equip the servant of God for every good work, we cannot dismiss any issue with the cavalier comment, "Oh, the Bible doesn't deal with that." And so, the question stands: How do we find ethical guidance for contemporary society in the ancient commands of the Bible?

Finding Applications in All Kinds of Scripture

▶ **Principle 1: In applying the Bible, we must expect to find applications in all kinds of Scriptures, not just in commandments.**

To be precise, we can identify seven partially overlapping places to find application in Scripture.[3] This broad list shows that while the Bible is not a set of instructions, the entire Bible is instructive.[4]

1. *Laws or rules* require obedience to specific commands. Some of these transfer to our culture easily, and some do not. For example, Moses said, "If . . . [a] bull has had the habit of goring and the owner has been warned but has not kept it penned up and it kills a man or woman, the bull must be stoned and the owner also must be put to death" (Ex. 21:29). Similarly, Paul told the Romans to greet one another with a holy kiss (Rom. 16:16). Later we will show how some of these rules apply today.

2. *Ideals or principles* guide a wide range of behavior without specifying particular deeds. For example, Jesus said, "Love your enemies. . . . Be perfect, therefore, as your heavenly Father is perfect," and "Seek first his kingdom and his righteousness" (Matt. 5:44, 48; 6:33). In Hosea the Lord said, "I desire mercy, not sacrifice" (Hos. 6:6), and Paul declared, "If it is possible, as far as it depends on you, live at peace with everyone" (Rom. 12:18). Principles neither command nor forbid one particular action, but they supply the basis for many acts.

3. *Actions in narratives* depict positive examples to be imitated and negative ones to be avoided. The Bible may tell us what to imitate, or we may have to see for ourselves. Paul and Peter tell us to live as Christ did, putting others first, sacrificing ourselves for others, and suffering patiently (Phil. 2:3–8; Eph. 5:25ff.; 1 Peter 2:18–25). Likewise, when the Israelites made a golden calf, Moses explicitly condemned their rebellion (Ex. 32). But when David shows courage in his battle with Goliath, the Bible lets us draw conclusions for ourselves (1 Sam. 17). Every narrative also teaches us something about God and his redemptive plan, and thus requires us to believe something about him.

4. *Biblical symbols and images* create new ways of seeing things, new opportunities to see life God's way, and act accordingly. Most symbols are concrete objects that represent an abstract concept. For example, the cross, as a symbol of Christ's work and our fellowship in

his sufferings, calls us to fidelity, whatever the price. It frees us from selfish calculations of the costs and benefits of obedience. It encourages us to do what is right and trust the results to God. The image of God as Father calms our fears when we feel hurt, worried, or lonely. The image of the sluggard in Proverbs warns us against laziness more effectively than a plain command could. We see him turning on his bed like a door on its hinges, crying out, "There is a lion in the road," and burying his hand in the dish, too lazy to raise it to his mouth (Prov. 19:24; 26:13–16). No one needs to add, "Don't be like the sluggard." We get the picture and resolve that we will never play the sluggard.

5. *Doctrines*, that is, the cardinal beliefs of the faith, require us to act according to our convictions. If we believe that Jesus is the only Savior, we must evangelize. If we believe that God created all people in his image, we must treat them with dignity. If we believe that the redeemed are new creations, then we must put off the old self and its desires.

6. In divine *promises,* God commits himself to do something in the future.[5] Promises tell us which deeds God approves and rewards, and which he disapproves and disciplines. They guide God's people by showing them how to live so as to rest under God's blessing, even if there are no guarantees of a trouble-free life.

7. *Songs and prayers* show us how to worship and pray. The Psalms are divinely sanctioned examples of the praise and thanksgiving of the believer. The prayers of the righteous show us what we should desire.[6] A few, such as that of the self-righteous Pharisee in Luke 18:9–14, show us how not to pray.

We see, then, that we can find applications in every text. In each one, some command, principle, action, symbol, doctrine, or promise will show how God's saving work liberates us from sin and the Fall. But how do we apply what we find to contemporary cultures? Is there a method for moving reliably from meat sacrificed to idols to gambling? By way of reply, let us think of a sidewalk and a bridge.

Applying Ancient Truths to Our Culture

The Sidewalk

▶ **Principle 2: Sometimes the application of a text is basically the same today as it was thousands of years ago.**

Spanning the gap from antiquity to the present may be no more draining than a stroll down the sidewalk. No mysterious terms or customs interrupt the process of communication. The Bible means just what it seems to mean, and the body of Christ has always understood it essentially the same way.[7] The church debates dozens of issues and gets all sorts of things wrong, but it is almost impossible to make some mistakes. Even casual readers must see that the God of the Bible offers salvation by grace through faith, that theft and adultery are immoral, and so on.[8]

Of course, it may still be difficult to fulfill a lucid command. For example, we know that coveting is as wrong today as it was in Moses' day, but the advertising media test us sorely, and we may not know how to avoid the temptation. Should we ban television from our homes—or throw out catalogues, like so much toxic waste, the moment they arrive? Again, we know that we should honor our parents, but may not know how to honor aged parents when they give poor counsel, or when foolish fears grip them. We should speak respectfully and show honor, but what next? So, although there is art in handling foolproof texts, we acknowledge that they exist, and move to harder ones.

The Bridge

The great intellectual challenge to the application of Scripture is *to bridge the gap between the cultures of the Bible and current cultures.* Though the challenge of doing what we know we should do may be even greater, still, we need to learn how to build a bridge from the past to the present, so that we at least know what obedience we owe.

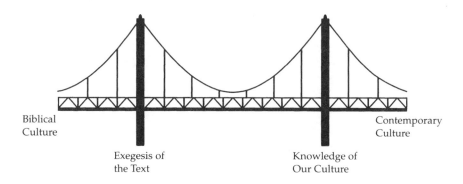

Biblical
Culture

Contemporary
Culture

Exegesis of
the Text

Knowledge of
Our Culture

The first support for this bridge is solid exegesis of the text (chaps. 1–8). The second is knowledge of our culture. To read devotionally, we must know ourselves. To study in order to teach others, we must know others. We must listen, long and true—to truck drivers, engineers, insurance agents, car salesmen, and mothers of toddlers; to young and old, rich and poor, simple and wise, male and female. We should read all kinds of magazines: *McCalls, Rolling Stone, Better Homes and Gardens, Fortune, Redbook, Field and Stream,* and *People.* And, yes, even take a glance at *Soap Opera Digest* or *Guns and Ammo.* Read not to condemn, but to learn what moves these people. What do they treasure? What do they believe? It is said, "You have to deal with the world as it is, in order to make it what you want it to be." We must expect to get our hands a little dirty, just as Jesus did when he ate and drank with tax collectors and sinners.[9]

The roadway, the span between the foundations, comes next. The span is constructed from a principle that applies to ancient life and modernity.

> ▸ **Principle 3: We bridge the gap between prophets, apostles, and Americans by applying established principles to new situations.**

Illustration: From Kisses to Handshakes?

Let us illustrate with Paul's command, "Greet one another with a holy kiss" (Rom. 16:16; 1 Cor. 16:20; 2 Cor. 13:12; cf. 1 Peter 5:14).

Step 1: Determine the original meaning. The adjective *holy,* along with the Bible's general opposition to sensuality, proves that Paul is not commanding romantic kisses. Research shows that a holy kiss was a standard greeting, given in secular society as well as the church, to demonstrate trust and affection. It was ritualized, and may have entailed no more than touching cheek to cheek on both sides. Further, only people of the same gender exchanged this "kiss."

Step 2: Find the principle.[10] Paul does not state the principle behind the holy kiss, but it does remind us that all Christians belong to the same family. We ought to feel brotherly love for them and give them some token of our affection (Rom. 12:10; Eph. 4:32).

Although the principle behind the kiss goes unstated, the text sometimes announces its principles. In the case of idol meat and gambling (above), the text was part of a long discussion of Christian freedom (1 Cor. 6–10). Most of Paul's commands there develop one of three explicit axioms in some way: (1) Everything is permissible, but not everything is beneficial (6:12; 10:23). (2) Everything is permissible, but we should not be mastered by anything (6:12). (3) Whatever we do, we should do it all for the glory of God (10:31). These principles govern Paul's discussion of freedom and sexuality, marriage and food. To switch to an Old Testament example, the principle "Be holy because I, the Lord, am holy" lies behind many regulations in Leviticus (11:44–45; 19:2; 20:7). As a general rule, a commandment rests on an abiding principle if it is grounded, as the last two are, in the creation order, the nature of God, the work of redemption, or the redeemed life that follows.[11]

Sometimes we must deduce the main principle. For example, many proverbs rest on the idea that calamity overtakes the fool. For example, the sage commands his son to avoid wicked men because they lie in wait for their own blood; they waylay themselves (Prov. 1:18). He should avoid harlots because they will rob his strength and give his wealth to strangers, and ruin him before the assembly (5:8–14). He must shun laziness because poverty comes on the sluggard "like a bandit and scarcity like an armed man" (6:11). The principle behind these sayings (and many more) is that evildoers are self-destructive. "The evil deeds of a wicked man ensnare him" (5:22; cf. 1:25–27).

Principles for behavior can be derived from doctrines, too. For example, Paul exhorted the Galatians not to observe Jewish holy days (4:9–11) or be circumcised (5:2–3) because some hoped to earn God's favor through them, and that is contrary to the gospel of justification by faith (2:16–17). Symbols can also supply principles. Using the cross as a symbol, Paul charged the Philippians to put each other first, because they are united to Christ Jesus, who put others first, even though it cost him his life (2:1–8).

Step 3: Apply the principle to a similar situation today. Here we need to know our culture and rely on Spirit-guided intuition and wise friends. To return to the brotherly kiss, we know that a literal kiss of greeting would cause a shock in North America today. The bridge-building question is: What greeting conveys acceptance and warmth in our society? Between women, a hug may do it; between men, a handshake. Sometimes a warm smile and a greeting will suffice. Our culture has developed other tokens of friendship, such as calling to chat on the phone or sending greeting cards (or E-mail?). By these somewhat ritualized actions, we live out the ideal of greeting one another with a holy kiss.

Step 4: If possible, verify your conclusions by comparing them to other Scriptures. It is impossible to prove that handshakes are the equivalent of holy kisses. But certain passages do confirm that Christians should be affectionate toward one another (Rom. 12:10; Eph. 4:32), and we know that love must prove itself in deeds.

So far, we have explored the simple case of the holy kiss. To solidify our grasp on the task of building bridges, let us take up the harder case of a bull with a habit of goring.

A Test Case: From Bulls to Tractors

In Exodus 21:28–29, we read, "If a bull gores a man or a woman to death, the bull must be stoned to death, and its meat must not be eaten. But the owner of the bull will not be held responsible. If, however, the bull has had the habit of goring and the owner has been warned but has not kept it penned up and it kills a man or woman, the bull must be stoned and the owner also must be put to death." Today, this law seems irrelevant to all but farmers and ranchers. Or is it? Let us follow the steps for building a bridge and see.

Step 1: Determine the original meaning. Here we ask how the command functioned in Israel. What did bulls do, and when might a bull gore a man? Bulls were beasts of burden, trained to plow, harvest, and thresh. They worked more efficiently than men, but could harm them while they toiled together on farms. Thus, the closest parallel to a bull in our culture is not a dangerous animal, such as an attack dog. The closest analogy is the work hazard, perhaps especially farm machinery like tractors, harrows, and threshers, since farm equipment, like bulls, toils in the place of humans and can harm them.

Step 2: Find the principle behind the specific command about bulls. The command regarding bulls lies in a passage in Exodus on injuries and accidents (Ex. 21:12–36). The teachings forbid and punish both killing and wounding, whether premeditated or accidental. Because the passage describes the prevention of accidental injury and death, it orders owners to kill their bulls if they gore someone to death. The bridging principle, therefore, is this: murder is forbidden, and so is anything that resembles murder, such as the reckless endangerment of others.

Step 3: Discover a similar situation today. I proposed that dangerous equipment of all kinds resembles the bull of antiquity. Like bulls, manufacturing equipment, explosive chemicals, heavy construction and engineering, and the airline and trucking industries all serve mankind, yet can cause accidental harm. Moses' command probably also applies to the careless operation of potentially dangerous equipment, such as a car. Perhaps a reckless driver is to his sheet metal as the reckless owner is to the horns of his bull. The text requires the covenant family to preserve life by preventing accidents.

In this third step, we became a little tentative, for it is hard to be certain that a bull is equivalent to manufacturing equipment. So we go the next step to verify this tentative conclusion.

Step 4: Compare our application to other Scriptures. This tests the soundness of the bridge. A mind that is saturated with Scripture is less likely to blunder. Further, when an application fits several biblical passages, we gain confidence in it.

We observe, therefore, the law's concern for safety in regulations concerning accidental death and quarrels (Ex. 21:12–13, 18–19) or blows to pregnant women (Ex. 21:22–23). It reappears in Deuteronomy 22:8, where Moses commands the Israelites to put a parapet (a low wall) around their roofs. Roofs were flat in Palestine, and people spent time on them (Josh. 2:62; 2 Sam. 11:2), even sleeping there on hot nights. Other texts treating accidental or negligent killing include Genesis 9:5 (by man or animal), Numbers 35:6–34 (accidents distinguished from murder; cities of refuge), and Joshua 20–21 (cities of refuge). Indeed, the Bible often addresses the preservation of life, perhaps because it is God's nature to give life and guard it (Pss. 37; 91; 121; Luke 12:7; 1 Peter 5:7). Taken together, these texts confirm that God does require us to take reasonable steps to prevent accidents.[12]

To summarize, when we encounter a command that seems far removed from our day, we ought not to discard it. Intuition will yield some insights effortlessly. Yet when intuition fails or should be verified, we follow this method: (1) Determine the original meaning. (2) Find the principle. (3) Apply the principle to a similar situation today. (4) Check your ideas against other Scriptures.

Principles and Commands Together

This chapter has assumed that broad principles and particular rules—for example, "Do not kill," and "Watch your bull"—are inseparable if we wish to grow in holiness. Like highways and residential streets, we must travel both if we wish to reach our destination, that is, a life filled with righteous thoughts, words, and actions. If principles are like multilane highways that traverse a vast domain, rules are like the smaller roads that get us all the way home.

To their own loss, many Christians read the Bible for principles, such as love and justice, and ignore its rules.[13] Others say that they take every command as universally binding law. It is better to see specific commands as inspired applications of universal principles. They push us to do something concrete. We may be able to apply those commands today just as believers did long ago. If not, they still function as signposts, pointing to correct applications for new situations today.[14]

Take the principle of caring for the poor. God cares for the poor (Pss. 14:6; 35:10; 112:9; Isa. 25:4; Matt. 11:5; Luke 4:18; 7:22) and condemns their oppressors (Amos 2:7; 4:1; 5:11; James 2:2–6). Therefore, God's children should protect them, be generous to them (Deut. 15:7, 11; Luke 12:33; 14:13, 21), grant them justice (Ex. 23:6; Lev. 19:15; James 5:4), and minister to them (James 1:27). But how can we concretely apply the principle "Care for the poor" today? How, for example, does it bear on panhandlers, who are quite possibly addicts? They may use your gift to buy another round of alcohol or drugs.

Israel's specific gleaning laws offer help. "When you reap the harvest of your land, do not reap to the very edges of your field or gather the gleanings of your harvest. Do not go over your vineyard a second time or pick up the grapes that have fallen. Leave them for the poor and the alien" (Lev. 19:9–10). Literal obedience to the rule would help few of the poor today. The rule fits a rural, agrarian society, whereas most of the poor live in the city today. Yet the law contains a vital principle: We should give to the poor without encouraging sloth or dependence. Even though we cannot apply it literally, the gleaning law is more than a husk to be discarded once we locate a kernel of universal truth. It is an inspired paradigm for care for the poor; it should stimulate our imagination to create new ways of caring for them.[15]

So it goes with many principles; their application varies from culture to culture. Yet once we locate a contemporary parallel, we must apply the principle if we respect the authority of Scripture. Thus, principles form the foundation, roof, and steel girders of the edifice of Christian ethics. Specific rules and the deeds that are approved in biblical narratives, finish the walls, lighting, and carpeting.

We have finished discussing the mental work of application now, but two matters remain that have more to do with the will. The first has to do with being imaginative. The second is the challenge of actually telling people what to do.

A Method for the Imagination?

Thomas Edison said, "Genius is one percent inspiration and ninety-nine percent perspiration." His maxim holds for Bible application. Sometimes ideas come unbidden, but the imagination is no tame beast that comes at our call. What then shall we do when we have general ideas about application, but nothing concrete comes to mind? If you are reading the Bible devotionally, this is rarely a problem. If you are preparing for a home Bible study, you can enlist your friends' help. Tell them, "This passage requires us to do this and that. Who here has had to confront this issue lately? What happened? What did you learn?" But if you teach more formally, or want to be well prepared for casual gatherings, you must give the imagination a boost from time to time. Here are some ideas:

1. Start your lessons well in advance, and then keep your eyes open for applications at work, at home, or on the news. Read widely. Listen to people; get them to talk about what matters most to them.

2. Immerse yourself in the fundamentals of Scripture. Return to the person of God, knowing that his image is our destiny (Rom. 8:29; Eph. 4:24; 5:1). Ponder mankind, fallen and redeemed. Master the fundamentals of Christian ethics—the Ten Commandments, the Sermon on the Mount, the meaning of love, righteousness, and gratitude. In your application, as elsewhere, you must dare to be boring (see chap. 9).

3. Try to see the passage from a new perspective. How would a

new Christian or a child take it? How will we view it from heaven? What might a nominal Christian say? How might unbelievers from various walks of life resist: a businessman, a homemaker, a student, a retiree? How does God see the issue?

4. If you have the resources, see how past Christian leaders applied the passage.

5. Assuming that the command is clear, ask, What obstacles prevent obedience? What excuses do we offer for disobedience?

Turning such questions over in the mind, we invite the bolt of insight to strike. Nourish your imagination with these exercises and it will grow stronger. Of course, try as we might, some lessons never soar. Then we take comfort in a crawl, if it is in the right direction.

Open Your Mouth

Like the duck pastor in the previous chapter, many teachers have a hard time opening their mouths and letting out a full-blooded command. They hate to tell people what to do. They will say something is wise, that God blesses it, or that we should think about it, but pure commands rarely pass their lips. I have battled this myself. Because my doctoral studies centered on the family, churches were already asking me to teach about marriage and parenting when I was 27 and childless after five years of marriage. Plunging into the task, I dispensed counsel and commands with élan. Then my wife became pregnant, and I began to stutter a bit, thinking, "I do not yet have one child; how do I dare to instruct people with three? What if my children become wild and rebellious, putting the lie to all I have said?" In time, self-doubt silenced me, and I refused every request to speak on the subject.

There is some merit in such hesitation. Jesus does want us to practice what we preach (Matt. 23:3). Besides, who trusts an obese nutritionist, a scabrous dermatologist, or a divorced family therapist? Yet caution can lapse into misguided silence. The Lord charges his watchmen to proclaim the whole truth and let the hearers be accountable for their hearing (Ezek. 3:16–19; 33:1–20; Matt. 13:9; Rev. 2:7, 11, 17). In the end, the value of the proclamation rests on the truth of the message, not the virtue of the messenger. Therefore, when you teach, you must articulate God's requirements, even if you are falling short yourself.

In short, to proclaim biblical commands, teachers need both boldness and humility. They need boldness to overcome an undue reluctance to speak, but they need the humility to recognize that they may—and sometimes will—fail to practice what they preach.

When you do state commands, be concrete. Press beyond vague generalizations about love and Christian service. Tell people about washing dishes, staffing church nurseries, and inviting obnoxious people to join them for lunch. If you think you are saying something they have never heard before, suggest how they might begin to do it.

Take the area of private devotions. First, the devotional life of most teachers is a disgrace. Second, while the Bible often shows the devotional acts of the righteous, it never outlines a program for private worship. So we have two excuses for remaining silent on the subject! Yet we dare not do so, because it is absolutely clear that believers should pray daily, and it is absolutely certain that many do not.[16]

So, if prayer comes up while you lead a study, you have no right to excuse yourself, saying, "My own devotional life is hardly exemplary; how dare I tell others how to live?" Nor can we say, "Wait till I work out my theology of devotion, and then I will speak." Of course, we despise the legalism that says, "Have daily devotions or God will punish you," or, "Have devotions or you cannot call yourself a serious Christian." But the excesses of legalists do not justify silence, either. Some people sincerely want to know what to do, and they may be hoping you can guide them. So, if devotions come up, we should silence our fears, gather our courage, and suggest a plan, even if it is as simple and minimal as this: "Above all, do *something*. Every Christian should read the Bible and pray a little every day. As for family devotions, God requires Christian parents to train their children in the nurture and admonition of the Lord, and family devotions provide one excellent means."

Then suggest some ways to conduct devotions effectively. I say something like this, when asked: "My family has family devotions most days, but not every day. We have them after dinner whenever possible, but sometimes we wait until bedtime. We switch formats from time to time, for variety seems to help the children. After some weeks with a devotional guide, we will read a book or two in the Bible and entertain any questions that come up." By presenting some rules ("Read and pray daily"), some options, and some testimony, I try to give directions without becoming a legalist.

We must avoid two misunderstandings. First, you need not have a detailed plan, or an application for every verse before you speak. Obligations typically flow more from an entire passage than from its parts. Second, we can apply the Bible without stating commands, by urging people to think about character, about their goals, and about a godly view of life. We truly apply the Bible when we urge people to praise God for delivering us from our folly and rebellion. We truly apply the Bible when we encourage them to rest in Jesus' mercy. A full description of Jesus' saving work and its consequences already begins the work of application.

Conclusion

Sometimes, sound applications come easily. A passage is straightforward, and it applies today much as it did long ago, or it obviously addresses a hot topic. On such an occasion, we may check our work but need not toil over methods.

This chapter presents a method for finding applications when they are less obvious. It urges, first, that students of Scripture look for application in all kinds of passages: laws, principles, narratives, doctrine, symbols, promises, songs, and prayers. Second, determine the original meaning of a text before applying it. Third, find the main principle of the text. Fourth, apply the principle to a similar situation today. Fifth, let particular rules and general principles interpret each other. Finally, speak. Avoid legalism and focus on Christ, but do not hesitate to tell people what to do.

With this chapter, we have finished all but the final step in the CAPTOR plan. Having gathered the data from our work in Context, Analysis, Problems, Themes, and Obligations, only the process of Reflecting on the main idea and its application remains.

Exercises

Find the main application in the passages below. Fill out one or two applications by (1) thinking of specific ways you or your friends could put them into practice, (2) listing some of the objections or obstacles to obedience, and (3) replying to them—and, if appropriate, proposing steps toward a faithful response.

1. Narratives
   a. Abraham's near sacrifice of Isaac (Gen. 22)
   b. Hezekiah's deliverance from the invading Assyrians (2 Kings 18–19)
   c. Peter's preaching to Cornelius's household (Acts 10)

2. Ethical texts
   a. Jesus' instructions for the disciples' first evangelistic mission (Matt. 10:1–16)
   b. The covenant law for the conduct of the king of Israel (Deut. 17:4–10)

3. Doctrinal texts
   a. The absence of condemnation (Rom. 8:1–4)
   b. The names of Christ (Isa. 9:6–7)

Notes

[1] For more on application and fallenness, see Bryan Chapell, *Christ-Centered Preaching: Redeeming the Expository Sermon* (Grand Rapids: Baker, 1994), 40–44, 263–66. We will return to this in chap. 12.

[2] For a more elaborate list of the challenges to application, see I. H. Marshall's list of eleven obstacles to application in "New Occasions Teach New Duties? 2. The Use of the New Testament in Christian Ethics," *Expository Times* 105 (February 1994): 131–32.

[3] This list is indebted to shorter lists by Richard B. Hays, "Scripture-Shaped Community: The Problem of Method in New Testament Ethics," *Interpretation* 44 (January 1990): 47–51, and Richard Longenecker, *New Testament Social Ethics for Today* (Grand Rapids: Eerdmans, 1984), 1–15.

[4] Richard Bauckham, *The Bible in Politics: How to Read the Bible Politically* (Louisville, Ky.: Westminster/John Knox, 1989), 6; Richard Pratt, *He Gave Us Stories: The Bible Student's Guide to Interpreting Old Testament Narratives* (Phillipsburg, N.J.: Presbyterian and Reformed, 1990), 313–14.

[5] Promises could be called a special kind of doctrine because they affirm something about God.

[6] See Gordon Fee and Douglas Stuart, *How to Read the Bible for All Its Worth* (Grand Rapids: Zondervan, 1982), 169–86.

[7] Here is another dream sermon (the first is in chap. 9, note 19): "Throughout church history, theologians have taken this passage to mean 'x.' Most of you have probably tended to read it that way, too. Today, I want to tell you that, all this time, everyone has been absolutely . . . correct."

[8] See Richard N. Longenecker, "On Reading a New Testament Letter—Devotionally, Homiletically, Academically," *Themelios* 19 (December 1994): 5.

[9] Alistair E. McGrath, "New Occasions Teach New Duties? 4. The Reformation," *Expository Times* 105 (April 1994): 198.

[10] For more on finding principles, see chap. 12 and Jack Kuhatschek, *Taking the Guesswork out of Applying the Bible* (Downers Grove, Ill.: InterVarsity Press, 1990), 57–61.

[11] William Larkin, *Culture and Biblical Hermeneutics: Interpreting and Applying the Bible in a Relativistic Age* (Grand Rapids: Baker, 1988), 108–9.

[12] In taking an example from the Law of Moses, I do not intend to make a statement about the continuity between the covenants, theonomy, and such issues. The assumption of this section is the modest one that Israel's civil law rests on abiding principles of justice.

[13] Consider, for example, the monomania for love in Joseph Fletcher, *Situation Ethics: The New Morality* (Philadelphia: Westminster Press, 1966). Many Christian feminists likewise decree that all texts suggesting male leadership must be subordinated to the framework established by Gal. 3:28. See Andreas Kostenberger, "Gender Passages in the NT: Hermeneutical Fallacies Critiqued," *Westminster Theological Journal* 56 (Fall 1994): 273–79.

[14] Richard Longenecker, *New Testament Ethics for Today* (Grand Rapids: Eerdmans, 1984), 27–28; Larkin, *Culture and Biblical Hermeneutics*, 104–7. For a simplified discussion, see R. C. Sproul, *Knowing Scripture* (Downers Grove, Ill.: InterVarsity, 1977), 106–8.

[15] Richard Bauckham, *The Bible in Politics*, 12–13.

[16] The proof rests not in a law, but in the pattern of the entire Bible. We see Abraham, Moses, Nehemiah, Stephen, and Jesus fervent in prayer. We see Daniel praying three times a day (Dan. 6:10) and David crying out "evening, morning and noon" in his distress (Ps. 55:17). We know that the faithful cry out to God day and night (Ps. 88:1; Luke 18:7), and that many Scriptures urge continual prayer (1 Chron. 16:11; Eph. 6:18; 1 Thess. 5:17; James 5:13).

11

Reflecting on the Point of a Text

Driving Toward the Goal

When I was starting out as a pastor, a member of my congregation told me that while he basically liked my preaching, my sermons often left him frustrated. "I don't quite know how to say this," he began, "but let's imagine that you're the quarterback of a football team. Your team marches down the field with beautiful drives, but someone keeps fumbling at the fifteen-yard line." These fumbles, I came to understand, were sermons that failed to make one point that my friend could take home. They contained many true statements but failed to connect with one central message. Even with interesting information or illustrations, my preaching sometimes brought him little profit because it lacked a single, clear objective.

Superior teachers are not afraid to make many points at one time, but they do take care to drive home one main idea. For teachers of the Bible, that one idea must flow from the particular verses that constitute the text of the day. Yet truly Christian messages must also cohere with the Christ-centered message of the whole Bible.

> ⬧ Principle 1: Reflection is the vital art of finding and applying the unique point of a biblical text and relating that point to the redemptive message of the whole Bible.

In this chapter, we will see how to plan lessons that do just that.

155

The Goal of Reflection

If we can compare Scripture lessons to football games, we can also liken them to meals. Some teachers offer up a snack when their students expect a dinner. They stroll into meetings with a few loosely organized ideas, a story, and an intriguing question, but the class goes home hungry. Others make students feel like gluttons after a meal at a bad smorgasbord. They generate masses of data and, in their enthusiasm, try to present everything. But zeal may backfire if leaders begin to think in terms of covering material rather than reaching people. The result, as one student put it, is like asking for a drink and having someone aim a fire hose at your mouth.

The goal of reflection is to discover and teach the main lesson of biblical texts. Reflection helps teachers plan lessons that nourish students and prevent both gluttony and starvation. It prompts over-eager owners of fire hoses and smorgasbords to distill their mounds of data, to sift through their masses of notes, and to develop unified lessons.[1] It diagnoses carelessness by testing whether teachers have located a human need and their text's solution for it. It coaxes the lazy teacher back to the study, for having a main point requires more than possessing an idea or two. Finally, it keeps private devotions honest by requiring them to meditate on the main lesson, not just on intriguing tangents.

We find the main point through a series of steps or questions. First, what is the topic of the text? Second, what does the passage teach about the topic, and what is the main point of the teaching? Third, how does the main point apply to your audience? Be specific here. Fourth, what is the redemptive focus? How does the text surpass a mere list of things to do and believe, and point to Christ?

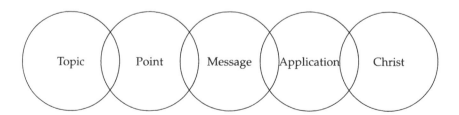

What is the topic? [Links with]
Not just a topic, a point; what is the message about that
    topic?
Not just a message, a specific application
Not just something to do or believe; something that points
    to our life in Christ

As they choose, research, and analyze a text, wise students and teachers of the Word often return to the question, What is the main point? For many texts, we see an answer readily. For others, we have to sift through the clues.

Establishing the Topic

The process of establishing the subject depends on whether we classify a text as a narrative or a discourse. The topic of a narrative or a story is usually obvious for the three subtypes, which we have labeled reports, speech stories, and dramas (see chap. 5). Reports and speech stories announce their topics. In dramas, the topic will be close to the crisis and climax of the story, that is, the moment of truth. The characters in a drama may also state the main issue in dialogue. To illustrate, the topic of the story of David and Goliath in 1 Samuel 17 is clearly the battle between the two main characters, David and Goliath. But the lengthy dialogue, in which each claims that his God will lead him to victory, shifts the focus from physical combat to spiritual warfare.

Topics may be less obvious in discourses such as letters, prophecies, psalms, and sermons. We ordinarily see the theme of a discourse in the first sentence, the last sentence, or in repeated words or phrases. For example, the repetition of the words *law* and *do* shows that the topic of Romans 7:14–25 is our ability—actually, our painful inability—to keep the law. Likewise, in Hebrews 11, the repeated phrase "by faith" announces the chapter's topic. In Hebrews 11:32–39, the sudden appearance of lions, swords (twice), flames, prison, torture, death (twice), jeering, flogging, stoning, and persecution introduces a new subtheme, the need for faith when facing the threat of violent suffering.

Establishing a Specific Theme

Once a topic is established, the lesson gains strength through a crisp statement of the theme. Many a lesson has drowned in a sea of vagueness. Wonderful as God's grace is, no heads snap to attention when a teacher announces, "The topic of today's lesson is the grace of God." An effective teacher would advertise something specific about God's grace. Precise, finely crafted theme statements make a topic sizzle.

Too many teachers make text after text sound the same. They reduce the Bible to ten or twenty lessons, retold again and again, on the love of God, holiness, prayer, faith, and a few more war horses. To be sure, we must adhere to the fundamentals of the faith and state them often. Yet if we ceaselessly repeat a few fundamental lessons, and interweave little that is new or specific, we serve the children thin gruel.

Not long ago, I watched a visitor smile and cry, and smile and cry, while I preached a sermon. As we spoke afterward, she explained, "One of my children died three years ago, and I have had doubts ever since. Week after week I go to church and hear that Jesus is the answer to all of our questions. But in three years, this is the first sermon that actually addressed *my* questions."

The family of God deserves more than the repetition of a few favorite slogans. Further, a high view of Scripture runs against the notion that dozens of texts say the same thing. Every text has a unique purpose or perspective, a distinctive truth or application. Good teachers let that truth emerge and use theme statements to prepare their audience for it.

To create a specific theme statement, you need both diligence and precision. Mediocre teachers simply know a few facts about their topic. They aim at nothing, and hit it, as the adage goes. Excellent teachers hone their knowledge. They answer the big questions: What is striking or unique about the author's message? How can we verify that it is true, that it makes a difference? Careless teachers have vague ideas about what they want to say. They seize on something interesting, even if it is a minor matter, isolated from the main point. Precise teachers attend to first things first. After discovering the unique thrust of their passage, they prepare to explain it, illustrate it, answer objections to it, and apply it.

Someone may wonder why I rate diligence and precision so highly; surely teachers most need love. Yes, but diligence and precision are the instruments of the truly loving teacher. Precision is an expression of love, for it distinguishes teachers who take pains to know what their students need, and to find scriptural answers for those needs.

A Method for Establishing the Theme

Skilled students of the Word often discover the theme of a passage intuitively. Here we provide clues for those times when intuition needs a nudge.[2]

> ▶ **Principle 2: Use every resource to ensure that you discover the theme of your passage.**

1. *Ensure that the theme of the passage fits its context.* Expect the theme of a passage to fit within its multichapter unit.[3] If not, your theme may be flawed. For example, David's battle with Goliath introduces David to the people of Israel as a hero and leader. This fits the context of 1 Samuel 13–16, where God has rejected faithless Saul and chosen David to be the next king. At first glance, the theme of Romans 7, our inability to keep the law, seems out of step with Romans 6 (we are no longer slaves to sin) and Romans 8 (there is now no condemnation). But it actually qualifies and clarifies Paul's teaching about sin, renewal, and mercy in Romans 6–8. Paul declares that although we are no longer slaves to sin (chap. 6), the power of sin is not yet exhausted (chap. 7). Nonetheless, Christ has freed us from condemnation and given us new life in the Spirit (chap. 8).

2. *Know where to find the theme.* As we saw earlier, the main point of a discourse typically comes in the first or last sentence of the text (see chap. 6). For example, in Matthew 6:1–18, Jesus states the theme at the beginning of the passage: "Be careful not to do your 'acts of righteousness' before men, to be seen by them. If you do, you will have no reward from your Father in heaven." In slightly different words, Jesus repeats this statement several times. He fleshes it out by sketching the dangers of performing three "acts of righteousness" before men: giving to the needy, praying, and fasting.[4]

In a narrative, look for the main point either at the high point of the drama or in the closing comments after the drama has been re-solved (see chap. 5). In Luke 5:17–26, we learn that Jesus does have the authority to forgive sins when the paralytic, still dangling on his ropes, gets up from his stretcher and walks at Jesus' command. Nar-ratives also close with statements that isolate the key issue. Thus, at the end of Jesus' controversial encounter with Zacchaeus, a chief tax collector, Jesus explains why he went to the home of a despised man: "The Son of Man came to seek and to save what was lost" (Luke 19:10).

3. *Notice repetition.* For thousands of years, people have empha-sized their main ideas by repeating them. If an idea matters to an au-thor, he will find a way to repeat it. For example, God's covenant promises are repeated more than once to all the patriarchs in Gene-sis, because they are so important. Repetition takes many forms, but it is especially prominent in poetic parallelism and rhetorical argu-ment. Chapter 6 already discussed parallelism. Here we note that rhetoric is a prominent method of developing a main point in the New Testament.[5] According to the principles of rhetoric, speakers or-dinarily state their proposition, or main point, both to open a dis-course and to sum everything up at the end. The epistles frequently do just that. When Paul tells the Corinthians to trust that they can serve God whatever their situation in life, he does so three times, so we cannot miss it: "Each one should retain the place in life that the Lord assigned to him and to which God has called him. . . . Each one should remain in the situation which he was in when God called him. . . . Brothers, each man, as responsible to God, should remain in the situation God called him to" (1 Cor. 7:17, 20, 24).

4. *Listen to dialogue.* Dialogue highlights the lesson of a drama, es-pecially when it appears just before or after the climax. As we noted above, the verbal warfare between David and Goliath before their physical combat indicates that their battle is spiritual, that "the bat-tle is the LORD's" (1 Sam. 17:44–47). Similarly, when the angel of the Lord stays Abraham's hand just before he slaughters Isaac, he reveals the point of the test: "Now I know that you fear God, because you have not withheld from me your son, your only son" (Gen. 22:12).

Context, location, repetition, and dialogue have the greatest weight, but the Bible leaves other hints that quietly lead readers to the main point. Authors have always written so as to make their thought accessible (until the advent of experimental literary methods in the twentieth century, at least). They hope to lead careful readers to their central concerns. Here are three clues:

5. *Notice unusual or extravagant details,* both in narratives of real events and in parables.[6] For example, the lengthy description of Goliath's massive, impregnable armor underscores the truth, when David slays him, that the Lord won the battle.

6. *Observe references to other Scriptures.* Quotations and allusions to other texts tell us that an author wants to locate his ideas within the stream of Scripture. Thus, Jesus' repeated quotations from Deuteronomy during his temptation show that he wants us to see his successful resistance to temptation as a reversal of Israel's failure to resist sin. Allusions invite readers to interpret one event in light of another. For example, in Judges 19 the tragic story of the Levite and his murdered concubine uses language, in verses 22–24, that is very similar to language used in the story of Sodom and Gomorra (Gen. 19:4–8). In both texts, wicked men stand outside a house and call for sex with a visiting male. In both, the host rebukes his "friends" and offers a woman instead (Gen. 19:7; Judg. 19:23). Thus the author intimates that Israel's wickedness has grown to Sodom's proportions. Ripe for judgment, Israel sorely needs new leadership.[7]

7. *Interpret irony.* In irony, the correct interpretation of words or events is the opposite of the apparent meaning. We call it verbal irony when a speaker intentionally says one thing, but means the opposite, trusting the audience to "get it." In dramatic irony, the narrator of a story lets his audience in on knowledge that is hidden from the actors in a story.

The gospels are filled with irony.[8] For instance, Jesus uses verbal irony when he tells the Jewish leaders that he dines with tax collectors and sinners because there is "more rejoicing in heaven over one sinner who repents than over ninety-nine righteous persons who do not need to repent" (Luke 15:7; see also 15:10; 5:32). Of course, the leaders are not truly righteous, but self-righteous, and in far greater need of repentance, as the subsequent parables of the lost son (15:11–32) and of the Pharisee and the tax collector (18:9–14) show.

Dramatic irony abounds in Jesus' final days. In John 11:49, Caiaphas, the high priest, determines that Jesus must die: "It is better for you that one man die for the people than that the whole nation perish." This is exactly true, as John points out, but not in the way Caiaphas intended (11:51–52). Later, the Roman soldiers mean to act ironically when they place a crown of thorns on Jesus' head, kneel before him, and say, "Hail, king of the Jews!" Their real thoughts are shown by the way they spit on him and strike him again and again (Matt. 27:27–31). Yet there is a second layer of irony, for, unknown to them, Jesus is exalted as king precisely in and through his suffering!

In passages like these, irony highlights an author's main point by inviting us to examine and reject the surface meaning of a text. As readers determine what the text does mean, they see matters as the author does.

We have listed seven things to consider or look for in order to detect the main point of a narrative or discourse: context, location, repetition, dialogue, details, references to other Scripture, and irony. As one might expect, several of these criteria may point toward the same theme. For example, the theme of Genesis 22, that God tests and approves Abraham, appears in dialogue near the climax (v. 12) and is repeated at the end of the passage (vv. 16–18). In Luke 15, the idea that God welcomes sinners who return to him is stressed through irony (v. 7), through allusion to another text (v. 7, alluding to 5:32), through repetition (vv. 7, 10, 20–24), and through extravagant details (vv. 20, 22–23). Using these guidelines, we can articulate very specific theme statements.

Bringing a Lesson to a Point

Precise theme statements represent a great advance over I-dare-you-to-keep-your-eyes-open utterances such as "Our topic today is holiness." But we aspire to more than an effective theme statement. First, we must connect our themes to the person and work of Jesus Christ, our Lord and Savior, lest we merely offer true ideas and sound advice. Second, we must probe our applications to find the one that completes our theme. The goal is to link the theme to its consequences in life. Books on preaching call this step the development of a proposition, but it works even if you never preach.

▶ Principle 3: The proposition brings a lesson to a point when it joins the central truth of a lesson to the central life application.[9]

Propositions may be either declarative or engaging. You can declare what ought to be done as a consequence of the truth: "Since x is true, we ought to believe or do y." Or, you can engage your hearers, by inviting them to decide it is true: "If x is true, then we ought to believe or do y." Let us see how this works with some passages that we have already examined.

The theme of 1 Samuel 17 is "David demonstrates that the battle is the Lord's by using the smallest weapons to defeat a Satanic foe fully prepared for combat." We must condense this theme statement if we want to connect it to the application and still have one manageable sentence. This is what we come up with: "Because the battle is the Lord's, we should face our foes with confidence, even if the odds seem to be against us."

Romans 7:14–25 presents a harder case because Paul's message is multifaceted. Paul says, "I have a double self. But my better self is incapable of preventing me from doing wrong (vv. 14–17) or making me do what is right (vv. 18–20). There is therefore a constant conflict within me; I delight in God's law, but sin works the opposite within me. From this conflict I cannot deliver myself, but, thank God, deliverance comes through Jesus Christ (vv. 22–25)."[10] We hear three topics—inability, conflict, and deliverance—any one of which could be the basis for a proposition.

1. *Inability.* Since our sinful nature bars us from obedience, we should give up on our efforts at moral self-control and receive release from our sins through faith in Christ Jesus.

2. *Conflict.* Even though our sinful nature frustrates our desire to obey God's law, we should still delight in his law.

3. *Deliverance.* Because our sinful nature keeps us from obeying the law, let us hope only in the mercy of Jesus, who has freed us from condemnation.

If all three propositions have validity, which one should we use? That might depend on your audience. Wise speakers shape their message to meet the needs of diverse audiences. The unbeliever needs the first message. Lawless believers may need the second. Hard-working Christians with a legalistic streak may need the third.

Does a Passage Have *One* Main Point?
Do I Have to Dwell on It?

The invitation to choose between three propositions for Romans 7 raises a vital question. Does every text have *one* main point? Or do texts have two or three chief points, so that we can dwell on whichever of them is most relevant? Are we obligated to discover and present the one point? Or can we acknowledge the main idea, but focus on something that strikes closer to home?[11]

That very issue once came up in family devotions at our home. While my three daughters (then six to twelve years old) ordinarily got along quite well, the house had recently been filled with howls, tears, and requests that my wife and I punish the wicked sisters whose infractions they reported to us. In this atmosphere, I read the story of Jesus' visit to the home of Mary and Martha (Luke 10:38–42). As I read Martha's line, "Lord, don't you care that my sister has left me to do the work by myself? Tell her to help me!" embarrassment spread over their faces. "I know why you're reading that," said the oldest, half wary, half confessional. "We have sounded a lot like Mary and Martha lately."

In fact, we were reading through Luke, and had read 10:25–37 the night before, so her surmise was incorrect. But now I faced an exegetical dilemma. The tension between Mary and Martha is only a circumstance that sets up the climax and lesson of a story on discipleship. Should I therefore say, "No, girls, these verses have little to do with your recent squabbles; the point is . . ."? That might be faithful to the text, but it would also waste a golden opportunity for healing. In fact, devotions covered two topics that night: (1) sisters may quarrel when one does not like what another is doing, and (2) listening to Jesus is the most important thing, even if someone thinks you should be taking care of business in the kitchen. But was I unfaithful to my principles when I talked about quarreling sisters?

One Main Point, Many Applications to Different Characters

First, notice that many texts have several interconnected points that revolve around the main theme.[12] For example, the *theme* of Luke 5:17–26 is this: By healing the paralytic, Jesus proved that he is the divine Redeemer who has the right to forgive sins (see chap. 5). The *proposition* of the story can be stated in different ways, however, depending on how we want to apply the theme. In fact, there is an application for each character in the story. Each suggests an application for those who stand in roughly the same place today.

The Pharisees. Inasmuch as the healing of the paralytic proves that Jesus has the power to forgive sins—a prerogative that belongs to God alone—the Pharisees should acknowledge Jesus' deity and believe in him. To this day, the miracle challenges doubters and skeptics to recognize the evidence for Jesus and believe in him.

The paralytic. Because his illness is connected to personal sin, the paralytic needs to complete his quest for healing by receiving the forgiveness Jesus offers. Even today, sin and trouble are connected. Pride and sophistication resist this, but sometimes we must face it to be healed.

The friends. Believing that Jesus had the power to heal, they acted boldly, tearing a hole in a roof to present their friend to the Lord. To this day, we should bring our friends to him, acting boldly if need be. Sometimes we have to break the rules of propriety to please God.

Jesus. The healing of the paralytic demonstrates both the compassion and the divine power of Jesus and summons doubters to faith and believers to confidence in his goodness.

Like the story of the paralytic, the parable of the lost son (or the "prodigal son") has one theme that can be presented several ways. The theme of all of Luke 15 is that God seeks fellowship with both "the righteous" and sinners. The proposition might read, "Because God seeks fellowship with both the righteous and sinners, all should come and enjoy his embrace." The main point is theocentric. God the Father welcomes all to his feast of celebration. God the Son has come to call all who are lost in either overt sin or the sin of self-righteousness. But this lesson can generate more specific propositions.

For prodigals. God will welcome you back, with a love so strong, so extravagant, so free, so forgiving, that it will upset "righteous" people. If you come to yourself, if you admit you have sinned against God and your fellow man, he will put his sandals on your feet, his rings on your fingers, and his robe on your back.

For the self-righteous. Since God welcomes sinners, we should welcome them too, even if they smell like they have been with pigs and look like they have been with prostitutes. Even today, "Christian" people who imagine they have done something to qualify for God's mercies should beware of judgmentalism. If God's grace is distasteful to you, if you measure how long and hard you have worked for him, beware, for you may find yourself outside the door! Yet the Lord even welcomes all who have regarded themselves as superior, even though they may have strayed the farthest of all by their pride.

One Main Point, New Applications to a Different Age

Second, in a very different vein, lessons may have a point today that differs from the original point, because of progress in God's plan of redemption. This is especially true for the Old Testament, but it is also true for parts of the Gospels and even Acts. For example, we know that the tabernacle, temple, and sacrificial system point beyond themselves to the atoning work of Christ. We know that the ministries of prophet, priest, and king suggest aspects of Jesus' ministry. We understand clearly that God chose Israel not as an end in itself, but as a step in the process of offering the gospel to the nations.[13]

One Main Point, Seen Through Many Eyes

Third, most historical texts feature several characters. Just as the colors of light emerging from a prism let us see what makes up the light entering the prism, so the characters in a narrative allow us to see the story, through their eyes, in several ways. Through them we can detect how the various witnesses to the drama perceived it. As we have seen, we should look first for the action of God, who is the main character. Then we explore how humans respond to his words and works, looking specifically for a believer, an unbeliever, and an undecided party. In the Gospels, for instance, we meet Jesus, the truly faithful one; the disciples, who are faithful but weak; the Jewish leaders, who are hostile; and the crowds, who are "well disposed" to Jesus, but faithless.[14] Besides them, we meet seekers, vacillators, friendly women, and more. But the three basic types of people continually reappear, and they represent the typical reactions people have always had to God's revelation: belief, unbelief, and hesitation. The characters in a drama give us angles for seeing the message today. We can read letters and prophecy the same way. Among the readers, both then and now, there are disciples, adversaries, and the uncommitted.

To summarize, faithful teachers stick close to the main theme of their passage, lest the text become a pretext for their own ideas. Yet the thrust of a lesson need not be identical to its theme. Weighing the needs of their classes, they might decide to focus on one aspect of the theme. Wise leaders pray for the capacity to discern what their students need to hear. At times they will need to hear more about something that lies near the main theme of a passage, but is not itself the chief idea. We conclude, therefore, that teachers may bypass the main point of a passage in order to attend to an important secondary idea.

Conclusion

This chapter has begun the final step in the CAPTOR plan, Reflection. Reflection is the art of finding and applying the unique point of a biblical text and relating that point to the redemptive message of the whole Bible. Building on a knowledge of a text's Context, Analysis, Problems, Themes, and Obligations, good teachers bring everything together by joining the main teaching and the main application in one statement. This kind of reflection helps to prevent some common mistakes among teachers: presenting too much raw data, reducing the Christian life to a series of beliefs and commands, and failing to establish a goal for a lesson.

Once we find the point of a text, we must present it to our hearers, yet teachers may dwell on a secondary idea, if it meets a clear need. While we always strive to preserve the diversity of Scripture throughout this process, we must also protect its vital unity. That unity, which will be examined in the next chapter, is the whole Bible's testimony that the one true God has redeemed fallen humanity through Jesus Christ, his only Son.

Exercises

Our exercises go back over a few passages that we have looked at several times already. Reread them, following the methods discussed in this chapter. For each text, find the topic, the theme, a proposition, and the redemptive focus.

1. Genesis 22:1–18

2. Romans 12:1–2

3. Galatians 1:6–9

4. Matthew 18:21–35

Notes

[1] Save extra ideas, which may fit into later lessons or answer questions that come up in discussion.

[2] Richard Pratt describes how five of the next seven clues are used in the Old Testament, in *He Gave Us Stories* (Phillipsburg, N.J.: Presbyterian and Reformed, 1990), 244–50.

[3] This generally does not hold for Proverbs or the self-contained oracles in the prophetic books.

[4] These three acts were the archetypal good deeds performed by pious Jews. As one apocryphal Jewish work put it, "Prayer is good when it is accompanied by fasting, almsgiving and righteousness" (Tobit 12:8; Tobit was probably written between 200 and 170 B.C.).

[5] See George A. Kennedy, *New Testament Interpretation Through Rhetorical Criticism* (Chapel Hill, N.C.: University of North Carolina Press, 1984); Burton Mack, *Rhetoric and the New Testament* (Philadelphia: Augsburg, 1990). Rhetoric appears in the New Testament because it was the core subject of a formal education in that day. Used in courts, public settings, and literature, it permeated the Roman empire, including Palestine. Because they were exposed to it so much, average people could hardly avoid knowing something about rhetoric, whether they studied it formally or not. This allowed Jesus and the apostles to use some of its techniques.

[6] Craig Blomberg, in *Interpreting the Parables* (Downers Grove, Ill.: InterVarsity Press, 1990), 45, 166, 176, passim, shows that extravagant details call attention to items with symbolic weight in the parables. See also chap. 2.

[7] Pratt, *He Gave Us Stories*, 246–47.

[8] Robert Fowler, *Let the Reader Understand* (Minneapolis: Fortress, 1991), 11–14, 156–75; Mark Allen Powell, *What Is Narrative Criticism?* (Minneapolis: Fortress, 1990), 30–32. The definitive work on irony may be Wayne Booth, *The Rhetoric of Irony* (Chicago: University of Chicago Press, 1974).

[9] These are called the consequential and the conditional forms. See Bryan Chapell, *Christ-Centered Preaching: Redeeming the Expository Sermon* (Grand Rapids: Baker, 1994), 142–43.

[10] This paraphrase is based upon that of William Sanday and Arthur C. Headlam, *A Critical and Exegetical Commentary on the Epistle to the Romans*, 5th ed. (Edinburgh: T. and T. Clark, 1902), 176.

[11] This is one of the most common questions students ask about interpretation.

[12] Two respected authors who argue that parables have several points or a cluster of points are Craig Blomberg, *Interpreting the Parables,* 166ff., and Kenneth Bailey, *Poet and Peasant* and *Through Peasants' Eyes,* combined ed. (Grand Rapids: Eerdmans, 1976), 1:107, 133, 205; 2:21, 55–56, 70–71, 87, 111–12, passim.

[13] See Geerhardus Vos, *Biblical Theology: Old and New Testaments* (Grand Rapids: Eerdmans, 1948); Willem Van Gemeren, *The Progress of Redemption* (Grand Rapids: Zondervan, 1988); Gerard Van Groningen, *Messianic Revelation in the Old Testament* (Grand Rapids: Baker, 1990).

[14] The language is from Jack Dean Kingsbury, *Conflict in Luke: Jesus, Authorities, and Disciples* (Minneapolis: Fortress, 1991), 28–31. In this book and his companion volumes, *Conflict in Mark* (Minneapolis: Fortress, 1989) and *Matthew as Story,* 2d ed. (Philadelphia: Fortress, 1988), Kingsbury analyzes the Gospels by telling the story of Jesus, the disciples, and the authorities separately. See also chap. 5.

12

Reflecting on the Redemptive Thrust of Scripture

The Right Focus

When I was in seminary, shortly before I preached for the first time in my regular church, the pastor showed me a plaque hung over the corridor that led from his study to the pulpit. It read, "Sir, we want to see Jesus" (John 12:21). Later, when I was a young pastor, one of my elders told me, "I believe we need to hear the gospel message, at least for a few minutes, in every sermon." Recently, in a church of two thousand, just before I climbed the steps to the pulpit, the senior pastor leaned toward me and said, "On an average Sunday, we have two hundred seekers in attendance."

Although they expressed it in very different ways, each leader wanted to see if I shared a vital conviction with them, a conviction I hope you share, too: every truly Christian message draws attention to Jesus Christ, Redeemer and Lord. Conversely, no matter how true, how moral, how informative, how stirring, or how practical a sermon may be, it is sub-Christian if it fails to present Jesus to this fallen world.

This chapter suggests two ways for teachers to focus on Christ: the "fallen-condition focus" and the "redemptive-historical focus."[1] The fallen-condition focus (FCF) is a more experiential path. As you prepare a message, it asks, "What aspect of the fallen condition of mankind does this passage address?" Then it shows how Jesus is presented in that text as the remedy for our experience of sin, immaturity, suffering, or brokenness. If the fallen-condition focus is an experiential perspective, the redemptive-historical focus (RHF) is a more theological perspective. The RHF begins by asserting that God has a gracious, sovereign plan to redeem his people. It asks, "What aspect of the divine plan does this passage reveal?" Then it shows how Jesus is presented in that text as the one true Redeemer.

> ▶ **Principle 1: Every passage in the Bible presents Christ both as the remedy for human fallenness and as the end point of God's plan of salvation.**[2]

Comparing and Contrasting the FCF and the RHF

Characteristic	Fallen-Condition Focus	Redemptive-Historical Focus
Source of authority	Scripture	Scripture
Theological emphasis	Doctrine of man: the Fall and sin	Doctrine of God: grace and sovereignty
Initial appeal	The experience of human need	The unfolding of the divine plan
Special insight	Every text shows how Christ meets a universal human need.	Every text manifests the need for a redeemer, the work of the Redeemer, or the consequences of redemption.
Final goal	To present Christ from every text	To present Christ from every text

Jesus and the Fallen-Condition Focus (FCF)

The FCF dwells on the person and work of Christ by observing the many ways in which people need him. By "fallen condition" I mean any aspect of human nature that requires God's grace. Even if it is indirect, every passage in the Bible points out some aspect of our fall-enness and some aspect of God's remedy.[3] The fallen condition in view may be an individual sin or a corporate sin. It includes greed, rebellion, hardheartedness, or any violation of the Ten Command-ments. Fallenness also covers the consequences of living in a sin-scarred world, such as living with illness, losing a loved one, or liv-ing under the authority of an evil person, whether at home or at work. Our frustrated longings are also part of our fallenness. This includes the quest for a better life, whether by finding a marriage partner or gaining more dignity at work. It includes the quest for higher moral attainment—more self-discipline or a more open heart. It also includes the quest for inner peace or a due self-acceptance.

We can illustrate the FCF by asking why we suffer. We commonly experience our fallenness through suffering, but we can suffer for many reasons.

1. We may suffer as a consequence of our own sin. For instance, drunkards commonly endure hangovers, lose their jobs, and live in poverty.

2. We suffer because we live in a sin-wrecked world. We suffer, for example, when a loved one dies, especially if it seems untimely. Likewise, we suffer when droughts or floods strike, simply because we live in a disordered world. In these cases, most likely, no sin has caused the suffering.

3. We suffer, even when we do not personally sin, if we are con-nected to evildoers. Citizens suffer from their leaders' foolish wars. Children suffer when their parents gamble away their money.

4. Christians suffer persecution and Satanic oppression. These are both consequences of the Fall, but Christians who are persecuted for righteousness' sake have not sinned. Indeed, they suffer precisely be-cause of their righteousness.

5. We can suffer from ignorance. People press the wrong buttons, choose offensive words, take harmful medications, and much more, all in ignorance, perhaps even with the conviction that their actions are proper.

Looking at the causes of suffering, we see that fallenness is a broader category than sinfulness.

> ▶ **Principle 2: Every passage of the Bible touches on some aspect of the fallen human condition and presents some part of God's remedy in Christ.**

As Paul says, every Scripture rebukes, teaches, corrects, and trains in righteousness (2 Tim. 3:16). In studying the fallen condition, we simultaneously find ourselves drawn to Jesus and to the universal need that links the ancient text and the modern readers.

Teachers who think in terms of an FCF concentrate their lessons on the biblical answer to a universal human question. It helps teachers escape the temptation to list all their thoughts on a text, possibly in a chaotic jumble of "ideas that seem important to me." If the FCF directs teachers to genuine issues, it convinces listeners that they need to hear the message. Once they see that a text addresses a common human problem, they will be more prepared for the biblical solution, which comes through the grace of God in Christ.

To grasp how the FCF works, we need to look at something concrete and particular. We can return briefly to Matthew 6:24 and the topic of money (from chap. 8) to become more specific. There Jesus says, "No one can serve two masters. Either he will hate the one and love the other, or he will be devoted to the one and despise the other. You cannot serve both God and Money."

The FCF, shared by both ancients and moderns, is the tendency to treat money as a rival to God. That is, the FCF is more specific than "People have problems with money." Almost every American will admit that his or her attitude toward money gets out of hand at times, whether by worrying, spending, or envying. The specific FCF of this passage is that money really does pose as an alternative god, even for believers, who might think they are above all that.

But Jesus' teaching suggests that the temptation to worship money is usually subtle (see especially the double warning "Watch out! Be on your guard against all kinds of greed" in Luke 12:15). That is, Money is not the kind of god that demands direct, exclusive worship. You need not bow down to it, and it is willing to make room for other gods. So money does not look so dangerous.

Consider another "What would you do for a million dollars?" question (see chap. 8 for the previous one). This time the pollster asked people if they would spend two years in jail, permanently move to a foreign country, never see their best friend again, or throw their pet off a cliff for a million dollars. Forty-two percent of those polled said they would do at least one of them for a million dollars. Although the poll was more of a joke than a study (especially for those who own parakeets), our very interest in such questions reveals our fascination with money. This is surely part of the fallen condition addressed in the text. But many of us suppress it, since we would like to store up treasures both in heaven and on earth. We wish we could serve two masters; we wish we did not have to choose between God and Money.

As the case of money suggests, sometimes we have to persuade people that the FCF of the text really matters to them. When, for example, the Bible insists on doctrinal purity, we may have to persuade people that doctrinal truth matters. Again, many Scriptures present God's remedy for human guilt. But a great deal of popular psychology denies the existence of real guilt. We only have feelings of guilt, it is said, and we should get rid of them as quickly as possible. We must show that while there is such a thing as false guilt, genuine guilt also exists. There is a remedy for it, and we need that remedy.

Jesus and the Redemptive-Historical Focus (RHF)

The RHF centers on Christ by observing how each text of the Bible presents some aspect of his person and work. The RHF examines the unfolding of God's saving plan in space and time. Within that plan, every prophecy, every event, every law, and every song plays its role. The essential insight of the RHF is that Jesus is the focal point of Scripture. On the first Easter, when Jesus met his bewildered disciples and explained his death and resurrection to them, he said,

> "Everything must be fulfilled that is written about me in the Law of Moses, the Prophets and the Psalms." Then he opened their minds so they could understand the Scriptures. He told them, "This is what is written: The Christ will suffer and rise from the dead on the third day, and repentance and forgiveness of sins will be preached in his name to all nations, beginning at Jerusalem." (Luke 24:44–47)

Earlier that day, Jesus told two disciples on the way to Emmaus that the Christ had to suffer and then enter his glory. "And beginning with Moses and all the Prophets, he explained to them what was said in all the Scriptures concerning himself" (24:27).

> ▶ Principle 3: Since Jesus himself says the entire Bible speaks of him, then every Christian lesson should, in its own way, present Jesus as Redeemer and Lord.

He fulfills all the hopes of the Old Testament and constitutes the center of the New.

Of course, Jesus said this even before the New Testament was written. So, when Jesus explained what "all the Scriptures" said about him, he had the Old Testament in mind. In what sense are all the Scriptures concerned with Jesus? What do the Proverbs or the narratives of wicked northern kings have to do with Jesus? First, Jesus was thinking of the Old Testament as a whole, not just of individual testimonies, when he spoke. In Luke 24:46, Jesus uses the expression "it is written," which ordinarily introduces an Old Testament quotation. But no quotation follows, indicating that Jesus was thinking of the Old Testament in its entirety.[4] When Jesus says that "Moses and all the Prophets" (24:27) or "the Law of Moses, the Prophets and the Psalms" (24:44) testify to his suffering and glory, he is making the same point, for the Jews used both phrases to refer to their complete Bible.[5] He is announcing, therefore, that the subject of the Old Testament as a whole is his suffering and glory for the forgiveness of sins.

Each portion of the Old Testament anticipates Christ's suffering and glory in its own way. Historical developments prepare Israel for the coming of the Messiah. Debacles show the need for a Savior. Triumphs hint at his future glory and kingdom. Some prophecies predict him specifically. A much larger number describe the people's failure to keep the covenant and warn of judgment, which Jesus came to remove. Or they promise the mercy that Jesus came to provide.

Few will deny that the New Testament centers on Jesus. Broadly speaking, the Gospels tell the story of his life, ministry, death, and resurrection. Acts recounts the spread of the gospel of Christ, and the Epistles explain and apply the work of Christ to the church and the world. Thus, every epoch of biblical history, every book of the Bible, and many individual passages disclose unique features of God's plan of salvation. The rest of this chapter will give a more specific, although still sketchy account of the way in which the whole Bible presents Christ.

Jesus and the Law (Genesis to Deuteronomy)

The books of the Law point out the universal human need for Christ in several ways.

1. As they describe the entry of sin into the world, and then its

spread and development (Gen. 3–6), the books of the Law call out for a redeemer. The first promise of a savior comes already in Genesis 3:15. Thus, from the outset, the reader of the Old Testament awaits the coming of one who will crush the head of the Serpent who introduced humanity to sin. But none of the patriarchs of Genesis, and none of the early leaders of Israel could be that savior, for they all sinned and died, and stood in need of redemption themselves.

2. Many people see no special problem with universal human sin. They reason, "We are only human, and God is merciful. If everyone is failing the course, good teachers curve the grades and lower the standards a bit. So it must be with God. He will forgive; that is his job!" The Law could hardly disagree more. It encodes God's own standards of justice and holiness, which flow from his very nature. Every violation of his law violates his good structure for the world. Therefore, universal sin produces universal guilt and liability to punishment. The Law constantly reminded Israel of that by establishing a system of sacrificial offerings for sin.[6] Day by day, year by year, the priests offered sacrifices for sin. The endless repetition of the rituals suggested that none of them actually removed human guilt. The blood of bulls and goats cannot atone for human sin (Heb. 10:1–4, 11).

3. Modern folk propose a second solution to the problem of sin. They imagine, "Perhaps we can do nothing to atone for past sins, but we can reform ourselves and live better. Our good deeds and good intentions will outweigh our errors." Again, the Law disagrees by demonstrating our bondage to sin. If people continue to sin after they know its consequences, it suggests that they are either weak and cannot change, or rebellious and refuse to change. Thus, the Law can inform, but it cannot transform. Indeed, far from restraining sin, the Law sometimes tempts us to sin. If the Law prohibits adultery, some will ask why; they will wonder what they are missing (Rom. 7:1–12). So, every study of the Law leads logically to a discussion of Jesus, the only one who can deliver his people from their bondage to sin.

Therefore, every time we read the Law, we encounter our weakness, guilt, and need of a deliverer. Every time we read about a sacrifice for sin, it turns our attention to Jesus, the final and perfect sacrifice.

Jesus and the Historical Books (Joshua to Esther)

Every leader of Israel—every king, priest, prophet, and judge— points toward Jesus in some way. Righteous leaders hint at his redemption; wicked ones suggest the need for a true leader. Of course, even the best had their failings, so that none could perfectly lead the people to God.

1. Israel's kingship illustrates the way Old Testament history leads up to Christ. The tale begins in the disastrous period of the judges. At that time there was no king in the land, and "everyone did what was right in his own eyes" (Judg. 21:25 NASB; also 17:6). So they asked for a king, one "such as all the other nations have" (1 Sam. 8:5). They got precisely that in Saul; like the kings of the nations, he was proud and self-serving, prone to mutiny from the start and an utter rebel and military disaster by the end.[7] After the relatively short glory days of David and Solomon, roughly half of the southern kings and every northern king led Israel astray, with some actively promoting the worship of pagan deities. Failed leaders such as Jeroboam, Ahab, Manasseh, and Ahaz teach us to yearn for a true king. They show us how Jesus, the good king, will not rule.

2. Israel enjoyed a few noble kings, but grave flaws marred even the best of them, such as David, Josiah, and Hezekiah, not to mention the thoroughly mixed reigns of kings like Solomon and Uzziah (2 Chron. 26:16–23). The righteous kings performed vital royal tasks. They protected Israel from her enemies, provided prosperity, upheld the law, and established justice. But Jesus perfectly fulfills all these missions, forever.

3. Other officeholders did little better than the kings. Many priests joined the evil kings in perverting the nation. They served other gods, sometimes alongside the Lord, sometimes pushing him out of the way for pagan deities—sometimes on the hillsides of Israel, sometimes even in the temple (Ezek. 8). The judges could not offer final redemption, either. Most of the prophets that we meet in biblical history were faithful. Yet, as a rule, the nation ignored them. Their words, by themselves, could not restore Israel's allegiance to the Lord. Like the prophets, even faithful priests had little effect, for their sacrifices could not remit sin and few heeded their good instruction.

4. Israel's history is essentially a downward spiral. After auspicious beginnings, first with Moses, then with king David, the nation kept declining, until first the northern part, and then the southern part of the kingdom suffered crushing military defeat and exile. From these travails the nation never fully recovered. In all these failures we recognize signs of the cosmic conflict between the seed of

the woman and the seed of the Serpent (Gen. 3:15). The sorrows of Israel show that Jesus is the one seed of the woman who can crush Satan's head.

5. The story of David's battle with Goliath illustrates several of these points. Israel faced an invasion largely because Saul's sins caused God to withdraw his favor. Saul himself should have fought the giant, since he was the tall, well-armed king (1 Sam. 9:2; 10:23). His cowardice allowed the rest to sink into fear, and no one answered the giant's taunts. Yet behind Goliath's taunts and murderous threats toward David, we detect a cosmic conflict between the forces of God and Satan; David certainly saw their combat that way, and with good reason (1 Sam. 17:45–47). The Philistines had repeatedly invaded and attempted to exterminate Israel (Judg. 14–16; 1 Sam. 4–6; 29–31). Goliath in particular intended to slay David, God's anointed and an ancestor of the Messiah. When David defeated Goliath, he simultaneously delivered Israel from an enemy—a vital, royal task—and faintly prefigured Jesus' defeat of Satan. Noble-hearted as he was, heinous sins lay in David's future, reminding us that even those who foreshadow the Redeemer need him too.[8]

Jesus and the Prophets (Especially Isaiah to Malachi)

1. We tend to focus on the small number of prophetic oracles that predict the coming of the Messiah. These are very important, but the prophets look to Christ in other ways as well. They call the people to covenant obedience and to the love of God. They warn of the price of infidelity. When the people plunged into sin, the prophets predicted a Messiah to bear their punishment and forgive them. Some texts, such as Isaiah 7, 9, 42, 49, and 52–53 predict this explicitly. A larger number promise that God will be merciful, without specifying how.

2. To illustrate, Hosea 1 and 2 compare the prophet's adulterous wife to Israel, whom God will punish for her unfaithfulness. Her daughter was called Lo-Ruhamah, for Israel would be "not pitied" before God. One of her sons was called Lo-Ammi, for Israel was "not my people."[9] Yet, at the end of Hosea 2, the prophet suddenly predicts that the Lord will restore his covenant with Israel and make her his wife forever. How and when this will take place, Hosea never says; only the New Testament does.

3. The careers of some of the prophets foreshadowed certain ele-

ments of Jesus' ministry. Like Christ, they fearlessly proclaimed the truth, even at their own risk. Others, notably Elijah and Elisha, performed miracles, such as multiplying food, healing lepers, and raising the dead (2 Kings 4–5, for example). Their works anticipated the greater works of Christ, the last and greatest prophet. He performed more miracles, multiplying more food and healing more lepers. When Israel rejected the prophets, it foreshadowed the greater rejection of Jesus (Luke 4:24; Matt. 21:33–40).

4. Like the prophets, Jesus threatened judgments (Matt. 23:13–29) and promised blessings (Matt. 5:3–11) to come. Like the prophets, he had supernatural insight into the thoughts of those around him (Mark 2:5, 8). His mighty deeds made the people conclude that he must be a great prophet, even the prophet for whom they had long waited (Luke 7:16; John 6:14; 7:40). Yet Jesus is more than a prophet (Matt. 12:38–41), for not even the greatest prophet's ministry will redeem Israel (Matt. 11:20–30).

Jesus and the Wisdom Literature (Job to Song of Songs)

1. The diverse wisdom books lead to Christ in several ways. Excellent as the Law of Moses is, these books, especially Proverbs, presuppose that it only begins to probe the human heart. Proverbs investigates the finer points of life—points that the Law cannot regulate.[10] Its critique of folly leads into counsel on the mind and attitude of the faithful. Jesus takes this aspect of wisdom to its highest level by probing the thoughts and motives of everyone (Matt. 5:21–48; 23:1–33).

2. Jesus' teaching is purer than the wisdom literature. Both Job and Ecclesiastes deliberately use partial falsehoods as a foil, to stimulate our desire for the truth. But Jesus' teaching is unalloyed. The darker aspects of Ecclesiastes and Job also show that our existence is unpredictable, brief, and vain, so that mere wisdom cannot grant a satisfactory life. Again, Jesus surpasses wisdom by opening the door to eternal life.

3. Because the psalms are so varied, they point to Jesus in several ways. Some predict aspects of his life and ministry. For example, the New Testament repeatedly cites the prediction in Psalm 118:22–23 that the people would reject Jesus, God's chosen cornerstone. Jesus himself used some psalms to explain his ministry. He used a psalm of lament to express his sorrow on the cross (Ps. 22 in Matt. 27:46).

He fulfilled the psalms that praise humans—once all mankind, once a king—with language that seems too extravagant for mere mortals (Ps. 45 in Heb. 1:5–6; Ps. 8 in Heb. 2:6–9).

4. Jesus also embodied the concept of wisdom. Solomon was the old covenant's wisest man, but in Jesus something greater than Solomon was here (Matt. 12:42). In Matthew 11 and Luke 7, Jesus compares both himself and John the Baptist to the prophets and to wisdom. That generation would not listen to their wisdom. Yet the wisdom of Jesus and John would be vindicated by their children (Luke 7:35). Jesus would reveal his wisdom to them (Matt. 11:25–27) and their deeds would vindicate his teaching (Matt. 11:19). Proverbs 8:22–31 personifies the wisdom that God used to create the world and form it well. The New Testament reveals that Jesus is the true, personal wisdom who joined with the Father in the creation of all things (John 1:1–14; 1 Cor. 1:24, 30; Col. 1:16; Heb. 1:1–4).

We see, therefore, that the Old Testament points to Christ in many ways. The Law demonstrates that we need a savior. The history of Israel demonstrates that the nation cannot save itself. Even the best leaders actively fail and passively fall short of the kind of leadership mankind needs. Jesus is the one true prophet, priest, king, and wise man of God.

Jesus and the Gospels and Acts (Matthew to Acts)

The Gospels, obviously, center on the person and work of Jesus in several ways. Whole books have been written about them. We mention a few that have the widest significance, showing, first, that Jesus fulfilled the Old Testament offices of king, prophet, priest, and wise man.

1. *King.* The Gospels constantly portray Jesus as the lord of a kingdom. John and Jesus both inaugurated their ministries by announcing, "Repent, for the kingdom of heaven is near" (Matt. 3:2; 4:17). As king, Jesus delivered the whole person, not just the soul. The miracles especially proved that Jesus was master of both nature and the supernatural realm. He healed the sick, raised the dead, and stilled storms. These signs were foretastes of eternity, when he will restore all things. Jesus also reigned by promoting justice and defending people against their adversaries. By casting out demons, Jesus de-

feated Satan, tied him up, and plundered his house (Luke 11:14–22; Matt. 12:28–29). A few healings liberated people from bondage to Satan (Luke 13:10–16). His deeds of regal power provided complete well-being. Some promoted faith (Mark 9:17–24; John 9:1–38), repentance, and forgiveness (Luke 5:17–26; John 5:2–14). Jesus even restored people socially, when, for example, he healed lepers and had fellowship with outcasts. Jesus reigned even in his death and resurrection, for by them he saved his people from the final enemy, death.

2. *Prophet.* The people of Israel saw Jesus as a prophet, and he accepted the title. He came as a prophet, announcing good news to the poor (Luke 4), and he died as all the prophets died, in Jerusalem, at the hand of the people who should have received him (Luke 13:3–35; cf. John 1:10–11). Yet Jesus distinguished himself from all other prophets. He spoke differently. They said, "Thus says the Lord," but Jesus said, "Truly I say to you." He combined the roles of prophet and judge when he read thoughts and evaluated hearts.[11] As a prophet, he also predicted his own death and resurrection and even explained their significance (Matt. 16:21–23; 17:22–23; 20:17–28).

3. *Priest.* From the midpoint of the Gospels onward, Jesus headed for Jerusalem. There, acting as a high priest, he would offer his life as the perfect and final sacrifice to remove the sins of the people forever. Jesus' priestly work was intertwined with his regal and prophetic activity. As king, he declared sins forgiven. As priest, he earned the right to make that declaration. As king, he silenced Satan, the accuser of the saints. As priest, he earned the right to silence him, by removing Satan's one quasi-legitimate complaint, that we are sinners and deserve to be punished. As prophet, he outlined the highest possible standards of righteousness, yet also comforted the guilty with the promise of mercy for the penitent. As priest, he offered the sacrifice to remove the penalty for sin from those who knew their guilt.

4. *Teacher.* Jesus is called teacher or rabbi sixty-five times in the Gospels, and he never refuses the title.[12] In unskilled hands, Jesus' ethical teaching, such as the Sermon on the Mount, can be reduced to mere law, as if he said, "Do this to serve God, to be a true disciple." Some even give it a legalistic twist, as if he said, "Do this in order to earn God's blessing. Do this and God will love you for it."

To prevent these errors, we must place Jesus' ethic in its context.

a. Jesus' ethic is given to his disciples (Matt. 5:1–2)—to people who are already in the kingdom and want to know how to conduct themselves in it, not to people who hope to do something to enter it (Matt. 5:3, 10, 12, and 45 all describe the kingdom as the present possession of disciples).

b. Jesus promises mercy to those who violate God's standards, if they mourn over their sin (5:3–5). He also promises strength to those who lack the capacity to obey (7:7–11).

c. The New Testament teaches that gratitude and the desire to honor God are the chief motives for obedience. No one is encouraged to obey in order to merit something from God. We do not obey in order to put God in the position of owing us something.

5. *Son of God.* Jesus is the Son of God, of one substance with the Father, and the exact representation of God's character (Heb. 1:1–3). Thus, Jesus uniquely manifests the character of God to humanity. To see him is to see the Father (John 14:9). If someone asks, "How can I know what God is like?" the best answer may be, "Read the Gospels, fixing your attention on Jesus."

6. *Son of Man.* Day by day, Jesus conducted himself as the one true man and quietly developed the contours of true humanity.[13] This process began already with the Temptation, when Jesus passed the tests that Adam and Eve had failed. Unlike them, Jesus resisted the urge to indulge his desires to take food or any other physical pleasure that was not his to enjoy. He also refused to put God to the test or to bow down to Satan, no matter what benefits Satan dangled before him. Throughout his life, Jesus modeled the loving acceptance we owe to the poor and the outcast, and the compassion and generosity we owe to the weak, and the courage we should show before the strong and malevolent.

7. *The true Israelite and covenant keeper.* Jesus was the one true Israelite, the only one to remain faithful to the covenant to the end. He resisted the temptations to which Israel succumbed in the wilderness (compare Matt. 4:4 with Deut. 8:3; Matt. 4:7 with Deut. 6:16 and Ex. 17:1–7; Matt. 4:10 with Deut. 6:13). He fulfilled the law of the covenant. Then, at the end of his earthly ministry, he voluntarily bore

the covenant curses that were due to fall on those who failed to keep the covenant.

The book of Acts describes the spread of the gospel of Christ, by which people from every nation come to God. In Acts we hear the apostles proclaim Jesus, the only name "given to men by which we must be saved" (Acts 4:12).

Jesus, the Epistles, and Revelation

To generalize, the Gospels *tell* the story of Jesus' life and the Epistles *interpret* it. The epistles of Paul have enjoyed the front row in Christian theology, but the other epistles all develop the message of Christ in their own way.

1. *Paul's epistles* especially explain how Jesus' death and resurrection atone for sin, granting forgiveness, and restore the family of God. For Paul, all doctrine relates to Jesus. He describes the God who saves in Christ despite his wrath toward sin. His anthropology begins with mankind's wickedness and inability to reform itself. He grounds his ethic in gratitude for the work of Christ and in a desire to live out our new identity in Christ.

2. *Hebrews* investigates Jesus as the great and final high priest, the perfect sacrifice, who cleanses his people from sin, once and for all. The author of this epistle also regards Jesus as the champion who defeats the great foe, Satan. Jesus sympathizes with us as we run the hard race of life, yet he blazes and clears the trail on which we run and waits for us at the finish line.

3. Martin Luther called *James* "an epistle of straw" because it lacks a theology of the cross. But James wrote for Jewish believers who contented themselves with mere knowledge of right doctrine, without practicing it. He wrote to shake up those who thought that doctrinal orthodoxy guaranteed a covenant relationship with God. Echoing Jesus' teachings at dozens of points, James presents Jesus as the Lord of our ethical lives, since true faith in Christ necessarily entails obedience and good works (James 2:14–26).

4. *Peter* sees Jesus' crucifixion both as an atoning sacrifice and as a model for Christian endurance of persecution (1 Peter 2:18–25). Jesus "bore our sins in his body on the tree" (2:24). But he also urges Christians to bear unjust affliction as Christ did—suffering silently, entrusting himself to the Father, who would soon vindicate him.

Jesus exemplified Peter's pastoral counsel for a persecuted church (2:18ff.; 3:14ff.; 4:12ff.).

5. If the gospel of John was written to inspire faith (John 20:31), *1 John* was written to assure believers that they do indeed have faith, even if trials and heresies surround them (1 John 5:13). The epistle proclaims Christ as the indwelling power that allows believers to pass the three tests of genuine faith: true doctrine, true love, and true obedience.

6. *Revelation* is a series of visions of Christ (1:12–18; 19:11–21) and his triumph over Satan and his allies: the beast coming out of the sea, representing godless political power; the beast coming out of the earth, representing false religious power; and Babylon, representing the seductions of wealth and pleasure (chaps. 12–14, 18–20). The visions repeatedly promise the overthrow of evil and gather both saints and angels to worship the Lamb, who will wipe every tear from their eyes. Full of titles of Christ, Revelation has inspired countless hymns. If Revelation is prophecy, as some say, it is prophecy in the sense that "the testimony of Jesus is the spirit of prophecy" (19:10).

Conclusion

A passage can lead us to Christ in many ways. We can meditate on the character of God the Father, as it led him to send his Son. We may ponder Christ's character and conduct as a model for our own. We could contemplate the role of gratitude to Christ or dwell on the gift of the Holy Spirit as we journey toward maturity. This chapter has emphasized two ways to ensure that all our expositions look to Jesus: the "fallen-condition focus" and the "redemptive-historical focus." Each is an aspect of reflection, that is, the art of finding and applying the main point of a biblical text and relating that point to the redemptive message of the whole Bible. These two methods keep us from preparing messages that contain true statements and good counsel but are ultimately sub-Christian because there is nothing of the Savior in them.

This chapter completes the CAPTOR plan for biblical interpretation, which features the elements of Context, Analysis, Problems, Themes, Obligations, and Reflection. With the presentation of methods completed, let me reemphasize that methods do no lasting good unless we yield them to the Spirit's goals. Teachers always need to drive home one main idea from every text. That one idea always bears witness to the Lord, who is the final goal of both Scripture and life.

Exercises

Take the same passages used in the exercises for chapter 11 and see how each text points to Jesus' person and work in one of the ways described in the chapter:

1. Genesis 22:1–18

2. Romans 12:1–2

3. Galatians 1:6–9

4. Matthew 18:21–35

Notes

[1] The term "fallen-condition focus" is taken from Bryan Chapell, *Christ-Centered Preaching: Redeeming the Expository Sermon* (Grand Rapids: Baker, 1994). The section on that subject depends on Chapell, although my concept of it differs slightly from his.

[2] For an explanation of the concept of a "passage," see appendix B, "Selecting a Text."

[3] Chapell, *Christ-Centered Preaching*, 40–44, 201–2, 231–36, 263–66.

[4] The Greek is *gegraptai*, "it is written." Luke 18:31 and 21:22 and Acts 13:29 also refer to "everything written," without looking to one text. Of course, Luke cites specific texts on other occasions: see Luke 4:17–21 (quoting Isa. 61:1–2) and Luke 22:37 (quoting Isa. 53:12). See also Acts 4:11 (quoting Ps. 118:22) and Acts 4:25–26 (quoting Ps. 2:1–2).

[5] In 24:27, "Moses" means the five books of Moses, from Genesis to Deuteronomy. "The Prophets" refers to Joshua through Kings, but it can include the prophetic books and wisdom literature. In 24:44, "the Psalms" stands for all wisdom books.

[6] Actually, many sacrifices expressed gratitude or fellowship with God, but within biblical theology, sin offerings have more prominence.

[7] Regarding rebellion in Saul from the beginning, see V. Philips Long, "The Art of Biblical History," in *Foundations of Contemporary Interpretation*, vol. 5 (Grand Rapids: Zondervan, 1994), chap. 6. For a more technical discussion, see Long, *The Reign and Rejection of King Saul: A Case for Literary and Theological Coherence*, SBL Dissertation Series, vol. 118 (Atlanta: Scholars Press, 1989).

[8] For an extended, if sometimes overly enthusiastic treatment of Christology in Old Testament history, see S. G. De Graff, *Promise and Deliverance*, 4 vols. (St. Catherine's, Ont.: Paideia Press, 1977–81), vols. 1–2.

[9] The names mean "not pitied" and "not my people."

[10] For more on wisdom, see appendix D.

[11] Dan Doriani, "The Deity of Christ in the Synoptic Gospels," *Journal of the Evangelical Theological Society* 37 (September 1994): 340–43.

[12] Robert Stein, *The Method and Message of Jesus* (Philadelphia: Westminster, 1978), 1–2.

[13] Michael Griffiths, *The Example of Christ* (Downers Grove, Ill.: InterVarsity Press, 1984); E. J. Tinsley, "Some Principles for Reconstructing a Doctrine of the Imitation of Christ," *Scottish Journal of Theology* 25 (February 1972): 45–57; Alistair McGrath, "In What Way Can Jesus Be a Moral Example for Christians?" *Journal of the Evangelical Theological Society* 34 (September 1991): 289–98.

13

Getting Started

Entertainment and Info-tainment

Entertainment adds spice to life. Christians usually refuse the entertainment of jazz bars, comedy clubs, and risqué movies, but we still love the diversions of a family movie or trips to a zoo, a concert, or even a public lecture. In fact, many Christians read books, take classes, hear speakers, and accumulate information as a kind of spiritual or intellectual entertainment. This is ordinarily no problem; a talk that omits serious analysis to make room for jokes and stories can still communicate the truth. Yet we must be wary of the info-tainment mentality, especially when it is misapplied to the area of skills.

Pure information, collected passively, proves useful if we call it into action at the appropriate time. Training in skills is pointless unless we practice them. Think of those televised aerobics programs. What good is it to watch a thigh-toning exercise while potato chip crumbs accumulate on your sweatshirt? What good is a gourmet cooking program if you never bring out the cookware? You cannot even smell the food, let alone taste it.

The same holds for training in Bible interpretation. It is vain to become a slightly more informed spectator—more aware, but just as passive as before. While there is useful information in this book, its goal is to present methods of study, and its program is almost worthless if never practiced. Rust never sleeps. A skill left idle will erode with time. We either use it or lose it.

Getting Started with Private Devotions[1]

The easiest place to start using the CAPTOR plan is in private devotions because you only have to persuade one person that it is worthwhile. First, resolve to change your private devotions for the better. Then ask yourself what a reasonable goal for your private reading might be. Do you want to read through a certain amount of the Bible in a month or a year? Or do you want to spend a certain amount of time in study, without worrying about how much you cover? I recommend the latter approach initially, because the CAPTOR plan seeks quality more than quantity, and quality takes time. For this reason, it is best to start with a short book, such as Philippians, Ruth, or 1 Peter, which you can finish before long. When you finish a book or two, move to a longer book, such as a gospel.

Second, get organized. Decide when, where, and roughly how long you will study. Then gather your materials: a Bible, pen and paper (or computer), and the basic reference works, such as a Bible with cross references, a Bible dictionary or encyclopedia, and a concordance. Consider telling a friend what you are doing, and ask to be accountable to him or her.

Third, get started, going through the steps covered in this book. Begin with the historical context for your book: Who wrote it? When and why was it written? Then move through analysis, problem solving, themes, obligations, and reflection. After a week or so, and then again after a month, stop and evaluate how you are doing. How much progress have you made? Do you need to make any adjustments?

Getting Started with a Group

Some people will advance most rapidly by studying with a group. That way they can share discoveries and climb over roadblocks together. One person's insight, question, or objection prods the others to deeper thought. Experts say the ideal size for a small group is six to eight participants, but you can start with a group of three to twelve.

A Bible study group needs three things: a dedicated leader, agreement about its purpose, and people who are committed to that purpose. The leader is usually the key. He or she needs several skills and several character traits.

The Leader's Skills

1. *Organization.* The effective leader shows up on time and gets the group started. He prepares a discussion sheet, including perhaps a few key facts about the passage, a short outline of the passage, and some open-ended questions.

2. *Discussion.* Effective leaders keep everyone involved. They encourage quiet people and ask talkative members to wait for others. They neither fear silence nor attempt to fill every pause, since they know it takes time to think through some questions. They also keep the group focused on the Bible and the topic at hand.

3. *Facilitation.* Effective leaders also try to find something positive in every honest question and comment. They listen and help people articulate questions and observations. They know when a discussion is complete and close it by summarizing the group's best discoveries.

The Leader's Character Traits

While every biblical virtue will enhance the work of a leader, Timothy and Titus single out the qualifications that especially apply to Christian leaders. Several fit the Bible study leader.

1. *Love.* Love of God, his Word, and his people motivates leaders to prepare to lead a group faithfully, week by week.

2. *Patience.* Godly leaders cannot be contentious or quick to quarrel. Gentle explanation and persuasion win people to the truth. A leader must also have patience with someone who talks rashly and too often, yet leaders know when to step in, for the sake of others.

3. *Humility.* Wise leaders do not promote themselves or their own agenda. They respect everyone's contributions, yet guard the truth.

4. *Honesty.* Honesty guides the excellent leader in several ways. Honesty means a leader admits his or her ignorance when he or she doesn't know the answers, instead of hiding under a cloud bank of empty words. Honesty requires the leader to tackle hard questions, without denying real differences of opinion. This is no invitation to contentiousness, but we get nowhere if we deny that Christians differ with the world and among themselves.

The Purpose and People of the Group

To be fruitful, the members of the group must agree that its chief purpose is to examine the Scriptures and apply them to life. Intellectual stimulation, fellowship, and food belong in second place. Recruit people who agree with the purpose of your gathering.

Larger Presentations

Those who are already teachers or who aspire to be teachers must remember that the CAPTOR plan is a research method, not an outline for public speakers (see appendix A). After you have gathered your material, you still need to find a fitting way to present it. This is not the place to begin to explain the art of public speaking, but here are a few widely accepted principles.

1. The introduction stirs interest in the subject. Whether you begin with an illustration or not, you must show your audience that your topic matters. An introduction might investigate some aspect of our fallen condition and stir interest in God's remedy for it (chap. 12). Expect, ordinarily, to state your proposition early on, so all will know how God's Word applies in this situation (chap. 11).

2. Let the flow of the passage, discovered during your analysis, dictate the outline of your message. As you develop your points, synthesize your research notes on analysis, problems, and themes to create a seamless exposition. You may wish to stop and apply your points frequently, or you may introduce your application at the end of each section.

3. The conclusion should drive home your main ideas. It is tempting to ad lib the conclusion, but choose your words carefully here too. Be sure to ground your talk in the grace of God and the person of Christ. Take care not to leave the impression that knowledge of ideas is sufficient, or that you are merely giving advice on morals or life management.

4. Focus on Christ, not human effort. Does the world really need more good advice? Most of the time, people know what they should be doing. The problem is not ignorance, but inability or unwillingness to do what we know. The world does not need one more ethicist; it needs a Redeemer who forgives our failings and strengthens us for grateful obedience.

Conclusion

This book began by presenting three reasons why serious Christians need to have a method for inductive Bible study. We hear troubling sermons but cannot determine the root of the error; we become too dependent on commentaries and lesson manuals; and our private devotions fall far short of our ideal. In the chapters that followed, you received a great deal of information about how to study and apply the Bible, and I know that, unless it was already familiar, you will forget much of it. But there is a simplicity to everything you have read, too. In fact, you can forget many details, but if you remember the acronym CAPTOR, you have still taken a large step. Whenever you want to unfold the meaning of Scripture, the basic steps are simple:

C	= Context	Establish the context in your book and in biblical culture.
A	= Analysis	Analyze the flow of thought or the flow of a story.
P	= Problems	Solve your problems—the words and customs that baffle us.
T	= Themes	Develop a theme, a big idea that runs through all of Scripture.
O	= Obligations	Discover your obligations, the way the Bible applies to you today.
R	= Reflection	Reflect on the main point and the work of Christ.

The next step is yours to take. May our Lord guide you as you gain skill in interpreting the Word; may your desire for obedience grow along with that skill. May he instill courage to lead others toward the rediscovery of biblical truth in an hour of great ignorance of Scripture.

The apostle Paul summons Christian leaders to become skilled workers in the Word, who correctly handle the Word of Truth (2 Tim. 2:15). May you read God's Word and study it well. Then, as you meditate on it, may you find comfort, challenge, and direction, both for yourself and others, and so prove to be, as Jesus says, a light for the world.

Notes

[1] I owe some ideas on starting a small group to Howard G. Hendricks and William D. Hendricks, *Living by the Book* (Chicago: Moody Press, 1991), 324–40.

Appendix A

A Model Lesson

The following pages illustrate how I put the CAPTOR plan into practice in my preaching and teaching. This model lesson is a slightly revised sermon that I prepared using the methods in this book. In the headings on the left, I label the steps I took so that you can recognize them. This is a written record of a real sermon and, like all my sermons, it uses CAPTOR as a plan for research, but diverges from it somewhat in the actual presentation.

Jesus Christ, a Ransom for Many
(Matt. 20:20–28)

Introduction and Fallen-Condition Focus Most of us are slow to serve. Oh, we will serve eventually, if it is necessary, but we would rather not. We much prefer that work and problems go away, by themselves, and that beauty and honor come to us, by themselves. Take a simple thing such as the end of the family meal. Stomach sated by tasty dishes, mind cheered by pleasant conversation, we gaze at the table feeling satisfied. We take it in, vaguely, that the table is a mess, that something needs to be done about it. But *we* don't want to do anything about it. We hope the correct child remembers it is his or her turn, and that he or she does not have to go anywhere first. Suddenly the phone rings, and several people jump up to answer it. After all, we can't clear the table when we're on the phone, can we? Yes, the phone is portable, but the noise of clanking dishes would be rude to the caller, who is, it turns out, an old friend from MCI or AT&T, eager to talk to us about their exciting new service plans.

It's the same way in a dozen arenas. Men put off projects around the house until three months after they become embarrassing. Then, when we finally lay down our drills and hammers after completing our projects, we expect our wives to rush to us, swooning and blushing with love, and throw their arms around us, proclaiming, "My hero!" That is, we not only want to avoid work as much as possible but also want to get as much honor as possible when we finally do something. These failings are nothing new. In our passage and its context, we also see the disciples slow to serve and eager for honor. We also see how Jesus answers both them and us.

Theme Statement   Jesus has a twofold solution to our reluctance to serve. He redeems us from the sin, and he offers himself as a pattern for new life. Jesus says, "The Son of Man did not come to be served, but to serve, and to give his life as a ransom for many." He knew that when he did these things, few people would be throwing their arms around him. He knew that if anyone would swoon, it would be he, and not with pleasure. As Christians, we know that Jesus came to give his life as a ransom for us. His life is the source for our life. But in this passage he also says that his life is a pattern for ours. This passage summons us both to believe that and to live like that.

Broad Literary Context   During Jesus' final trip to Jerusalem, the topic of service comes up several times. In fact, the issue of service, including the desire to avoid it or to receive honor for it, dominates Matthew 19–20.

Broad Context, Part 1: The Pharisees in 19:1–12   The discussion begins in 19:3, when some Pharisees ask Jesus, "Is it lawful for a man to divorce his wife for any and every reason?" In other words, "Do I have the right to treat my wife almost any way I please? What is the absolute minimum I owe my wife? Can I divorce her as soon as she becomes displeasing to me?"

Historical Context   Some rabbis of the day said a man could divorce his wife for almost any reason: for burning his meals, for "twirling in the street" (which perhaps suggested wantonness), for becoming impertinent, and perhaps even for becoming unattractive and displeasing in his sight. So, Matthew 19 begins with the question, "How little can we give?"

Brief Application

This is still the motivating question for many people who seek divorce today. They want to know, "How little can I give? How briefly can I be faithful to my marriage vows? Can I leave my marriage as soon as marriage begins to look like a bad deal for me? When I seem to be giving more than I'm getting?"

Broad Context, Part 2: The Rich Young Ruler in 19:16–30

Next, in 19:16, a rich young man approaches Jesus and asks, "What good thing must I do to get eternal life?" In other words, "If I do something great, can I count on a reward?" He assumes that one must keep the commandments. He wants to know, "What great *extra* deed can I perform to gain credit before God, so that if I should sin, he will see this great deed, forgive me, and grant me eternal life?"

After some discussion, Jesus finally tells him, "Fine, there may be just one thing." But we quickly see that the "one thing" is everything: "If you want to do something, sell all your goods, give them to the poor, and follow me."

Now that is a great deed, not because it is so extraordinary to give something away, but because it says that a rich man must love God and his kingdom enough to give up his wealth. That gift would be great not because it is meritorious but because it would show that he loved God more than his wealth. It would show that he had given God his heart.

But this rich man cannot perform *this* deed, for money is his god, and he goes away grieving.

Here again, we see a very common attitude toward service. Sometimes we say, "Lord, What can I do for you? I will do anything. Just name it." The Lord names it. Then we say, "Well, I meant anything but *that.*"

Application

As the rich man departs, Jesus comments, "It is hard for a rich man to enter the kingdom of heaven." But Peter is not listening. He is still watching the rich young man trudging away, and a thought occurs to him. The rich man refused to make the sacrifice for the sake of the kingdom, but, Peter blurts, "We *have* left everything to follow you! What then will there be for us?" (19:27).

In fact, Peter has a point. The Gospels tell us

Historical Context   that Peter, James, John, and Andrew owned
                         their boats. A fishing boat from the first cen-
tury A.D., roughly the time of Jesus and his disciples, was discovered
intact off the Sea of Galilee in 1989. I have ridden across the Sea of
Galilee on a somewhat larger replica of that boat. It was a substantial vessel, capable of holding a lot of fish, and would have taken a
lot of capital to buy or build one of those boats. The mere fact that
they owned boats placed them in what we call the upper middle
class. So Peter's question is genuine.

Jesus says Peter will be rewarded, both in this life and in the life to
come (19:28–30). Peter and the others who followed Jesus will "sit on
twelve thrones, judging the twelve tribes of Israel." But Jesus warns
them to beware of pride, for "many who are first will be last, and many
who are last will be first." What is the danger? Pride of service.

Pride of service is the subject of that dreaded

Broad Context,   parable of laborers working in a vineyard
Part 3: The   (20:1–16). In that parable, you recall, the ser-
Workers in the   vants all received the same pay, one full day's
Vineyard in   wages, whether they worked one, three, six,
20:1–16   or twelve hours. When those who worked all
                         day saw the people who worked only an hour
getting a whole day's wages, they thought they should get more.
When they didn't, they grumbled against the master, who did, after
all, still give them what he had promised.

The story warns us against serving the master

Application   to get something for it. Beware of waiting for
                         the reward you think you deserve—the reward
you think he owes you. With such an attitude you may be last in the
kingdom, for you love your reward as much as you love your master.

Actually, this message strikes closer to home than the first. Most
Christians are a *little* like the rich young ruler. *Occasionally* we say,
"Lord, I'll do anything for you," and then take it back. But most of
us have truly given ourselves to the Lord. We are too dutiful to take
back our offers to God. So we are a little like the ruler. But we are a
lot like Peter. We *frequently* hope for generous rewards. We hope
God notices and repays every good thing we do. And we hope the
work does not break our backs, or our schedules. Jesus knows this.
He knows we want to give the minimum and get the maximum. To

lead Peter and us to maturity, he tells more about his view of service and his way of service. As we learn what he will do, we discover how it will save us and how it will guide us.

Immediate Context (20:17–19) That is what Jesus does when he predicts his crucifixion, now for the third time in Matthew. The first time, he said that he had to go to Jerusalem and suffer many things at the hands of the elders, chief priests, and teachers of the law, and that he had to be killed and on the third day be raised to life (16:28). Later, he predicted that the Jews would do to him "everything they wished," and that he would "suffer at their hands" just as "Elijah" (that is, John the Baptist) had suffered (17:12). Now he foretells, in more detail than ever, that he must soon be betrayed, condemned, mocked, flogged, and crucified. Then, on the third day, he will be raised to life (20:18–19).

Exposition, Part 1: A Mother's Request (analysis, historical context, and problem solving combined) (20:20–23) The next sequence of events is amazing. Shortly after Jesus finishes warning about excessive interest in rewards, as soon as he finishes describing the price he would soon pay to open the kingdom for his disciples, the mother of James and John approaches him with a request. The request shows that neither she nor her sons particularly care to hear what Jesus has to say about crucifixion. It is as though they were thinking, *We don't know about this crucifixion business, so can we please get back to what you were saying about sitting on twelve thrones and judging the twelve tribes of Israel?* So she asks, in language that comes close to a command, "Grant that one of these two sons of mine may sit at your right and the other at your left in your kingdom" (20:21). To paraphrase, she says, "Now, Jesus, you can choose whichever you want for right and left, but please say the word."

The right and the left were the positions of closest proximity to the king. She is asking that Jesus grant her sons the positions of highest honor, next to himself, in his kingdom. While it is somewhat foolish and selfish, the question also shows faith. The phrase "in your kingdom" assumes that Jesus *will* reign and that James and John *will* sit on thrones, just as Jesus said. On the other hand, they think it will come soon, without the cross. Yet they believe the promise enough to ask *which* thrones they will occupy. The question "Where will I sit?" is a *believer's* question.

Application
As for them, so too for us, the hope for honor in the kingdom is not entirely wicked. To be good at something and receive recognition for it is good. The problem comes when we are not content with honor. We want *high* honors; we want to be honored more than anyone else. Sometimes the desire for high compliments is innocent. We like to hear our children say, "You're a great daddy, a great mommy." But it feels even sweeter to hear, "You're the best daddy, the best mommy in the whole world!"—especially if they are over ten years old and are no longer expected to say such things.

To desire honor as a parent is one thing, but to long for honor at work, on the social scene, in music, or in sports, can be another. High aspirations can be very good or they can have a decidedly selfish tinge. Suppose we want to be the best musician or athlete, not just "pretty good," but great—"the best." It is possible to have an innocent desire to be the best, but that desire turns sour if we are also thinking, "I want everyone else to fall *below me.*" Further, we would like our excellence to come naturally, without much effort. If possible, we would still like to have plenty of time left over.

Resume Exposition (20:22–23)
Jesus' reply addresses James and John, and so we assume that they were behind their mother's request. Perhaps they thought that Jesus would find it harder to say no to a dear older woman who might have been his aunt. But Jesus looked past the mother to the sons. With both kindness and severity, Jesus told them, "You don't know what you are asking. Can you drink the cup I am going to drink?"

This is the point: Whenever we ask for greatness, we ask for the troubles that go with it. To ask for wealth is to ask for responsibilities, anxiety, and envy. To ask for high position that makes you the center of attention is to ask that everyone *want* your attention. They, in turn, give their attention to every word you say, until casual talk becomes impossible. To ask for high position is to ask for great labor and suffering. To share in Christ's glory, one must share in his suffering, for that is what the image of the cup signifies.

Theme
In the Old Testament, the "cup" Jesus describes signifies judgment, wrath, and retribution. For example, in Jeremiah 25:14–17, after the Lord promises to repay the nations and their great kings for their wicked deeds, he tells Jeremiah, "Take from my hand this

cup filled with the wine of my wrath and make all the nations to whom I send you drink it. When they drink it, they will stagger and go mad because of the sword I will send among them." Jeremiah reports, "So I took the cup from the LORD's hand and made all the nations to whom he sent me drink it."

A few verses later (25:27–29), the Lord Almighty orders the nations to drink the cup Jeremiah holds: "Drink, get drunk and vomit, and fall to rise no more because of the sword I will send among you. . . . You must drink it! See, I am beginning to bring disaster on the city that bears my Name, and will you indeed go unpunished? You will not go unpunished, for I am calling down a sword upon all who live on the earth, declares the LORD Almighty." In Isaiah, too, the Lord promises to punish Israel for her sins by making her drain the cup of his wrath to its dregs, bringing ruin and destruction, famine and sword (Isa. 51:17–18). Babylon made the nations drink "the maddening wine of her adulteries," and at the end God will require her to drink "a double portion from her own cup" (Rev. 18:3–6). So the cup is a biblical symbol for the principle that the guilty will not go unpunished.

When Jesus says he will drink the cup of God's wrath, he is promising to bear the divine punishment against human sin when he goes to the cross. So, when Jesus asks, "Can you drink the cup I am going to drink?" and they say, "We can," Jesus could easily have replied, "You have no idea what you are saying." James and John could not drink the cup as Jesus did. Yet one day they would participate in it. James was the first apostle to be martyred (Acts 12:2), and John endured exile in his old age on the prison island of Patmos (Rev. 1:9). Of course, they could hardly even imagine such things, and Jesus allowed their claim, "We can," to stand. He only replied, "You will indeed drink from my cup, but to sit at my right or left is not for me to grant. These places belong to those for whom they have been prepared by my Father."

Exposition, Part 2, A: Jesus' Way and the Gentile Way (analysis, contexts, and problems regarding the unique work of Christ) (20:24–27) When the other ten disciples overheard James and John's question, they became indignant (20:24). Perhaps they wanted everyone to be equal; perhaps they had wanted to ask the same question themselves. But Jesus sensed their dismay and called them all together to instruct them. He began by comparing two ways, the Gentiles' way and his way: "You know that the rulers of the Gentiles lord it

over them, and their high officials exercise authority over them"
(20:25). The terms for "lord it over" and "exercise authority" are not
pejorative in Greek. Jesus simply states a fact; since ancient times,
the world has measured greatness by the number of one's servants.
Ancient Graeco-Roman society counted the number of slaves one
possessed. Today, we judge success by the size of the staff someone
commands. We ask where we stand and where others stand on the
organization charts. We ask who takes orders and who gives them.
So it goes with the Gentiles, with the world, then and now.

But Jesus interrupts his brief social analysis. "Not so with you,"
he thunders. "Put off your dreams of rising to the top." He describes
his way in three parallel statements. They have the poetic form called
climactic parallelism, in which three successive remarks culminate
in the strongest statement:

	Whoever wants to become great among you
Analysis	must be your servant,
	And whoever wants to be first
	must be your slave—
	Just as the Son of Man did not come to be served,
	but to serve,
	and to give his life as a ransom for many.

Problem/Exposition:
Defining Service

We must not smooth over what Jesus says
here. The word "service" has lost its edge in
our language, as we talk about service de-
partments, parts and service, legal services,
financial services, and the service sector of the economy. One can rise
high, one can get rich, by offering "services" for a handsome fee. But
Jesus is not thinking of such rewarding forms of service. He means
the kind of service a slave might render. The service of a slave—that
is his way to greatness. But what precisely does it mean to serve just
as the Son of Man came to serve?

Problem/Theme:
Defining "Son of
Man" and
"Ransom"

First, Jesus is "the Son of Man." That is his
favorite self-designation in the Gospels. Second, there are two sides to his service. One
aspect we can imitate; one we cannot. We
will look at the service we cannot imitate
first.

"I did not come to be served, but to serve" states Jesus' mission
and identity. "I came" implies his preexistence. He was somewhere
else and he came to our world to accomplish something. Jesus often

says he came on a mission. He describes his mission in different ways, but there is a common thread to the statements. He says, "I have not come to call the righteous, but sinners to repentance" (Luke 5:32); "For the Son of Man came to seek and to save what was lost" (Luke 19:10); "I have come into the world as a light, so that no one who believes in me should stay in darkness. . . . For I did not come to judge the world, but to save it" (John 12:46–47). Paul summarizes everything when he says, "Christ Jesus came into the world to save sinners" (1 Tim. 1:15).[1]

Jesus says he came to give his life "as a ransom for many." A ransom is a purchase price. It is the payment someone makes to recover a king or a general who has been captured in war, or to buy back a friend or relative who has somehow fallen into slavery. When the Bible says that Jesus gave his life as a ransom for many, it means that he gave his life in order to purchase their freedom. He exchanged his life for the life of many others. He drank the cup of God's wrath that they were scheduled to drink. He came to drink the cup that was set at our table. He drained the cup of the wrath of God. That is his gift to us, and we need to do just two things to receive it: provide the sin that made it necessary, and say, "I'll take it. I will receive the gift." This is not really something we do. Like a child, we say, "Jesus, I will trust you to do this for me."

Jesus' gift of himself as a ransom for many is unique and unrepeatable. Yet we notice the term "just as." He says that we should serve "just as" the Son of Man came to serve. So Jesus' life, Jesus' service, is a pattern for ours. But how can that be?

Exposition, Part 2, B: Jesus' Way and the Gentile Way (analysis, contexts, and problems regarding the imitation of Christ) (20:24–27)

Actually, Jesus often said that his life was a pattern for his disciples. He went to the cross and said, "Take up [your] cross and follow me" (Mark 8:34). He washed his disciples' feet and said, "Wash one another's feet" (John 13:14). He enjoyed table fellowship with outcasts and sinners, and expected others to do the same (Luke 14–15).

Application

If a disciple understands this, he must commit himself to it. There is a moment for the Twelve and for us when the light dawns, when we say, "Now I get it." Jesus says to us, "I give my life for you. My death redeemed you. Now, if you call me Savior and

Lord, you must do as I have done for you. If you want to be great, you too must become a servant."

It is so easy and so deadly to be abstract here. We profess, "I want to serve," but somehow our service also takes care of our agenda, our needs, our honor.

I think of a young man who once attended a Bible study I led. One evening, when we were talking about our goals in life, he professed, rather eloquently, that his purpose in life was to serve the Lord, to show the love and service of Christ in his actions toward all who were around him. It was really a fine statement. Yet the rest of us sat there dumbfounded. We could hardly think of one shred of evidence that verified the man's lofty claims. In fact, he was a very selfish person; most of his life was structured around his own advancement or ease at home, at work, and in social relations. His great words were vanity.

Theme
Jesus' service was concrete. He washed feet that needed to be washed. He cured people who needed to be healed. He went to the cross when there was sin and a need for atonement. We too need to be concrete in our service.

Application
At home, we need to get up and help clear the table instead of looking for a way out. If a coat sprawls on the floor, pick it up. If towels lie moldering in heaps, hang them up instead of yelling at your spouse or children to do something about it. More broadly, ask yourself, "Am I doing something for someone for which I can gain no pay, no favors, no praise?" And when the chore is done, neither boast about your toil, nor blame others who made it necessary. Let it be your secret.

In the church, be sure you do something small, ignoble, invisible. Don't hide behind "gifts" theology: "I can't help plan the picnic, it's not my gift." Let me give you a test: For those of you who do *not* have small children, when was the last time you took a turn in the church nursery? For anyone, when was the last time you volunteered for the cleanup detail after a church dinner, picnic, or retreat? When was the last time you did something that no one notices, that never gets a reward, that has no prestige?

At work, are you willing to put in the time necessary to bridge the gap between an acceptable and an excellent report, between an interesting presentation and a convincing presentation, between a good try and success? Of course, we cannot always work harder and longer. We have other obligations. It can even be harmful to do our best at everything. Sometimes we just need to get a job done. But when an issue really matters, service means the willingness to put in extra time, even if no one notices.

In the home, at work, or in the church, check and see if you are doing anything for which you can gain absolutely nothing in return. That is the mark of service. Some of you may disagree with these examples. Fine. They are illustrations, not laws, not an exhaustive code. But this I know: an abstract commitment to service, without concrete deeds, is cowardice and hypocrisy. It is less than worthless.

I saw this in myself recently. While I was working on this very passage, some youth workers asked me if I would be interested in speaking at an area-wide junior high retreat in November. My unspoken, emotional reaction to the invitation was, *This is beneath my dignity. I don't 'do' junior high; I do adults.* The unwritten rules of Christian etiquette prohibited me from saying such a thing, of course. People do not say no when they want to turn down an invitation; they say, "I will pray about it" or "I will have to check my schedule." *Then* one can say no.

But junior high is the one age I don't understand, and kids that age know it. They can smell it. When I was in my early twenties, I worked with a junior high group for about a year. It was an unmitigated disaster. Twelve kids came; their only discernible reason for attending was to torture me. Eighteen years later I was still recovering. So I said no. Not even, "I'll pray about it." Just "No." It was too far from my comfort zone.

But the people in charge were students whom I knew well from my seminary, and they were not going to take no for an answer. They persisted, along these lines:

YOUTH LEADER: "Your daughter [a seventh grader] can come for free."

DAN: "No."

LEADER: "You could meet her friends. It would be good for you to know what junior high kids are like as your kids enter that age."

DAN (softening): "That's a good point, but the answer is still no."

YOUTH LEADERS (hopefully): "We'll pay you lots of money!?"

DAN (laughing): "That's interesting, but it's a lie."

YOUTH LEADERS (snickering): "The food is really good."

DAN: "That's another lie."

YOUTH LEADERS: "We can get you an isolated cabin, a quarter of a mile from the main building."

DAN (softening further): "Well, maybe I'll think about it."

YOUTH LEADERS (earnestly): "We're asking you because we think you are the one to deliver the message they need. Please."

So they wheedled and pleaded for several weeks, until I finally relented and said yes. As soon as I did, I marveled at how long it had taken me to agree to speak. I compare my hesitancy to Jesus' willingness to come and redeem us—and he was *completely* out of his comfort zone. If we were in his shoes, I suppose some of us might have said, "I don't 'do' crucifixions." Yet Jesus came without pleading, without the promise of a pleasant, isolated speaker's cabin, without perks.

Conclusion (final statements on main point and main application) Like the disciples, we want to avoid work whenever possible and gain the maximum reward for all we do. We want glory without suffering. Jesus came to forgive our lazy indifference, to redeem us from such sins. But Jesus also came to establish a new pattern. Like our master, we must learn to count the number we serve, not the number serving us. The world thinks that the great wield power while the small serve. But disciples learn to recognize that Jesus is Lord even as he washes their feet (John 13:1–9). We worship the Son of Man for dying a slave's death, to ransom us from destruction.

An admirer once asked Leonard Bernstein what was the most difficult instrument in the orchestra. He replied, "Second fiddle. I can get plenty of first violinists, but to find one who plays second violin with as much enthusiasm, now that's a problem. And yet, if no one plays the second part, we have no harmony." Bernstein put his finger on it: the willingness to subordinate oneself for the sake of the whole. Jesus set the pattern for service by perceiving our true needs, identifying with the needy, and meeting their true needs.

How can we combine humility and greatness, as he did? It flies against our nature. The two sides of our text remain as the two sides of our answer. First, we must love the Lord who redeems us from our refusal to serve. He ransoms us from bondage to that sin and all others. Second, we take his life as the pattern for ours. That means that we forget the selfish quest for greatness and honors. Jesus has already given us all the greatness we need. We can observe the people around us, and then do whatever we can to genuinely serve them. Then greatness will come, when we are not even looking for it.

Notes

[1] In some other statements concerning his purpose, Jesus said, "For this I came into the world, to testify to the truth" (John 18:37), and, "I have come to bring fire on the earth" (Luke 12:49).

Appendix B

Selecting a Text

The Need for This Skill

There is no formula for determining the appropriate length of a text—the number of verses needed for a good lesson. The simplest idea is *to choose a passage that makes one main point or tells one story.*[1] Texts may be self-contained or have complex relationships with other passages. They may have subpoints and side interests. Yet, a well-chosen text will make one main point. The ability to choose a text helps teachers by providing a solid foundation for application and reflection. Application is most effective if it makes one specific point, based on one text, and then defends it by addressing any doubts that hearers may have, and enhances it by presenting motives and steps toward obedience. Selection of a true text obviously helps reflection too, for one can hardly join the central truth to the central application if one has chosen a text so large that it contains several main points and applications. Short texts create the opposite problem.

Some may think that they can trust the chapter, verse, and paragraph divisions of their Bible. Those divisions can indeed be useful, but they have limits. Whole chapters are often too long, for they contain several units of thought. But a single verse is usually too short to convey a complete idea with precision. Moreover, you dare not blindly trust the paragraphs or section headings, for they vary from one version of the Bible to the next. Besides, none of these divisions belong to the original text. They are useful for reading and reference, but even a casual reader can see problems, such as verses that begin in mid-sentence and chapter divisions that interrupt the flow of thought. Verse divisions often break sentences into pieces, and chapter divisions often sever the parts of a unified discourse. For example, the discussion of the Christian home spans Ephesians 5:18–6:9, and the new chapter heading in Isaiah 53 senselessly places the song of the Suffering Servant in two chapters (52:13–53:12). Many biblical narratives include several chapters. Since we cannot trust the chapter, verse, and paragraph divisions in our Bible, we need to know how to recognize a right-sized text.

Obviously, one can err in this process in only two ways—by selecting too many verses or too few. New teachers often try to cover too many texts or topics in one lesson. While multichapter lessons can provide beneficial overviews, surveys often bury the audience under an avalanche of information. The many points become shallow and generalized because there is no time for development. Illustration and precise application shrink or disappear, and unity is lost.

On the other hand, a fragment of a text yields only a fragment of a lesson. Texts become indecipherable without the development of reasons and consequences that the rest of a paragraph provides. Removed from their context, they can be used for moralistic lessons or the mere presentation of information. Favorite notions, unintended by the author, can easily be read into an isolated text. Or we may notice a key word and use it for a topical study through the whole Bible, instead of a true exposition of a text. Of course, intensive study of one verse, even of one phrase or word, has its place. But it is difficult to understand what an author intends by looking at just one or two sentences.

The main unit of thought in a discourse, where an author wants to inform or persuade his audience, is a paragraph. Authors ordinarily need at least one paragraph, spanning a cluster of related sentences (probably a minimum of five verses), in order to convey complex ideas with precision.[2] A narrative unit may span a group of paragraphs— whatever it takes to tell a whole story, as defined in chapter 5.

Finding a Text—General Principles

1. *Right-sized texts have a prominent and coherent idea.* Somewhat like Goldilocks, we want texts that are not too long, and not too short,

but just right. But how do we find a text that is "just right"? One sentence will rarely convey a complete idea, because most sentences need a context in which to make sense.[3] But an entire chapter may present so many ideas that coherence becomes elusive. Ordinarily, a right-sized text will have one to five paragraphs. A paragraph is a cluster of sentences marked by coherence and prominence.[4] *Coherence* means that all the sentences deal with one main idea or action. *Prominence* means that one idea is stressed, so that all the others develop, explain, or prepare for that chief idea. The goal, therefore, is to locate a group of verses in which one idea or theme has prominence and the subpoints develop it.

2. *Unified texts commonly have a distinct vocabulary.* The repeated use of special terminology often signals a unit of text. The topic of Mark 7 is obviously "tradition," for the term appears five times in Mark, all in 7:1–13. Does the passage therefore end at 7:13? No, the special vocabulary of things clean and unclean begins in 7:2 but continues to verse 23, after which it, too, leaves Mark's vocabulary. In Mark 7, vocabulary alone could disclose the limits of the text. (Confirming the clue given by vocabulary, Mark 7:24 begins, "Jesus left that place. . . .") In 1 Corinthians, Paul repeats the term "wisdom" some sixteen times from 1:17 to 2:13, and then it disappears until chapter 8, so we know that wisdom is the theme in chapters 1 and 2. Similarly, Paul repeatedly speaks of "righteousness" in Romans 6, indicating that that is his theme.

3. *Unified texts often repeat key phrases or ideas.* Genesis 1 repeats the phrase, "There was evening, and there was morning—the 'nth' day." In the Sermon on the Mount, the repetition of a key phrase delineates several sections. Jesus' phrase "Blessed are . . ." marks the Beatitudes (Matt. 5:1–12). When he stops using it, we know the section is over. Later, the words "Your father, who sees what is done in secret, will reward you," unites the section on hypocrisy in Matthew 6:1–18. The section also uses terms such as *Father, seen/unseen, secret,* and *know* again and again.

Inclusion (also called inclusio), a special type of repetition, is the use of the same phrase or idea at the beginning and end of a section. The statement, "'Everything is permissible for me'—but not everything is beneficial" appears at the beginning and the end of Paul's long discussion of Christian freedom in 1 Corinthians (1 Cor. 6:12; 10:23). In Matthew 19:30 we read, "But many who are first will be last, and many who are last will be first." A parable about reversals follows, and concludes, "So the last will be first, and the first will be last" (20:16). Parallel concepts may also create an inclusio. For example, the passage including the parable of the rich fool (Luke 12:13–21) begins and ends with a question about who will get an inheritance.

4. *Consult the larger context to see how your passage fits within it.* Every passage contributes something to the larger section. The themes of large sections are usually clear; a text chosen for study should contribute a definite idea to them. For example, Romans 1:18–3:20 describes the sinful condition of the human race. Each text in the section develops the form, origin, or significance of human sinfulness. Every coherent text belongs somehow to the larger section in which it falls. If you cannot see a connection to the larger unit, you may not have a proper text.

These four principles apply to all texts. Some more specialized principles apply to the main kinds of text—narratives and discourses.

Finding a Right-sized Narrative

Narrative texts tell one story, typically in one place, at one time, and with one set of characters. We have seen that a story is over when the action has come to an end, when the tension has been released, when the protagonist "wins" and the antagonist suffers a defeat. Now we add that when time or location or characters change, a new story is probably beginning.

1. *New characters.* Rarely will all the characters change from one passage to the next; often only one or two shifts occur. Some characters, such as Saul in 1 Samuel or the Pharisees in the Gospels, come and go. But one change of character may mark a new story, if that character is central.

2. *New geography.* Throughout the historical books of both testaments, new events begin when the main actors move to a new place.

3. *New time.* Sometimes a book mentions a specific time interval (for example, "six days later"). A new episode may begin by referring to the last story: for example, "After such-and-such happened . . ." Kings and Chronicles mention times in the reign of a king. The Gospels may establish time in reference to Jewish holidays. Even a vague indicator of time, such as "after this," "then," or "one day," may indicate the start of a new event.

4. *Summary remarks.* Large sections often close with a summarizing remark. For example, "So the word of God spread. The number of disciples in Jerusalem increased rapidly, and a large number of priests became obedient to the faith" (Acts 6:7). Especially in the Old Testament, the summary may also come in the middle or the beginning. The statement "Day after day Saul searched for him, but God did not give David into his hands" (1 Sam. 23:14) summarizes 1 Samuel 21–23. (See also 1 Sam. 15:34–35; 18:30, or 1 Kings 13:34–35; 2 Kings 17:40–41.) Summary remarks may delineate one story or a series of related stories that should be studied for several weeks.

Finding a Right-sized Discourse

No one sign marks the beginning of a new unit in a discourse. Look for any of the following signs that an author is taking up a new subject in his letter, speech, or prophecy:

1. *Terms of address.* To list a few examples, authors address their hearers and readers as "brothers," "dear friends," "you foolish Galatians," "O Israel," or "my son."

2. *Questions.* Rhetorical questions get the reader to respond to the teaching just presented. For example, the question "What, then, shall we say in response to this? If God is for us, who can be against us?" opens a section of reflection on God's gracious salvation (Rom. 8:31–39). Questions also present imagined objections to prior teaching. "What shall we say, then? Shall we go on sinning so that grace may increase?" in Romans 6:1 begins a section on sanctification in 6:1–14. (The inclusio, "What then, shall we sin. . . . By no means" in verses 15, echoing verses 1–2, also distinguishes the section.) The question "Is any one of you in trouble? . . . Is anyone happy?" (James 5:13) prepares us for a text that tells us how to respond to the joys and sorrows of life.

3. *Acts of communication.* Biblical writers often urge their audience to listen, pay attention, or use their ears to hear. They also pause to tell their hearers what they are doing and what they want to accomplish, using such phrases as "I want you to know," "Don't be deceived," "I do not want you to be ignorant," "I write in order to," "What I am saying is this," and so on. Similarly, authors sometimes tell the reader what they are doing: "I plead with you," " I urge you," " I appeal to you."

4. *Formulas for the conclusion to a unit of thought.* "Therefore," "so," and "now" are common; others are listed in chapter 6. These terms may start a new unit or wrap up an old one. Individual authors develop their own styles and clues for the end of a section. For example, at crucial points the author of Hebrews uses the formula "Therefore + since or seeing that such-and-such is the case + let us do such-and-such."[5]

5. *Multiple markers.* You can be fairly certain that a new unit is beginning when two or three markers appear together. Consider the phrase, "Therefore, I urge you, brothers" (Rom. 12:1). It contains a formula of conclusion ("therefore"), an act of communication ("I urge you"), and a direct address ("brothers"). They verify our hunch that a new unit begins in Romans 12. Notice some other sentences that show multiple signs that a new sentence is beginning. "My dear children, I write this to you so that you will not sin" (1 John 2:1). "What good is it, my brothers, if a man claims to have faith but has no deeds?" (James 2:14). "I do not want you to be ignorant of this mystery, brothers, so that you may not be conceited" (Rom. 11:25).

Art and Science

While these clues will enable you to choose texts well on most occasions, we must not think of choosing a text in the same way we think of slicing a loaf of bread—as a simple, automatic procedure performed to create bite-sized pieces. Sometimes teachers must color outside the lines a little to allow odd connections between ideas to show. For example, the later parts of a book will often allude to the earlier. Thus, the many parallels between Paul's ministry in Acts 13–19 and Peter's in Acts 2–12 show that God is at work in both men.[6] Two narratives may also be intertwined, so that each story interprets the other.[7] For example, in Mark 5:21–43, the account of a woman with a flow of blood "interrupts" the story of the raising of Jairus's daughter, so that the healing of the woman gives hope for an even more miraculous healing of the dead girl.

Sometimes texts can plausibly be divided or kept together. For example, one could take Romans 12:1–13:7 as one unit, on the Christian's response to the gospel. Or, one could study 12:1–2 as an overture to the Christian's life, and then examine 12:3–8 on the believer in Christian society, 12:9–16 on the believer and individual Christians, 12:17–21 on the believer and individual non–Christians, and 13:1–7 on the believer and non-Christian society. Still, the selection of texts is not the wax nose of exegesis; there are many certainties.

Conclusion

The body of this book focused on the proper interpretation of set or assigned texts. But students and teachers of the Word must often choose texts themselves. You certainly cannot trust in chapter, verse, and paragraph divisions in the Bible to do the work for you. If your chosen text is too small, it is easier to take it out of context and fall into subjective and moralizing interpretations. If it is too long, your lesson may have too many points and lose its focus. This appendix has presented specific suggestions for establishing textual units that tell whole stories and present complete ideas. The choice of a text is an art as well as a science, and many passages can plausibly be divided several ways. Still, some choices of textual divisions are better than others, and wise selection does promote coherent lessons.

Exercises

1. What are the textual units of 1 Samuel 16–22? Defend your reasoning.

2. Determine the textual units of a short Pauline epistle such as Philippians, Galatians, or Ephesians.

3. Divide Matthew 5 into two series of lessons—one to be presented in three or four weeks, and one for which you have roughly eight to ten weeks. Do the same for the life of Abraham, Jacob, or Joseph.

Notes

[1] John Beekman and John Callow, *Translating the Word of God* (Grand Rapids: Zondervan, 1974), 279–80.

[2] William Klein, Craig Blomberg, and Robert Hubbard, *Introduction to Biblical Interpretation* (Waco: Word, 1993), 158–60. The number five comes from George A. Kennedy, who believes the shortest conceivable New Testament text is five or six

verses, for it took at least that long, by Greek standards, to develop a persuasive argument. See his *New Testament Interpretation Through Rhetorical Criticism* (Chapel Hill, N.C.: University of North Carolina Press, 1984), 34.

[3] John Lyons, *Introduction to Theoretical Linguistics* (Cambridge: Cambridge University Press, 1968), 412–23.

[4] Peter Cotterell and Max Turner, *Linguistics and Biblical Interpretation* (Downers Grove, Ill.: InterVarsity Press, 1989), 193–95.

[5] Hebrews uses a present participle in the Greek and translators render it different ways.

[6] Both ministries start with an impulse of the Spirit. In each case, a long sermon follows the healing of a lame man near a temple. Both suffer unjust imprisonment that ends through a supernatural release. See Glenn Barker, William Lane, and J. Ramsey Michaels, *The New Testament Speaks* (New York: Harper and Row, 1970), 300–301.

[7] This practice, known as intercalation, occurs perhaps a dozen times in the Gospels, most often in Mark. For a study of intercalation and many other artistic features of Mark, see Robert Fowler, *Let the Reader Understand* (Minneapolis: Fortress, 1991), 142–47.

Appendix C

Advanced Principles for Discourse Analysis

In a nontechnical book, one can only introduce complex concepts and skills. This appendix introduces readers to a more thorough study of the relations between propositions. The appendix first introduces the kinds of relations that all languages use. Then it describes relations between propositions in the New Testament.

Common Relationships Between Propositions in All Languages[1]

Every coherent discourse has a main theme, a leading idea that it attempts to explain or prove. Within a whole book, longer sections develop the main subpoints of the theme, paragraphs develop the sections, and sentences and clauses develop the paragraphs. Whatever their culture and language, most people relate one idea to another in certain universal ways.

Single propositions and large themes relate to each other in one of two ways: they either add to or support one another. When ideas add to one another, they develop the theme. One can add chronologically, by describing events. Events may be sequential (for example, "Paul went to Athens, and then to Corinth") or simultaneous (for example, "While Jesus was leaving Jericho, two blind men called out to him"). One can add all sorts of nonchronological propositions. For example,

214

one can add reasons: "I took the job because the work was more interesting *and* because it reduced my commute from an hour to five minutes." Or one can add circumstances: "I was feeling ill *and* had just gotten home when the phone rang." One can also add conclusions, means, circumstances, and so on. One can also add nonchronological ideas. We can add alternatives in either/or statements. Or we can list a series of conjoined ideas ("and" statements). For example, "When on vacation, I like to sleep in and eat out."

When ideas support one another, one idea is the head and the other supports it in one of three main ways: the supporting proposition may clarify another, argue for it, or orient the reader to it.

A proposition may clarify the main theme either with or without restating it. Restatement clarifies a proposition by putting the same idea in different words. More often, a supporting proposition gives a little more information—by expanding, illustrating, or giving a specific instance of the main idea. For example, a general statement can be clarified by stating a specific instance of the general idea. "She loves to sing" might be specified as "She especially loves to harmonize with her family during the holidays." Authors can also restate the main theme by summarizing a series of statements that amplify it.

Without restatement, authors can compare or contrast the main idea to other ideas. They also describe the manner in which an event takes places or how a proposition is true. Propositions may argue for their theme by supplying the reasoning that led to it or by describing the consequences that follow from it. Linguists specify six kinds of logical argument, six ways of reasoning from cause to effect.[2] They are:

1. *Reason-result.* A result is given, with the reasons for it. "The pork chops burned because I set the oven too high."

2. *Means-purpose.* This describes actions taken to achieve desired results, without stating whether the result came to pass or not. "Jason rushed out to get some fried chicken."

3. *Means-result.* This describes how (the means by which) a result actually came to pass. "Jason saved the day by running out and getting some fried chicken."

4. *Condition-consequence.* The conditions are stated under which a proposed consequence could be actualized. "If I make pork chops in that oven again, I will set it lower." In English, these are often if-then statements, with *then* left implicit.

5. *Concession-contraexpectation.* The result is unexpected, as it overrides factors that pointed in another direction. "Even though I ruined the pork chops, we still had a nice time." From Paul: "While we were still sinners, Christ died for us."

6. *Grounds-conclusion.* A writer draws conclusions on the basis of certain facts. The conclusion may be a new proposition. "Since we have been justified by faith, we have peace with God." Or it may be a command: "Since you have been raised with Christ, set your hearts on things above."

Finally, propositions may support a theme by orienting readers to it. ("Finally" orients the reader to this paragraph, by identifying it as the last in a certain series.) They may support the main idea by supplying its time ("In the time of Herod king of Judea there was a priest named Zechariah" [Luke 1:5]) or its location ("Now the Philistines gathered their forces for war and assembled at Socoh in Judah" [1 Sam. 17:1]). Or they may indicate other attending circumstances, other incidental things that were happening at the same time. A proposition may introduce an idea by giving the setting or background or otherwise preparing the reader for what is coming next. We think of Pauline phrases such as "I urge you," "I remind you," "I want you to know," "What I mean is," and so on. Consider the first sentence in 1 Corinthians 7, "Now concerning the things about which you wrote, it is good for a man not to touch a woman" (NASB). It orients the reader to the first proposition, "A man should not 'touch' (sexually) a woman," in two ways. First, the proposition is identified as a response to a letter. Second, it is evaluated: "It is good."

Notes

[1] This section depends largely on two semitechnical books, *Translating the Word of God,* by John Beekman and John Callow (Grand Rapids: Zondervan, 1974), chaps. 17 and 18, and *Linguistics and Biblical Interpretation,* by Peter Cotterell and Max Turner (Downers Grove, Ill.: InterVarsity Press, 1989), chap. 6.

[2] Beekman and Callow, *Translating the Word of God,* 300–309.

Supplement: Relations of Propositions with Reference to New Testament Greek

This section is for people who read New Testament Greek. It describes the most common English and Greek words that indicate relations between two propositions in the New Testament. Remember, propositions can be related implicitly, without the words below. In that case readers must use their judgment. Readers of Greek will also recall that certain linguistic constructions have a built-in ability to suggest some of the relations below. For example, a simple infinitive can connote purpose and a simple dative can connote means. The Greek words cited appear at least fifteen times in the New Testament.

The relations described here do not apply just to propositions that are next to each other. Further, any proposition can relate to one or more others. For example, in the statement "Unless your righteousness surpasses that of the Pharisees and the teachers of the law, you will certainly not enter the kingdom of heaven" (Matt. 5:20), the first clause states a condition for the second. But, taken together, they introduce the rest of the propositions of chapter 5, which explain how a disciple actually exceeds the Pharisees and the teachers of the law in righteousness. The six propositions introduced by "You have heard that it was said" all stand in a series, opening six paragraphs on righteousness. But each of those propositions also contrasts with the second proposition in their paragraph, as each one begins, "You have heard that it was said . . . But I tell you . . ."

Name	Definition	Key words (Greek 15+)
Propositions that add to one another		
Series	Each proposition or phrase makes an independent contribution to a larger idea.	*and, in addition, moreover, furthermore;* καί, δέ, τε, τε . . . καί, καί . . . γε
Progression	Like a series, except that each idea adds to the preceding one, building to a climax.	*and, then, also, moreover;* καί

Continued on p. 218

Name	Definition	Key words (Greek 15+)
Alternative	Propositions express two theoretically viable possibilities in a given situation or argument.	*or, either . . . or, on the one hand . . .* εἰ, μέν . . . δέ, ἤ, ἀντί
Contrast	Like alternative, except that two possibilities exclude each other; one affirmed to deny the other.	*but, not . . . but, on the contrary;* ἀλλά, δέ, οὔτε, μήτε, καί (rare)

Propositions that support a main idea by logical argument

Name	Definition	Key words (Greek 15+)
Reason or ground	The truth of one proposition rests on facts or arguments. Assertion comes first, then reason for it.	*since, for, because;* γάρ, ὅτι, διό, διότι, διὰ τοῦτο ἕνεκα, ὅθεν, διά + accus.
Inference	One or more propositions; events lead to conclusion. As above, except proof precedes conclusion.	*therefore, so, thus, so then, consequently, if then;* οὖν, ὅθεν, ἄρα
Greater-lesser	Argument by analogy. Proposition supported or explained by appeal to similar, but more or less weighty, parallel case.	*(How) much more, since, so then, if,* etc.; πολλῷ, μᾶλλον, πόσῳ, μᾶλλον
Means/ purpose	One action is performed in order to attain another. Describes the means to an end, without saying if the end is realized.	*in order that, that, so that, to;* ἵνα, ὅπως, μή, ὥστε, τοῦ + inf, εἰς τό + inf, εἰς
Reason/result	Result given, along with reasons that caused or prevented it.	*that, so that;* ἵνα, μήποτε
Instrument/ way to end	Result stated, along with the means for attaining it. Goal or result attained by certain means.	*by, by means of;* ἐν, σύν, πώς, dative case alone

Continued on p. 219

Name	Definition	Key words (Greek 15+)
Conditionals	An action or idea and one actually or theoretically consequent to it.	*if … then* (*then* often implicit); εἰ, ἐάν, ἄν
"Real"	Condition viewed as a genuine possibility in this case.	*if;* εἰ + indicative verb
"General"	Condition viewed as applying to all people who fit a certain set of conditions.	*if any, whoever, whenever;* ἐάν, ὅταν, ἄν + subjunctive
"Contrary to fact"	Condition seen as unfulfillable because conditions cannot be met.	Marked by sentence content and *if* (ἐάν) + subjunctive.
Concession	The main idea stands in face of contrary facts, arguments, or sentiments.	*nonetheless, nevertheless, yet, even though, in spite …;* ἔτι, πλήν

A simple adverbial participle can suggest several of these causal relations, including anything that could be translated "because" and concessions.

Propositions that support a main idea by clarifying with restatement

General-specific	One proposition states whole. Another develops it by illustrating or giving details regarding some parts.	Usually no explicit marker.
Specification/Interpretation	Proposition clarifies or explains meaning of a prior one, by expanding it with more or more exact information.	*that is, I mean;* relative pronouns; τοῦτ̓ ἐστιν, and ὅ ἐστίν, γε, ναί
Summary	One proposition restates several by summarizing them.	Can be introduced many ways.

Continued on p. 220

Name	Definition	Key words (Greek 15+)
Propositions that support a main idea by clarifying without restatement		
Comparison	An idea, action, or thing followed by another that clarifies it by likening it to another.	*even as, similarly, likewise, just as, illustrate;* ὡς, παρά, οὕτως, μᾶλλον, καθάπερ, ὥσπερ, ὁμοίως, ὡσαύτως
Manner	Proposition or event and how or in what way it is true or occurs.	*how, in this way;* participles, πώς, simple dative
Propositions that orient the reader to the main idea		
Introduction	Any proposition that prepares readers for major idea coming next.	No special terms; can be introduced many ways.
Time	States the time, duration, or occasion of main idea. This type of relation does not describe sequences of events.	*when, then, next, and;* ὅτε, ποτέ, ἄρτι, ἄχρι, μέχρι, ἐπεί, οὔπω, μηκέτι, οὐδέποτε
Location	Where main event takes place or where main idea is true. This relation is different from sequence of equal events.	*where, wherever,* places; ἐκεῖ, ποῦ, ὅπου, ὧδε, οὗ, πόθεν, ἐκεῖθεν, place names
Circumstances	Anything that takes place or is true at same time as main idea, yet is less important than main idea.	No special terms; can be introduced many ways.
Relations arising in historical texts and dialogues		
Q and A	Statement of a Q and perhaps its answer. May be a real Q, a rhetorical Q, or an internal deliberation.	Question mark; subjunctive marks deliberation and some rhetorical Q's, τίς accented
Situation-response	Statement of response to an event or idea.	Determined by context.

Name	Definition	Key words (Greek 15+)
Propositions that bear no direct relation to surrounding propositions		
Affirmation	Propositions stand alone, without support or explicit consequences.	May have performative verb. *I tell, urge, promise,* etc.
Aside-resume	Comment interrupts flow of thought or events, to which writer returns.	Parentheses, dashes

Appendix D

Applying the Genres of Scripture

This appendix supplements the chapters on application by offering guidelines for applying specific types or genres of Scripture. It suggests basic points to ponder when you prepare to apply each genre of Scripture. The appendix begins with comments on historical, theological, and ethical texts. Then it discusses the more specific genres of prophecy, wisdom, promises, and songs and prayers.

Whatever the genre of the text, find its message by following the normal rules of exegesis, as outlined in the rest of this book. Then ask a series of diagnostic questions:

1. Does this passage primarily require faith or action? Does it primarily address the mind (with information) or the heart (with a command)?

2. What type of text is this? Broadly speaking, is it history, theology, or moral instruction? Are you reading prophecy, wisdom, a song, a prayer, or a promise?

3. What important issues of the Christian faith and human life surface? List them and sketch what the passage says about them.

I. Application of Historical Texts

About one third of the Bible is historical narrative. Each narrative fits somewhere in God's plan of salvation. Within that plan, the Old

Testament describes God's work with Israel, while the New Testament describes the spread of salvation to the nations. In some ways, the entire Bible is one narrative, but here we consider the application of shorter, individual narratives, ranging from a few verses to a chapter or two.

Biblical history differs from ordinary history in that God is the main character in each narrative. These narratives never merely record what happened—they describe God's ways in history. They describe his action in establishing and maintaining a covenant with his people.

A. Begin with Basic Questions

You will probably have to deduce the answers to these questions; rarely are the answers given explicitly.

1. What does this passage reveal about God? About his ways with people?

2. What does it show us about covenant life—the life God blesses or judges?

3. Is there behavior here that we should avoid? Behavior that we should imitate?

4. How does this passage describe the covenant community and its life together?

B. Observe the Story's Major Characters

1. List all the characters in a narrative. Try to see the story through the eyes of each one. Expect at least one lesson and application for each person or group.

2. Look for these characters and areas of application: God or God's representative, a faithful believer, an unfaithful believer, an unbeliever, and an undecided or ambivalent party. Do not just look for individuals. Groups, tribes, and even nations can be one of the parties.

Narratives may have just two characters or a large cast. Moses and Elijah encountered God alone on desolate mountains. But in the account of David and Goliath, we have God, a protagonist (David), a faithful ally (Jonathan), several antagonists (Saul, David's jealous brothers, Goliath, the Philistine army), and two semineutral groups, the Israelite army and the Israelite women who cheer David. The various human participants can be categorized as faithful, unfaithful, or neutral observers.

3. God is a character in every narrative, even if only implicitly. Since he acts according to his unchanging nature, his past actions show us what he ordinarily does in similar circumstances today.

4. The faithful characters usually reveal the way one ought to respond in similar situations today. The unfaithful show the opposite. The neutral party may show the many ways in which people try to avoid commitment.

C. Locate Examples of Behavior and Attitudes to Imitate or Avoid

1. Not everyone agrees with the idea of seeking examples.[1] But the New Testament often exhorts readers to imitate the righteous and avoid the life of the wicked.[2]

- Jesus commanded his disciples to follow his example (John 13:15; Matt. 16:21–25; 20:28).
- Peter and Paul present Jesus as an example in their letters (Phil. 2:3–11; 1 Tim. 1:16; 1 Peter 2:21).
- Paul regards himself as an example to his churches (1 Cor. 11:1; Phil. 3:17; 4:9; 2 Thess. 3:7).
- Other leaders should be examples to the congregation (1 Tim. 4:12; Titus 2:7; 1 Peter 5:3).
- Hebrews 11 commends the faith and perseverance of many Old Testament heroes.
- Paul and Hebrews both forbid Christians to rebel as Israel did (1 Cor. 10:6–11; Heb. 4:11).

2. The Old Testament rarely mentions imitation, but its stories quietly illustrate God's laws.

- Deuteronomy's record of the blessings for obedience and the curses upon sin invites us to evaluate subsequent narratives as instances of blessed or cursed conduct (Deut. 28–32).
- The book of Ruth shows the blessing that obedience to the law brought to some Israelites during the period of the judges.
- Judges encourages believers to read its story as a warning against the consequences of rebellion (Judg. 2:16–23).

• 1 and 2 Samuel portray David as a flawed yet often exemplary king, whose fidelity to God is the standard by which to measure later monarchs (1 Kings 11:4, 6; 14:8; 2 Kings 16:2).

3. The people of God—first Israel, then the church—are often urged to imitate God or to imitate Christ, and to live lives worthy of him, worthy of membership in his family.

4. The idea that Christians should follow the examples set forth in the Bible has suffered widespread abuse. The quest for examples has led some to reduce the Bible to a morality tale. It is certainly foolish for Christians to think of imitating the individual acts, verse by verse, of Abraham, Moses, David, or Peter (below). But we cannot let abuses prevent the proper use of examples.

D. Guidelines for the Proper Use of Biblical Examples

We cannot repeat every good action described in Scripture. Sometimes the imitation of Christ is the height of virtue; sometimes to attempt to imitate him would be the height of blasphemy.[3] Therefore, we need some guidelines for imitation.[4]

1. Do you have reason to believe the author intended the action of a protagonist or antagonist to set an example or precedent? Does the action clearly keep or violate any commandment?

2. Does the action establish a pattern? For example, the Bible later cites God's simultaneous punishment of Egypt and deliverance of Israel as a model of his ways (Pss. 78; 80; Hos. 2:15; 12:9; Amos 4:10; Mic. 7:14ff.). Jesus' prayers are also meant to be patterns for the prayers of disciples.

3. Is the lesson gained from the example consistent with the rest of biblical ethics? Does it illustrate biblical commands? Does it express biblical virtues and ideals?

4. Do the actions of a hero inspire moral courage or excellence? Do the actions of villains instill revulsion toward wickedness?

5. Does the narrative establish the shape of covenant life? Does it describe the proper way of life in the family and the kingdom of God?

6. Look for moral lessons that emerge from the complete story, not from particular acts such as traveling to a specific place or getting a specific object. When examining an action, ask if the reasons for it are universal and permanent or local and temporary. Further, if a

character's actions flow from substantial ignorance of biblical revelation, imitation is less likely to be intended.

7. When God's agents had unique power and knowledge, we cannot imitate them. We cannot dry up the skies or call fire from heaven like the prophets; we cannot read thoughts, forgive sins, command demons, or heal on our own authority, as Jesus did.

E. Illustration

1. The story of the paralytic (Mark 2:1–12; Luke 5:17–26) features four characters: Jesus (God the Son), the paralytic and his friends (faithful men), the scribes and Pharisees (unbelievers/antagonists), and the crowd in the house (neutral). All four groups teach us something.

2. The passage reveals several things about Jesus. We ought to believe and rest in them.

- He is the Messiah promised in the Old Covenant. He fulfills the prophecies of Messianic miracles in Isaiah 35:5–6 and 61:1.
- He is tender and compassionate. The Gospels often say that Jesus' compassion moved him to action (Matt. 9:36; 14:14; 15:32; 20:34; Luke 7:11–15). He spoke warmly to the paralytic, calling him "friend" and "son."
- Jesus saves both by healing bodies and by forgiving sins. He is the Redeemer, for as the Son of God he possessed the right to forgive the paralytic with a word.
- We can imitate Jesus' compassion, directness, and interest in the whole person. We cannot imitate his remission of sins and his reading of minds, for they flow from his divine prerogatives.

3. The paralytic and his friends show the character of true faith—something all can learn from.

- These men exercised their faith together: "Jesus saw their faith" (Luke 5:20). Like them, we often advance much further when we exercise faith in community.
- Faith fights through obstacles. They did not, as the saying goes, "wait for a door to open." The door did not open, so they tore a hole through the roof. We should not take this as a justification for the reckless destruction of property (tearing a hole in a

roof was not as destructive then as it would be today), but as an illustration of persistence.

• Faith and imperfect knowledge can coexist. Even while the men acted obediently, they did not know exactly what to seek. The men sought physical healing and Jesus granted it, but first he forgave the paralytic's sins.

4. The scribes and Pharisees portray some traits of unbelief. They deny Jesus' deity, and consequently they criticize his forgiveness of sins. When Jesus proves that he does have the right to forgive by healing the man, they do not rescind their accusations. This group gives us limited insight into contemporary unbelief, however, for the scribes and Pharisees were a strict and knowledgeable religious group that has no close counterpart today.

5. The crowd's amazement is instructive, too. In Jesus' miracle and forgiveness they saw enough to confess his deity. But they only marveled at "remarkable things." This is typical of those who have seen enough to come to faith, but only admire Jesus from a distance.

F. Concluding Observations

1. There are two bases for applying biblical narratives today: God is the same today as yesterday, and, in their spiritual nature at least, people are fundamentally the same, too.

2. On the other hand, cultures change constantly. Languages and customs develop, historical events alter social structures, and knowledge is gained and lost. Therefore, we must be cautious when we apply ancient narratives to modern life. Lessing errs when he sees an "ugly, broad ditch" between past acts and present ethics, so wide that no one can cross.[5] There is a ditch, but we can cross it if we travel with care. This may involve a commitment to refashion our world so that it reflects the positive structure and values of biblical societies.

II. Applications of Theological Texts

A relatively small portion of Scripture strictly presents doctrine. Yet almost every text contains some theological truth. As always, we use the ordinary means of interpretation to establish the meaning of a theological passage. Then we can think about application.

A. Begin with a Knowledge of the Basic Areas of Doctrine

Examine your text for both central and tangential doctrinal instruction. Look for doctrinal instruction especially in the following areas:

1. God—Father, Son, and Holy Spirit
2. The covenants and saving work of God
3. Creation—as created, fallen, and perfected in eternity
4. Humanity—as created, fallen, restored, and perfected in eternity
5. This world and its patterns of behavior
6. The covenant community and its life, whether Israel or the church
7. Other topics, including Scripture, angels, demons, and final things

B. Guidelines for the Application of Doctrine

The application of doctrine begins with a question: what are the implications of the doctrinal truths of this passage? If the doctrine is true, what follows? Let your mind range over the whole of life, not just outward and individual actions.

1. How does this speak to the mind? What should Christians believe? What falsehood should they reject? What must we watch for in ourselves, in the church, in the world?

2. How does this speak to the heart, to our emotions and feelings? If the doctrine is true, what fears or anxieties should we put away? What comfort or encouragement should we receive?

3. How does this passage affect our attitudes and our speech, whether to God or mankind?

C. Illustrations

1. Genesis 1:26–27 and 2:15 declare that humanity is created in the image of God and commissioned to rule and care for the creation. If this is true, what actions and attitudes follow?

- How should we act toward creation, considering our commission?
- What should our attitude be toward others, if God formed every

person in his image? Specifically, what does this imply about our treatment of children, the elderly, and our peers? How does creation in the image of God affect the way we treat the rich and influential? The poor and powerless? Unbelieving neighbors and coworkers? Irritating people? Morally flawed people?
• How should we think about ourselves and our capacities, our successes and failures?

2. Galatians 1:6–10 teaches that anyone who preaches a gospel different from the gospel of Christ stands condemned. For most of this passage, we can simply state Paul's teaching and then ask, "If this is true, what follows?"

• Notice Paul's emotions of astonishment and anger as he describes the false gospel of the Judaizers. If Paul is so repelled by falsehood, what should be our attitudes toward heretical teachings? Toward orthodox teachings?
• Paul says the Judaizers' gospel is no gospel at all. What, therefore, should we say when we encounter "gospels" that require the performance of works for salvation?
• Paul says that if anyone—even he or an angel—should preach a gospel different from the one he preached, that person should be eternally condemned. What then if we hear someone preach another gospel? Should we denounce them? Should we try to persuade them? Should we be willing to break fellowship with someone who perverts the gospel?
• Paul concludes by saying that no one who tries to please men is a true servant of Christ. Surely it is not always wrong to please others. What does Paul mean?

3. The "What follows?" question cannot resolve every practical question about application. For example, it cannot tell us how to distinguish fundamental doctrinal errors, over which we must be willing to contend, from minor errors, which we should resolve quietly or even ignore (see John 17:20–23).

D. Theology and the Christian Life

Theology proper is the study of the triune God. Whenever a text reveals God's nature, we should pause, because we are the children of

God, members of his family. For example, in the Exodus, God delivered poor slaves in Egypt. He loved wanderers. Therefore, Israel
must show compassion to the poor and to wanderers (Deut.
26:1–15).[6]

E. Conclusion

We apply doctrine by finding the main doctrinal teaching and then
asking, "What thoughts, emotions, attitudes, and actions are consistent with the truths of the passage?"

III. Finding Applications in Ethical Texts

As we saw in chapter 10, every passage has ethical implications, but
only a modest portion of the Bible is overtly ethical. A great deal of
chapter 10 explained the application of specifically ethical texts, but
it did not cover every point.

A. Basic Principles

1. We readily grasp the thrust of many biblical commands, such
as "You shall not steal" (Ex. 20:15), "Love your enemies and pray for
those who persecute you" (Matt. 5:44), "Hate what is evil; cling to
what is good" (Rom. 12:9), and "[Speak] the truth in love" (Eph.
4:15). For such commands, the test lies in the doing more than the
understanding. At that level, even the clearest passages pose challenges. For example, how does one speak the truth in love? In America, Southern culture emphasizes politeness and propriety, but politeness sometimes masks the truth. Northern culture emphasizes
telling the truth, but sometimes uses the truth to wound, punish, or
manipulate others.

2. Other commands are harder to apply. Only rarely can we directly apply a command that is embedded in a narrative. We have
no obligation to obey God's command to Abraham, "Take your son
. . . [and] sacrifice him" (Gen. 22:2), and no obligation to heed Jesus'
command to his disciples, "Let down the nets for a catch" (Luke 5:4).

3. A few commandments even seem to contradict other Scriptures. When God commands Israel not to associate with the nations
of Canaan (Josh. 23:7), or when Jesus tells his disciples, "Do not go

among the Gentiles or enter any town of the Samaritans" (Matt. 10:5), we notice a tension with the missionary impulse of the New Testament. The next section suggests how to resolve such tensions.

B. Guidelines for Applying Difficult Passages

1. Determine the original meaning.

- Are you sure you have understood the text correctly? For example, it seems impossible to obey the King James translation of 1 Thessalonians 5:22, which reads, "Abstain from all appearance of evil." After all, many good or innocent deeds appear to be evil to someone. But check another translation (or the original language, if you can) and the difficulty evaporates. The NIV reads, "Avoid every kind of evil," and the NRSV reads, "Abstain from every form of evil." These translations are more accurate, and obedience is within reach.
- Would additional knowledge of the culture shed light on the text?

2. Has the redemptive-historical situation changed? If the passage is in the Old Testament, ask if God was governing his covenant people in a different way. Further, did the original audience lack knowledge that later believers have?

For example, Jesus told the disciples not to go to the Samaritans (Matt. 10:5) partly because they did not yet know that the gospel was for all the nations. They still regarded the Samaritans as half-breeds and heretics. With such a disposition, the disciples were not yet equipped to have an effective ministry among the Samaritans at that time. So Jesus did not send them yet.

3. If a command no longer applies to us literally because of changes in our culture or the time in salvation history, seek the principle expressed in the command. See the discussions of bulls and gleaning in chapter 10.

4. Consult parallel Scriptures. Compare your command to other, clearer instruction. For example, we know we should not apply Matthew 10:5 ("Do not go among the Gentiles . . .") literalistically because Matthew 28 clearly teaches that Jesus' followers should make disciples of the nations. The correct application of Matthew

10:5 today is not, therefore, to bring an end to mission work. But it does imply that we should not send evangelists to those whom they despise.

We still need to explain the unique features of some special genres of Scripture and their bearing on application. As always, the main principles of interpretation should be your starting point. A precise discussion of any of these genres could take an entire chapter. Here we offer a few specific principles for applying wisdom, prophecy, promises, and songs and prayers.

IV. Prophecy

A. The Basics

1. The main tools for interpreting prophecy are the same as those for any other genre. A knowledge of the historical background and terms and a familiarity with Hebrew poetry are especially helpful. Analysis of literary contexts is not so important, because prophetic oracles may be self-contained. As a result, two neighboring texts may have little bearing on each other.

2. Prophets both foretell and forthtell. By "forthtelling" we mean that prophets declare God's view of all things, not just the future. In fact, prophets see and announce God's view of the past, the present, and the future with equal ease. Prediction does not constitute the essence of prophecy. Only a small percentage of Old Testament prophecies describe the Messiah or even the new covenant era. The prophets speak chiefly to their own time and their near future.

3. The prophetic message is not entirely original, for it largely reapplies the law to Israel. The prophets are spokesmen for God's covenants, reminding the people of their obligations to him. They state and enforce the blessings for obedience and the curses for disobedience, as stated in Deuteronomy 4 and 28–32.[7]

4. Prophecies take many forms: woes, hymns, reports of visions, predictions of disaster or salvation, and more.

5. One prominent form is the lawsuit. In it the prophet "prosecutes" the people for failure to keep their covenant with God. He summons the people and charges them with violating the standards (called "covenant stipulations") of their king. He cites the evidence against them and renders his verdict.

B. Applying Prophecy

1. You need not find a future fulfillment of prophecy to apply it. Prophets often spoke about circumstances and events of their own day or in their near future—now in our distant past. To apply such passages today, ask if the church or our culture resembles the scene the prophets witnessed. Given what they said about the past, what would they say about the present?

2. The prophets remind us that we stand in a relationship to a redeeming God. They share the Bible's double emphasis on both orthodoxy (right doctrine) and orthopraxy (right practice).

V. Wisdom

A. The Basics

1. The books of Job, Ecclesiastes, and Proverbs are called "wisdom literature." Books such as James and 1 Timothy occasionally operate like the wisdom literature.

2. Wisdom can be defined as skill in the arts of life. The Hebrew term for "wise" often describes men who are competent in any skill, including manual labor (Ex. 31:3, 6; 35:35; 36:8; 1 Kings 7:14; Isa. 40:20; Jer. 9:17; 10:9; Ezek. 27:8) and even political intrigue (2 Sam. 13:3).[8] Wise animals are those that know how to live well (Prov. 30:24–28).

3. Wisdom, especially the wisdom of Proverbs, is partly a gift of God and partly the result of the labors of people who cultivate, preserve, and express what is commonly known, in a way that makes us pause over it and see it afresh.[9] It is "the discipline of applying truth to one's life in the light of experience."[10]

B. Types of Wisdom

The wisdom books are different from each other in crucial ways.

1. Job contains wisdom for the dark days, the storms and tragedies of life. It refutes the simplistic notion that justice prevails in this life.

2. Ecclesiastes is wisdom at sunset on a hot summer day. The author of Ecclesiastes had it all; he should have been a happy man. But as he cynically watches the sun set on his worldly joys, he laments

the transience, the thinness, the vanity of it all. Only occasionally does he point out the right way of life.

3. Both Job and Ecclesiastes contain a great deal of falsehood that serves as a foil for the truth. At great length, Job's miserable "comforters" present flawed interpretations of his suffering. The "vanity" sections of Ecclesiastes describe life and "wisdom" as one views it strictly "under the sun," that is, without the perspective of eternity. Like brackish water to a thirsty man, their half-truths stimulate our desire for pure truth. We apply these sections by taking them as patterns of thought that the faithful should avoid. The sound sections of Ecclesiastes and parts of Job generally function as proverbs.

4. The book of Proverbs describes wisdom for a sunny day, a normal day. They say, "Live this way and life will, ordinarily, go well for you."

C. Proverbs

1. As a genre, a proverb is a short, clear, memorable statement of truth learned through the distillation of extended human experience.

2. Individual proverbs appear in the New Testament, as well as the Old. The Gospels, for example, contain many proverbs, such as, "The worker is worth his keep" (Matt. 10:10) and "A tree is recognized by its fruit" (Matt. 12:33). Paul utters proverbs such as "Bad company corrupts good morals" (1 Cor. 15:33). If we isolate them just a little, some of James's statements sound like proverbs: "Be quick to listen, slow to speak and slow to become angry" (1:19) and "Friendship with the world is hatred toward God" (4:4). Like other proverbs, these statements are pithy, arresting, and self-contained, so they can be used in different settings.[11]

D. How Not to Apply Proverbs and Wisdom

1. Proverbs are not promises. Proverbs describe life as it is in brief, graphic bursts, using figurative language to catch the attention and remain in the memory. They make their mark by being bold, without stating exceptions, qualifications, or nuances. Consequently, proverbs articulate probable truth, not absolute truth; general truth, not automatic rules; tendencies, not guarantees from God. They are the way of wisdom, even shrewdness, in the world, not the way of

guaranteed success.[12] The following proverbs illustrate this point.

- "Commit to the LORD whatever you do, and your plans will succeed" (Prov. 16:3). This is generally true, but it does not cover plans to rob a bank. Selfish and misguided schemes do not automatically succeed if they have been consecrated to God.
- "He who works his land will have abundant food" (Prov. 28:19). Yes, but warfare, droughts, floods, and insect plagues do sometimes bring famine even to the diligent.

2. Proverbs are not strictly law. They are, in part, advice given to a young man starting out in life (Prov. 1:8; 2:1; 3:1; 4:1). They do not dictate the proper course of action in every situation. Some simply indicate the situations the wise never enter.

For example, the wise stay far from a contentious woman, for they know that she will not be restrained; a home in a desert or on a rooftop is better than a home with her (Prov. 21:9, 19; 27:15–16). This does not mean that the man who decides his wife is contentious should move up to the roof to get some peace. Rather, the proverb warns a young man to be careful whom he marries.

3. No single proverb should be read as the whole truth about a subject, as a famous pair shows: "Do not answer a fool according to his folly, or you will be like him yourself" (Prov. 26:4). "Answer a fool according to his folly, or he will be wise in his own eyes" (Prov. 26:5). Only in juxtaposition do these two proverbs tell us what to do when a fool spouts folly. Sometimes we must hold our tongue; to engage the fool is to sink to his level. At other times, we must break the bubble of his ridiculous confidence for his own good. The wise know which to do when.

E. Wisdom and the Whole of Scripture

1. Wisdom rests more on the theology of creation than that of redemption. Unlike Paul's epistles, wisdom does not rely on redemptive history or a prophetic revelation. Even the language of wisdom reflects this. It does not say, "Thus says the Lord," but rather, "I saw . . ."

2. The potential for wisdom to become calculating, as it counts the costs and consequences of every action, is held in check by the law

and God. Thus, Proverbs knows that gifts open doors (18:16). Yet, it does not recommend the use of bribes, for it follows the law by scorning those who use bribes to pervert justice (17:23, cf. Ex. 23:8; Deut. 16:19). So, wisdom subordinates itself to God's wisdom and to covenant law. As Derek Kidner says, "You have to be wise to be really good," but you also have to be godly, as God defines godliness, to be really wise.[13]

3. Wisdom refines the law. The law does not cover everything; some details of character and judgment are "small enough to escape the mesh of the law," yet they are decisive in personal dealings. Such details are wisdom's field.[14]

F. Wisdom in Theological Context

1. Wisdom invites those who love life and hope for good days to hear her (Ps. 34:12–14; 1 Peter 3:10–12), but she does not counsel happiness at any price. She says repeatedly that the fear of the Lord is the beginning of wisdom (Prov. 1:7; 9:10; 15:33; Job 28:28; Ps. 111:10). The wise act righteously because wickedness brings its own punishment with it (Prov. 26:27). But, more importantly, they know that God rewards good and punishes iniquity, that he brings peace and calamity (Prov. 5:21–23; 15:29; 16:6–7; Job 9:22–24).[15]

2. God is wise, and he gives wisdom to his people when they ask for it (1 Kings 3:9; James 1:5). But the idea of praying for wisdom can be misleading. For some things we can only pray. For others, such as our daily bread, we must both pray and work. Wisdom falls into the second class; we must both raise petitions and pay attention to the voice of the wise (Prov. 8) and to the scenes of life around us. The wise display their wisdom in their beautiful lives (James 3:13); therefore, the discerning will watch the life of the wise and take notice, just as they observe the way of the fool and take warning (Prov. 5:1–14; 6:6–11).

G. Profiting from Wisdom

Pursue the excellent life, as wisdom defines it, both by observing life and by mastering Scripture. Adopt the wise man's mentality. Keep your eyes and ears open. Let anyone who is wise instruct you, whether experts, peers, or beginners. Let them teach by their words and their ways, so you too can say, "I have seen . . ."

VI. Promises[16]

A. The Basics

1. A definition: A divine promise is a statement by which God commits himself to do (or not do) something in the future. Promises guide behavior by telling us what acts God approves and rewards and what acts displease him and deserve discipline.[17]

2. To apply promises correctly, one must learn to recognize them and know how to determine whether they apply or not.

Proverbs are not promises, but general statements about the ways of life. For example, Proverbs 22:6, "Train a child in the way he should go, and when he is old he will not turn from it," is a proverb, a general rule, not an absolute promise that all faithful parents will have good children.

- A large number of New Testament promises hold for Christians only. Consider the promise that nothing can separate us from the love of Christ (Rom. 8:35–39), or the promise that God will complete the good work he has begun in us (Phil. 1:6).
- Some statements function as promises even though they are not, technically speaking. For example, after Peter made his confession, Jesus said, "I tell you that you are Peter, and on this rock I will build my church, and the gates of Hades will not overcome it" (Matt. 16:18). This is a theological pronouncement, but it functions as a promise that, while individual churches may perish, the church of Christ will never die.

B. The Recipients of Promises

1. God makes some promises to individuals, some to groups, and some to all. Promises made to biblical figures should not automatically be taken as promises for us. God's vow to give Abraham a son does not mean that he will give us sons. All believers enjoy the consequences of God's promise to Abraham, but not as a direct promise to us.

2. Some promises to individuals do have a secondary application to us. Thus, God promised Joshua that he would never forsake him, and would go with him wherever he went, as he prepared Israel for war with the Canaanites (Josh. 1:5–9). This promise to Joshua does

not guarantee us victory in battle or physical protection. Yet Hebrews 13:5 applies the same promise (also found in Deut. 4:24) to believers under the threat of persecution.[18]

3. If a promise is given to a group, we must determine whether we belong to that group. We can assume that promises given to the church as a whole apply to us. But we cannot assume that promises made to Israel apply to the church. For example, the promise of material blessing for Israel if she tithes (Mal. 3:8–12) applied to that nation, not to other nations today. But the principle for the church remains that it is good to give generously to God, and that he rewards those who do.[19]

4. Many promises to bless or to curse are conditional; that is, the promised blessing only accrues to the faithful, while the curse falls only on the impenitent. This applies especially to Old Testament promises, although it is not alien to the New Testament (e.g., Rom. 11:22).

- In Genesis 8:20–22, God promises absolutely that he will never destroy the world and its rhythms again, no matter what mankind may do.
- In Deuteronomy 28, the Lord promises that he will bless Israel, but only if the people are faithful to his covenant.
- Jonah states what appears to be God's unconditional promise or threat to destroy Ninevah. Yet when the Ninevites repent, he relents (Jonah 3:4–10; cf. Ezek. 18).

5. The Bible clearly expects us to act on universal promises. The promise "Everyone who calls on the name of the Lord will be saved" (Rom. 10:13) summons everyone to call on his name.

C. Compare Promises to the Rest of Scripture

It can be difficult to determine whether a statement is a promise or a proverb, and whether a promise is limited or universal. We confirm or deny that we have a universal promise by consulting the rest of Scripture.

1. We know that the promise "Never will I leave you; never will I forsake you" is universal, because it appears several times, without conditions, and in several biblical settings. It is given to the church in Hebrews 13:5, to Israel in Deuteronomy 31:6, and to Israel's

leader in Joshua 1:5, 9. Jesus makes similar promises to his disciples in Matthew 28:20, John 14:23, and Acts 18:10.

2. Mark 11:24 seems to be a universal promise about prayer: "Whatever you ask for in prayer, believe that you have received it, and it will be yours." But this promise is limited by other statements about prayer. Specifically, God hears our requests if we ask according to his will (1 John 5:14). He will not grant requests that aim only to gratify our own desires (James 3:3). If we remember these qualifications, we will not fall into the errors of the health and prosperity gospel and its fantasy that every earthly blessing is ours for the asking.

VII. Songs and Prayers

A. The Basics

1. In the Psalms and other biblical prayers, the authors speak to God in the first person.[20] The Psalms and other biblical prayers are the personal words of believers to God. But how can human words spoken to God still be God's Word for us? How can someone else's expression of faith guide our expressions of piety?

2. The Psalms adopt a poetic style, filled with images and metaphors, and an emotional tone. They speak the language of the heart. As Luther put it, the storm winds of life "teach us to speak with earnestness, to open the heart and pour out what lies on the bottom of it. . . . What is the greatest thing about the Psalter but this earnest speaking amid these storms and winds of every kind? Where does one find finer words of joy than in the psalms of praise and thanksgiving?" Where does one find "more pitiful words of sadness than in the psalms of lamentation?" The Psalter, he concludes, is the book where all the saints find words that fit their situation.[21] Thus the Psalms inform the emotional life of the believer.

3. The Psalms shape our sensibilities, not just our emotions. The habit of meditating on them shapes our sensibility, so we treasure gratitude, praise, humility, awe, justice, and righteousness, as the psalmists do.[22]

4. The language of the Psalms is general, not specific. Writers grieve over distress and enemies, but they never spill details such as, "My wife has died, my back and teeth hurt, and my foes have stolen all

my camels." The lack of detail allows us to identify with the psalmists. Specific lists of troubles do not create a gulf between their afflictions and ours. We can identify their distresses with our own.[23]

B. Types of Prayer in the Psalms

There are several types of psalms, each with a recognizable form and a function in Israel's life. Scholars have differed in their categories, and some psalms defy classification, yet the main categories do help explain and apply the Psalms. Here is one list:

1. *Lament.* There are sixty or more individual or corporate laments in the Psalms. We can use laments to express any kind of distress to God. Laments pour out a complaint about an oppressor or physical or spiritual affliction. Laments direct each cry to God, and then petition him to help. Psalms of lament expect God to hear and deliver, and almost always end with a note of confident praise. Some psalms of lament are Psalms 3, 22, 31, and 94. See also 2 Samuel 1:19–27.

2. *Thanksgiving.* About fifteen psalms laud God, especially for his deliverance of his people in times of trouble. Typically, these thank God, describe a season of distress, and then recount his merciful provision. See Psalms 18, 34, and 107 and Exodus 15:1–18.

3. *Praise.* Psalms of praise are similar to psalms of thanksgiving, but they exalt God for his character and his work as creator, redeemer, provider, and ruler, without focusing on one particular act of deliverance. These are especially appropriate for worship and song, and include Psalms 8, 100, 103, 104, and 145–47. See also 1 Samuel 2:1–10. Some of these psalms focus on Zion (for example, Pss. 46, 48, and 76). They may seem a little strange unless we recall that Zion was king David's city, the home of the temple and thus the focal point of God's presence.

4. *Wisdom.* Instructive, meditative, and speaking in the third person, these psalms resemble wisdom literature. They contrast the just and the wicked, give advice for conduct, and urge people to fear the Lord. Like wisdom, the anchor of these prayers is law and human experience, more than God's salvation. See Psalms 1, 32, 34, 37 49, 111, and 112.

5. *Psalms of vengeance or imprecation.* Many psalms ask God to bring evildoers to justice, but a few, known as imprecatory psalms, harness our anger, channel it to God, and call stoutly for him to send his covenant curses upon the wicked. Since the call for judgment

stands at the center of these psalms, they can make us uncomfortable. How shall we apply psalms that declare the blessing of those who slay the children of the Babylonians (Ps. 137:7–9) or declare of evildoers, "I hate them with perfect hatred" (139:22)?

The truth at the core of imprecation is that faith in a just God requires his judgment on an unjust world. Our sense of justice and of God's righteousness generates a desire for retribution. The call for judgment is directed to God, and the final disposition lies in his hands.[24]

- The imprecatory psalms describe those who embody evil. The possibility of repentance is not even an issue. In these cases, the rejection of the wicked is a statement of loyalty to God (Ps. 139:19–22); the psalmist hates those who have a settled hatred for God.
- If the psalmists' tone of hatred and revenge seems out of place, stop trying to identify and pray with the psalmist, and try to hear him. See if you resemble the wicked in any way.

6. Some experts list psalms of salvation history, of celebration and affirmation, of covenant renewal, of trust, and of royal enthronement. Psalms of trust and renewal seem natural to us, but we must work to appropriate royal psalms.

7. While this section dwells on the psalms, Scripture contains many other prayers. Other petitions refrain from selfish request and first attend to the God who hears and acts (Neh. 1:5–11; Dan. 9:4–19; Matt. 6:9–13; Eph. 1:17–19; Phil. 1:9–11). The petitions within these prayers dwell on great things—on the Lord's salvation and the need for godliness—not petty, egocentric desires. On all these points, they are a good model for us.

C. Applying Songs and Prayers

1. Biblical prayers teach us how to pray. All Christians pray, but how many have learned how to pray? Lacking instruction, we utter petitions and little more. Or we repeat the Lord's Prayer, or the prayers we hear from parents or leaders. By contemplating the variety of prayers in the Bible, we gain variety in our prayer life. We learn to present our sorrows, joys, and perplexities, not just our needs! Biblical prayers help us break out of stale habits.

2. Biblical prayers deepen our worship, both public and private. They invite us to consider why we love God. Their imagery, such as "The Lord is my shepherd," is universal, and it still speaks to us. The dense language and poetic forms slow us down, and we contemplate.

3. Biblical songs and prayers teach us to relate honestly to God. They invite us to express every emotion, positive or negative, subdued or overwhelming. They encourage us to take every experience to God, to lay every burden before him, and to remember his presence especially in the hour of need.

Biblical prayers nourished Jesus and the apostles, Augustine, and Calvin and Luther, and they will nourish us too, if we let them.

Conclusion

This appendix has supplemented the general discussion of application by presenting some guidelines for applying texts that have an ethical or a theological emphasis, and some proposals for the genres of narrative, prophecy, wisdom, promise, and song and prayer. The points only amount to rough navigational charts and can never replace the pilot, the teacher.

Notes

[1] Sidney Greidanus, *Sola Scriptura* (Toronto: Wedge Publishing Foundation, 1970).

[2] The New Testament commands imitation of God eleven times and imitation of a human being seventeen times.

[3] John Murray, *Principles of Conduct* (Grand Rapids: Eerdmans, 1957), 177.

[4] See William Larkin, *Culture and Biblical Hermeneutics* (Grand Rapids: Baker, 1988), 109–12; Richard Pratt, *He Gave Us Stories* (Phillipsburg, N.J.: Presbyterian and Reformed, 1990), 311–33.

[5] Gotthold Lessing, "On the Proof of the Spirit and of Power," in *Lessing's Theological Writings,* trans. and ed. Henry Chadwick (Stanford: Stanford University Press, 1957), 31; James Barr, *The Bible in the Modern World* (New York: Harper & Row, 1973), 39–41.

[6] Bruce C. Birch and Larry L. Rasmussen, *Biblical Ethics in the Christian Life,* rev. ed. (Minneapolis: Augsburg, 1989), 29–30.

[7] Meredith Kline, *By Oath Consigned* (Grand Rapids: Eerdmans, 1968), 51–54; Kline, *The Structure of Biblical Authority,* rev. ed. (Grand Rapids: Eerdmans, 1972), 57–62.

[8] Gerhard von Rad, *Wisdom in Israel* (Nashville: Abingdon, 1972), 20. For an evangelical introduction to wisdom literature, see Derek Kidner, *An Introduction to Wisdom Literature: The Wisdom of Proverbs, Job and Ecclesiastes* (Downers Grove, Ill.: InterVarsity Press, 1985).

[9] Von Rad, *Wisdom in Israel,* 3–5.

[10] Gordon Fee and Douglas Stuart, *How to Read the Bible for All It's Worth* (Grand Rapids: Zondervan, 1982), 187.

[11] For more on the one hundred or more proverbs that some find in the Gospels, see Ronald A. Piper, *Wisdom in the Q Tradition: The Aphoristic Teaching of Jesus* (Cambridge: Cambridge University Press, 1989).

[12] Fee and Stuart, *How to Read the Bible,* 196–99; Derek Kidner, *Proverbs: An Introduction and Commentary* (London: Tyndale, 1964), 36–37, 52.

[13] Kidner, *Proverbs,* 31–32, 13–14.

[14] Ibid., 13.

[15] Roland Murphy, *Wisdom Literature and Psalms* (Nashville: Abingdon, 1983), 31–32.

[16] See Jack Kuhatschek, *Taking the Guesswork Out of Applying the Bible* (Downers Grove, Ill.: InterVarsity Press, 1990), 125–44.

[17] Promises could be called a special kind of doctrine because they affirm something about God's activities.

[18] Kuhatschek, *Applying the Bible,* 133–36.

[19] Ibid., 127–36.

[20] In a survey of the first ninety psalms, I found that the author speaks in the first person in over seventy. In most cases, he uses a first-person pronoun in the first verse. See Paul Ricouer, "Toward a Hermeneutic of the Idea of Revelation," *Harvard Theological Journal* 70 (April 1977): 1–19.

[21] Martin Luther, *Word and Sacrament,* vol. 1, ed. E. Theodore Bachmann, trans. Charles M. Jacobs, in *Luther's Works,* 55 vols. (Philadelphia: Fortress, 1955–1986), 35:255–56.

[22] Birch and Rasmussen, *Biblical Ethics in the Christian Life,* 45.

[23] Roland E. Murphy, *The Psalms and Job* (Philadelphia: Fortress, 1977), 17–19, 42–43.

[24] See Murphy, *Psalms and Job,* 45ff., and Fee and Stuart, *How to Read the Bible,* 182–84.

Appendix E

A Basic Christian Home Reference Library

This appendix describes the start of the reference shelf for the Christian who wants to engage in the kind of Bible study this book describes. These reference books belong in the home of an elder, deacon, Sunday school teacher, or Bible study leader. Whatever other books you may have, these are the basic works that you will consult over and over to establish contexts, solve problems, and develop themes. Of course, good new reference works come out regularly; the works recommended here are the best affordable ones in print today.

Bible Translations[1]

Effective Bible study begins with several accurate yet different translations of the original Greek and Hebrew. The chief issue is the theory of translation that guides each version.[2] Option one, *a literal translation,* stays as close as possible to the exact words and phrases of the original language. Although a good literal translation still makes sense in English, it sounds farther removed from both our culture and our diction. Option two, *a free translation,* seeks to transfer ideas from one language to another, without being so precise about the original words and phrases. Free translations update both the language and the cultural references of the original language. They feel more contemporary, but they sacrifice some accuracy. Option three, *dynamic equivalence,* translates words, phrases, and idioms into equivalent words, phrases, and idioms in English. They update the language but not the cultural references. Translators generally prefer the path of dynamic equivalence today. Ideally, you should have a literal, a free, and a dynamic equivalent translation. Consult all three when a verse or phrase is perplexing. The following chart locates some popular versions of the English Bible according to the three options.

Literal	Dynamic Equivalent	Free
NASB, [N]KJV, RSV,	NRSV, NIV, NAB,	JB, GNB, NEB, Phillips, Living

New study Bibles appear every few months, so I will not recommend any one version. I do advise this: use one before buying it. Are the notes informative? Where you are able to verify the accuracy of the notes, are they sound? Is the cross referencing system thorough and helpful? Try using it a few times before deciding whether to buy it.

Bible Dictionaries

Chapters 4 and 7 stressed the value of dictionaries and encyclopedias. If you have just twenty-five dollars, spend it on a good one-volume dictionary. The best ones hold a wealth of background information on names, places, terms, and customs of Bible times, and on the authors and settings of the books of the Bible themselves. Some good options are:

The New International Dictionary of the Bible. Ed. by J. D. Douglas and Merrill C. Tenney. Grand Rapids: Zondervan, 1987.
The New Unger's Bible Dictionary. Ed. by Merrill F. Unger. Chicago: Moody Press, 1988.
The New Bible Dictionary. Ed. by J. D. Douglas. Downers Grove, Ill.: InterVarsity Press, 1982.

Bible Encyclopedias

The next step, costing 50–150 dollars, is to purchase a Bible encyclopedia. Below are three good options. Baker is the simplest and the International Standard Bible Encyclopedia is the most thorough and technical of the three.

Baker Encyclopedia of the Bible. Ed. by Walter A. Elwell. 2 vols. Grand Rapids: Baker, 1992.

International Standard Bible Encyclopedia. Ed. by Geoffrey W. Bromiley. 5 vols. Grand Rapids: Eerdmans, 1979–88.

Zondervan Pictorial Bible Encyclopedia. Ed. by Merrill C. Tenney. 5 vols. Grand Rapids: Zondervan, 1975.

Other Reference Works

1. A concordance. This is the first of the rest of your tools. Unless you know Hebrew or Greek, get one that is based on the translation of the Bible you use most, and has a system for finding the Hebrew and Greek terminology.

2. A handbook of systematic theology. Here are three good options:

Berkhof, Louis. *Systematic Theology.* 4th ed. Grand Rapids: Eerdmans, 1941.

Erickson, Millard. *Christian Theology.* Grand Rapids: Baker, 1983–1985. (There is also an abridged version.)

Grudem, Wayne. *Systematic Theology: An Introduction to Biblical Doctrine.* Grand Rapids: Zondervan, 1994.

3. A Bible atlas contains dozens or hundreds of maps of the biblical world, supplying far more detail than the few maps a typical study Bible has.

4. Commentaries deserve discussion too. Since commentaries are costly, buy them as you need them, rather than purchasing whole sets. Observant teachers should never need to buy devotional commentaries. No matter how insightful an author may be, if he lives in another place and time, the local teacher who knows his or her audience has the advantage. Look instead for commentaries that in-

form you in the areas that the CAPTOR plan would teach you to expect information. Finally, as with study Bibles, it is wise to borrow a commentary from a library to determine its value before buying it. Look for the following categories of information:

a. Historical background, including social customs, geography, the state of religion and secular history at the time, and the setting of the book.
b. An analysis of the flow of your passage, including its place in the larger context of the book.
c. The meaning of the original Greek or Hebrew, covering the meaning of words, grammatical constructions, idioms, plays on words, and subtle emphases of the original text.
d. Reference to other biblical passages that bear on your text.
e. For debated passages, an outline of the interpretive options and their strengths and weaknesses.
f. The main point of a passage, at least for the original audience.

This appendix has listed quite a few books, but fear not: you need only five books, costing less than one hundred dollars, to begin a study library. You need two good translations (with cross references), a Bible dictionary, a concordance, and a systematic theology.

Notes

[1] For a short but profound study of styles of translation and the strengths and weaknesses of each, see Gordon Fee and Douglas Stuart, *How to Read the Bible for All It's Worth* (Grand Rapids: Zondervan, 1982), 29–42. The following paragraph follows the wording of page 35.

[2] The second issue is the text that the translation is using. Generally, the newer the translation, the more likely that it relies on more ancient, more reliable manuscripts. The King James Version and other older translations simply did not have access to the most reliable of the handwritten copies of the New Testament that circulated before the invention of the printing press.

Scripture Index

Daniel M. Doriani (M.Div., Ph.D., Westminster Theological Seminary; S.T.M., Yale Divinity School) is senior pastor of Central Presbyterian Church, Clayton, Missouri. He previously was dean of faculty and professor of New Testament at Covenant Theological Seminary. He is a frequent speaker at conferences and seminars, and author of *Putting the Truth to Work: The Theory and Practice of Biblical Application*. Dr. Doriani presents the CAPTOR plan of interpretation in one-day seminars in local churches.